"Comparable to a John Grisham-st
to find out what happens in the end."
★ ★ ★ ★ ★ AMAZON REVIEW

"A powerful, gripping, true story of personal triumph
over a Catholic group gone rogue."
★ ★ ★ ★ ★ AMAZON REVIEW

"A non-fiction book that reads like fiction. I admire anyone who can go
through what Mr. Sullivan did and come out even remotely sane."
★ ★ ★ ★ ★ AMAZON REVIEW

"I hate this book and I love it."
★ ★ ★ ★ ★ AMAZON REVIEW

"I think this book is especially beneficial to anyone
who has been hurt by church or religion."
★ ★ ★ ★ ★ AMAZON REVIEW

"Fascinating, eye-opening book that tells the truth
and damn the consequences."
★ ★ ★ ★ ★ AMAZON REVIEW

"It is vital to know that one can go through hell…
and not only learn how to survive but to thrive."
★ ★ ★ ★ ★ AMAZON REVIEW

"Compelling read, challenging the reader to examine his/her
own thoughts about hope, love, and acceptance."
★ ★ ★ ★ ★ AMAZON REVIEW

"You will never look at a priest the same way again."
★ ★ ★ ★ ★ AMAZON REVIEW

"You will experience every human emotion possible reading
this book….Reminiscent of the Oscar winning 'Spotlight.'"
★ ★ ★ ★ ★ AMAZON REVIEW

# VATICAN
## INTERVENTION

### By Andrew Lee Sullivan

Andrew Lee Sullivan © Copyright 2016
Publisher's Cataloging-In-Publication Data
(Prepared by The Donohue Group, Inc.)

Names: Sullivan, Andrew Lee.
Title: Vatican intervention / Andrew Lee Sullivan.
Description: [Phoenix, Arizona]: [Receiving Love Press], [2016]
Identifiers: ISBN 978-0-9980552-0-6 | ISBN 978-0-9980552-1-3

(paperback)

Subjects: LCSH: Sullivan, Andrew Lee. | Catholic men--Italy--Rome--Biography.
| Abused men--Italy--Rome--Biography. | Miles Jesu (Religious order)--Corrupt
practices. | Cults--Italy-Rome. | God (Christianity)--Love. | Monasticism and religious
orders--Vatican City. | LCGFT: Autobiographies.

Classification: LCC BX4668.3.S85 A3 2016 (print) | LCC

BX4668.3.S85 (ebook) | DDC 271.7092--dc23

The catalog record for Vatican Intervention (paperback/ebook) is available in the OCLC
(WorldCat) and SkyRiver databases.

# DISCLAIMER

Vatican Intervention is presented solely for educational and entertainment purposes. The author and publisher (or future publisher) are not offering it as advice. While best efforts have been used in preparing this book, the author and publisher (or future publisher) make no representations or warranties of any kind and assume no liabilities of any kind with respect to the accuracy or completeness of the contents and specifically disclaim any implied warranties of merchantability or fitness of use for a particular purpose. Neither the author nor the publisher (or future publisher) shall be held liable or responsible to any person or entity with respect to any loss or incidental or consequential damages caused, or alleged to have been caused, directly or indirectly, by the information or programs contained herein. No warranty may be created or extended by marketing representatives or written marketing materials. This personal memoir is neither a guide to practice therapeutic prayer nor an instruction on how to break free from a cult. Vatican Intervention is based on a true story and names/ events may have been changed to protect people when appropriate.

## ACKNOWLEDGMENTS

Thanks, Mom, for the dozen writing books shipped to Ukraine. They helped me make the shift from expository to narrative writing. May you rest in peace. Dan, your concise advice and orientation launched me in the right direction. Show—don't tell. After two opening chapters stuffed in the garbage, I finally got it, I think. I'm grateful to all my friends, ex-members of Miles Jesu, who helped my memory and enriched my understanding. I appreciate the many hours of interviews, scribbled notes, and laughs. Thank you Olha for your unwavering years of encouragement. More than once I felt like giving up. You were always there for me.

## DEDICATION

I'd like to dedicate my memoir to the members of Miles Jesu, past, present, and future. I pray that my testimony may advance healing and inner growth. May love abound. May the truth set us free.

# CONTENTS

# INTRODUCTION

This is a true story. It's pieced together from my memories, letters, a personal journal, critical documents and thirty-two interviews of thirteen witnesses. It took seven years, a mountain of crumpled papers, and about twenty-five hundred cups of coffee to complete. Human life squeezed my writing into barely workable time slots before the crack of dawn.

These pages recount the turning point of my life in Rome, Italy. The cult. The entrapment. The implosion of love. The Vatican whistleblowing. I didn't fudge the time line, nor compress multiple events into fabrications, nor create composite characters except for a single instance. No. Here's the real story, as ugly, improbable, and beautiful as it gets.

I did weave in some misdirection surrounding identities. Eighty-three names appear: forty-nine real, thirty-four pseudo. A handful of names required some biographical muddying. Two pseudo names demanded a high degree of biographical fiction. They wanted no possibility of recognition. Their livelihood demanded anonymity. A secondary character was removed from the text altogether.

Granted literary wiggle room, the scenes and words of significant conversations represent reality. Because the memory has inherent limits, I often consulted others to assure accuracy. There were a few instances when memories clashed. Luckily these didn't touch upon matters of importance and I simply followed my own recollections. The bottom line: I've gone to great lengths to tell a true story, faithful to external facts and reflective of my sincere inner journey.

# CHAPTER ONE

Midnight, a few blocks from the Vatican, a city bus idled at the stop below my open window. I tossed and turned, trying to get some sleep at the Casa del Clero. More noise. Someone knocked loud enough to demand my attention, but careful enough to avoid the notice of other hotel room guests.

My roused mind raced to identify the cause of the intrusion. I knew who waited in the corridor. Gelson, you're so predictable! I finally made you jump, at least for damage control. Why did I have to threaten to expose everything to the Vicariate to salvage my emotional health? Stupid! Why did I let anyone know my whereabouts!

"Father Sullivan. Father Sullivan!"

"Yes. What do you want?"

"It's Father Gelson with your brother, Anthony."

Peeling away the covers, planting my feet on a cold marble floor, I shook my head and massaged my face.

"It's not a good time to talk," I yelled. Father Marcus Gelson was the superior of my Catholic religious community. Anthony Sullivan, my younger brother and a community member for 23 years, stood next to him.

Gelson plowed ahead.

"Andy, just let us in. It won't take long."

A cornered animal panics. It vacillates between escape or attack until one mode of survival yields to the other. Terror rushed through my body as I reluctantly moved to the door and reached for the knob.

The door swung inward; Father Gelson looked tired, his handsome New Orleans face strained by impossible responsibilities.

"Hello, Father Sullivan. How are you? I just learned of your situation," he lied, then embraced me with a strained smile and kiss. The pungent stink of cigarettes enveloped me. Anthony slipped in. I grumbled something and arranged a few chairs. It felt like vultures had landed.

Gelson sat down and faced me.

"Since it wasn't possible for Rick to come, I thought you wouldn't mind if your brother Anthony came along."

Anthony just sat there, silent. Rick Wolowicz, a pharmacist community member was on my side of the fight.

"That's fine," I said.

But it wasn't fine at all, as if I really had a choice in the matter. Why pull Anthony into this? Underneath the pleasantries, a power play manipulated the encounter. Rick would defend me. But where was he? Anthony's presence reinforced Gelson's position. My brother innocently accepted the role of a malleable witness to everything Gelson would say. Anthony would back him up and lend credence to each critical statement. I'd been through it all. I knew how to play the game. My blood brother's presence was aimed at swaying me and I felt sorry for his exploitation.

The element of surprise also played to their advantage. Why visit me in the middle of the night when my mind fumbled in the dark? Anthony knew that as a morning person I hardly functioned at night. "Andy, you said you might want to record our meeting. Anthony brought a tape recorder if we need it." With a slight nod of the head, Anthony acknowledged the fact, ready to record. But I'd mentioned recording a meeting with Rick present precisely to document an objective voice of opposition.

"No, that's okay. We don't need to record anything."

If Gelson offered to record the meeting, it wouldn't need documenting. I was tired and couldn't think straight.

Getting down to business, Father Gelson reached into the breast pocket of his slick suit coat and whipped out a twice-folded sheet of paper. Looking me in the eyes, he handed it to me.

"Here, maybe this is the best way to start. Go ahead and read this first." Not missing a beat, he kept talking. "We already discussed your needs and don't want you to come back to live in the community."

Trying to sound compassionate, he drew out these last words. He repeated them, wrapped them in silence, and hoped for maximum impact.

Cushioned with a sympathetic opening and closing, the core of the letter spelled out Gelson's position. It reassured me of financial support upon the condition that I live with another community member, wherever that may be. Otherwise, I'd be considered illegitimately absent and the community no longer financially responsible for me. Besides, it required that I allow the community to participate in my diagnosis and treatment.

I'd appealed to Father Gelson for material support with a hand-delivered letter. His response came from Father Jerry Kroll, a general government advisor and friend, I thought. The letter lacked both official letterhead and a signature. It hardly nurtured trust.

After I finished reading, I sat on the edge of my bed and stared at the floor, anticipating the complementary pitch. Marcus broke the silence.

"Andy, you don't have to go back to the community. We just want you to get better, no matter what it takes."

"So what does that mean in my case?"

"You would live with another member of the community, not at Via Tespi."

He said this with emphasis. Rightly so, I'd just escaped from three and a half years of house arrest there. He continued,

"We will do whatever is necessary to find out what is wrong with you. You can go to therapy at the best place possible, probably in the States. You don't need to worry about money anymore or where to live. We want to help with everything."

"What do you mean 'go anywhere to figure out my problem' and how to cure it? I know exactly what is wrong with me! I'm already going to the best kind of therapy possible for emotional deprivation disorder here in Rome. I know what I'm doing, with good advice from people in the Vatican."

*Why couldn't he just listen to me? Did he want me out of Rome where I wouldn't damage the community any further?*

Although I didn't say it, I knew exactly how Gelson's plan would play out. Once he found someone gullible enough, a puppet psychiatrist would be manipulated to say whatever my superiors wanted to hear. After discarding inconvenient advices, prejudice and ignorance would then shape a damaging therapy, justified by twisted religious principles. Not long afterwards, my "treatment" would be disrupted, reassessed, and changed to fit the community's purposes. Most likely, a public scolding would blame me for the change. I had witnessed the community's attempts to cure people, all futile efforts that invariably resulted in deeper emotional trauma. Accepting Gelson's offer would be like surrendering to the perfumed hand of a blind man heading toward a cliff. No thanks. I've been there.

Anthony jumped in with his two cents, a slight variation of Gelson's position.

"You don't need to worry about finding the money to cure yourself. Andy, you can go the States. We'll do whatever it takes to find out what is wrong with you. We want you to get better and have the best treatment possible, no matter how much it costs or how long it takes, no matter where you need to go to get cured."

I ignored him. Same old thing.

Gelson looked at me with sympathy and pleaded with a soft voice. "Andy, I'm begging you to trust me. I promise that we will do everything to help you."

"How can I trust you to help me? You're never around for my needs. I've tried to let you know many times how I'm doing. You never had time to listen. You couldn't even read anything I passed on to you. You're always busy with your own crises and trips to see exorcists."

I began shaking and abruptly exploded with the full force of my voice.

"Miles Jesu had twenty-eight years to discern what was wrong with me! Since nobody had the slightest idea how to help me I went to the external supervisors over Miles Jesu in the Vicariate of Rome. It's impossible to receive the help I need in the community. So, I submitted a thirty-four-page request for exclaustration to Cardinal Ruini."

An exclaustration is a permitted lengthy leave of absence from community life for a grave reason, such as the preservation of health or vocation discernment. Under normal circumstances, the request is a few pages long, requiring a few days to grant. Taking care of its own, the community mostly foots the bill. The request is usually submitted to the head superior governing the particular institute of consecrated life.

"How many pages?"

"Thirty-four," I said.

I'm sure the repercussions of my request slammed back and forth like a church bell in his skull. *What the hell did Sullivan write? This could have a devastating ripple effect in the Vatican and put the Institute into jeopardy.* Accustomed to managing crises, Gelson kept his outward composure fairly well.

I continued, "Father Gelson, I know you're trying to help me. I trust your good will. But you have no idea how to help. I know much better than you how to cure my emotional condition. You want to help, but I have a complete lack of trust in your competence." Gelson scrambled for something, anything to say.

"You've always had problems trusting in superiors. Andy, you have to trust in someone."

"But I do trust in someone."

"Who's that?"

He probably expected me to give the name of my psychotherapist. But I spun the conversation in another direction.

"I trust in Thomas Walsh. For the past year and a half, Tom was always there for me. I poured out my soul to him. He was always there at my worst moments. He was there with his hand on my back when I cried my guts out. He knows me inside and out. Tom became my first real friend in life. He became a father to me. You say that I have to trust in someone. I do trust in someone."

Gelson found himself unexpectedly in an awkward situation. Thomas was Judas as far as Gelson was concerned. Since he could neither discourage nor congratulate me for trusting, the very point he pressed, Gelson changed the subject.

Did he realize yet that I was beyond his reach?

"I understand that the bill for the Casa del Clero is due?" he asked, touching upon another tender nerve.

"Yes, why did you all make me struggle and sweat it out to the last minute? It's due tomorrow. I sent email after email explaining my situation, and a hand-delivered letter. I've gone through an ordeal trying to get money. Why did you show up only now, after I threatened to give the Vicariate a record of my unanswered requests for help?"

Father Gelson knelt down at my feet.

"Andy, like I said, I just learned of your situation. I am begging you to trust me. I can go downstairs right now and pay the bill. Would you like me to do that?"

"No, I only want the bill paid. I don't want a show of it. If someone can come tomorrow during normal working hours and pay the bill that will be enough."

Still on his knees, he grasped my hands, his last straw to earn credibility in my eyes. I'm surprised he didn't bend down and kiss my feet. I'd seen that many times. Ostentatious humility.

But the community's manipulative psycho-games no longer made me jump. I plainly wanted normal and dignified treatment, without empty theatrics.

"No, please just pay the bill at the front desk tomorrow morning," I said. Not before Gelson insisted again did he finally agree.

The second hand clicked past one, weariness finally catching up with everybody. We looked at each other with nothing left to say. I tried to put an end to things.

"Well, I guess that's it. I think it's time to go to bed."

Happily, Father Gelson and Anthony consented, as if waving the white flag. They failed to recruit me back into the community.

At that, we all stood up to say goodbye. They each gave me a friendly bear hug and kiss saying that they loved me, a community custom that automatically took over. They cracked open the door, stepped quietly into a poorly lit corridor, and disappeared. Liberated; I closed the door behind them.

Shaking all over, I walked into the bathroom and mixed a gin and tonic. With a drink in hand, I looked in the mirror. My middle-aged grey hair stood out, disheveled and unkempt. My cheeks carried that usual slightly plump Italian pasta look. Someday I'd worry about losing weight. It seemed that the bags underneath my eyes sagged a little lower. Suddenly, playfully, I lifted my glass, smiled, and congratulated the guy in the mirror, "Good job, Andy! You deserve a stiff drink!" I laughed at my reflection, threw a funny face, and turned around.

Shuffling back to my bed, plopping down, I stared at the locked door. It comforted me. I liked it locked. Then, like a sledgehammer between the eyes, the dreadful consequence of their visit hit me. I shook my head in disbelief.

"You freaks! I got to get the hell out of here!"

I again raised my drink in the air, saluted their departure, and toasted my late night guests, wherever they were, "You won't find me next time."

Poor Marcus and Anthony were victims like everybody else.

The encounter made me realize how much Marcus Gelson and I had polarized. I'd grown emotionally and left him behind. I now felt and thought very differently than him. For the first time in my life I stood up to authority for something essential in my life, albeit wobbly, but decisively.

Their desperate visit reminded me of the terrifying price of growing up emotionally overnight. Having suffered the consequences of emotional immaturity my entire adulthood, I finally woke from a living nightmare. Extraordinary emotional growth opened my eyes to an environment that stifled and choked off human growth. This epiphany grabbed me by the throat and throttled me. I lived in a holy mafia that had systematically traumatized me for twenty-eight years.

I'd grown too big for my britches and the Institute couldn't handle me. If I were to grow up completely, I had to disentangle myself from this smothering environment, no matter the risk.

Dawn jostled Rome awake with clear skies, spring air, and Mediterranean sunshine. Highways and narrow streets were clogged with the miniature cars Italians like so much. Tourists equipped with fat wallets, water bottles, and funny looking hats flooded the byways and cobblestoned piazzas of the city.

Across town, a twenty-minute car ride east from Saint Peter's Square, stood Saint John Lateran Basilica and the accompanying offices of the Vicariate. This mini bureaucracy purred within the hollows of an ancient Papal palace, complete with ceiling frescos and an Egyptian obelisk out front. In Rome, you weren't anybody without your obelisk.

It was not the Vatican, but the Vicariate that assumed the hands-on governing of the Catholic Church in the city of Rome. As the Pope immersed his hands in global matters, he routinely delegated a cardinal to run his own diocese. Currently, His Eminence Cardinal Ruini reigned. The deputation lent a great deal of power to the bustling officialdom of the Vicariate. These offices pulsated authoritatively as a practical modern working center, executing the daily grunt work of resolving the church problems of Rome.

Father Tonello worked in a Vicariate office near the junction of two long corridors up on the second floor. Nothing about his office stood out. Unpretentious basics occupied its space, a desk, a computer, a few chairs, and a table to support the overflow of active documents. The plain room reflected Father Tonello's 'just do it' attitude regarding the assignments that filtered down to his desk from superiors, mostly from Bishop Moretti across the hall.

With eagle eyes, Father Giuseppe Tonello clicked with a quick mind. He sported a neatly trimmed black beard, looking more like a lumberjack than the chancellor of the world's most prestigious diocese. Prone to speak exactly what he thought, a rare quality for someone in his power position, he tolerated little nonsense. His attitude didn't soothe much, but it produced results. That's what kept him his job.

This morning Father Tonello mulled over two alarming letters on his desk. Addressed to Cardinal Ruini, they dealt with crises that were sensitive, urgent and proper to the cardinal's jurisdiction, implying a delicate situation for someone close to the cardinal. Tonello derived his first logical conclusion: the documents meant another load of work was about to fall on his head.

In effect, the letters functioned as a viewing window on the hidden life of Miles Jesu, a sixty-seven member, developing religious community within the Catholic Church. Since its beginning in 1964, Miles Jesu had dodged the radar of episcopal scrutiny for forty-three years. Like a ping pong ball, the erratic group had bounced its headquarters six times since its founding. Originally established in Phoenix, Arizona, Miles Jesu had finally come to rest in Rome, directly under the nose of Cardinal Ruini.

The letters exposed for the first time ever to an external episcopal supervisor the bizarre inner world of Miles Jesu. Before speculating on their possible impact, Father Tonello compared the letters and noted their distinguishing points of interest.

The hefty letter bore my signature as a priest in the diocese of Rome. Because Miles Jesu superiors were incapable of processing my vital health need, I had gone above their heads. Letting loose an avalanche of thirty-four pages, I desperately appealed to Cardinal Ruini for an exclaustration from Miles Jesu. Mindful of canon law, my letter explained the grave reasons behind the request: emotional immaturity prevented me from assuming adult relationships and responsibilities: the damaging environment of Miles Jesu exacerbated my deteriorating condition.

The next letter pleaded for emergency intervention from Church authorities. A recently erected, consecrated institute in Rome was imploding, resulting in much suffering among its members. This five-page eye-opening letter communicated a distress signal that cried for rescue. It carried the weight of ten signatures, plus two anonymous supporters, all members of Miles Jesu.

Considered together, the letters represented two sides of the same coin: a personal crisis on the one side; an institutional crisis on the other. They projected an image of ecclesial tragedy with causalities strewn about in all directions.

Apart from their different contexts, the letters in unison exposed shocking details of life behind closed doors: sexual abuse, drug addiction, emotional trauma, power abuse, cover up, deception and coercion of recruits, flagrant disregard of cannon law, unqualified and dysfunctional leadership, psychological manipulation, obsessive focus on recruiting and fundraising, an atmosphere of fear, ultra-authoritarian governing, cult dynamics.

By the time Father Tonello finished reading he looked distressed. The shrewd administrator sat there stroking his beard, staring off into space. His eyes darted about as he thought things through. He gently touched his lips and shook his head in dismay. The 'no games' but now head-scratching chancellor had read enough. Still, he couldn't hold himself back from glancing once more at the list of signers.

Shaking his head, he wondered out loud, "Who are these people?"

Whatever the viewing angle of the letters, the signatures said everything. Combined, my exclaustration request and the twelve intervention supporters suggested a veritable cross section of the heart of Miles Jesu. Multi-layered trustworthiness stood out like hard-earned medals on a veteran's chest: eleven past founders of communities, ten past superiors, and eight priests, deacons or seminarians. The ranks numbered five former personal secretaries of the General Director, three past members of the general government, three past provincials, a member of the secret vanguard of the Institute, and an accumulative one hundred and eighty years of experience living in Miles Jesu communities worldwide. The two letters certainly merited credibility.

Tonello moved the pages forward on his desk, like pushing away a half-eaten bowl of beans. As distasteful as it was, the moment of processing had arrived. For the next few days, Tonello would tinker with the two time bombs near his keyboard and chew the fat with Moretti across the hall. The situation required a drastic and quick response.

# CHAPTER TWO

Twenty-eight years ago, apart from my quick farewell that morning the day started just like any other. Mom served Dad his usual breakfast: bacon, sunny side up eggs, buttered toast, instant coffee. It didn't look like much for a big man. Bite by bite, it disappeared from a flimsy TV table as Dad paused and nibbled while he gently rocked away. The TV broke the silence with the same old headlines; this guy killed that guy, bookended with weather reports and morning traffic updates.

I jumped out of bed, splashed water on my face, grabbed my prayer book, and knelt facing the back door. Nobody ever used that forgotten door at this sleepy hour. I lit a red devotional candle, bent to the floor, and rested my head in the palms of my hands. Half way through my routine, the wonderful smell of bacon floated everywhere.

By the time I finished praying, Dad finished eating. Normally, I'd then wait for the front door to close before abandoning my little sanctuary and venturing forth into the living room. I didn't understand why I acted that way, why I avoided Dad. There was an incommunicable distance between Dad and me. It wasn't that we were enemies, we just lacked bonding. We never shared the secret thoughts hidden deep inside of us. Vulnerability and closeness seemed beyond us. So our conversations circled around superficial things, the weather, sports, school, and more of the same.

Paradoxically, while not particularly fond of his presence, I exhausted my energies trying to experience the slightest gesture of his warmth for me. Did he feel any? And if I did happen to experience some fleeting moment of closeness, inexplicable tears would well up in my eyes, wiped away before anyone might notice.

This particular morning, June 21, 1979, the routine rituals made room for a farewell. With closed eyes and alert ears, I crouched in my prayer nook and strained to hear my father walk down the hallway. Soon enough, Dad made his move and I hurried to the front door, appearing as casual as possible. I had to say goodbye to my father. Within a couple of hours, I'd leave forever to join a new Catholic religious order called Miles Jesu.

We met a few feet from the yellow and green spray painted piano in the family room. This masterpiece of unashamed graffiti stood defiantly as the quickest, cheapest, and most uncultured job ever done on a piano. No precision was required for its freehanded chaos. It was Dad's idea, along with the dud hand grenade tacked to the wall and the suspended plastic shark in a nearby aquarium.

"Good morning Dad." I rested my right hand on the highest keys of the piano and felt the ambivalent sentiment of a farewell.

"Oh, hi Andy. I guess today's the big day."

"Yea, I just wanted to say goodbye, Dad." As we embraced, I kept talking. "We're going to drive to Phoenix this morning and from there fly to Washington D.C. in a few days."

"Well, it looks like you know what you are doing."

He knew I was a fiercely independent person and responsible about my comings and goings.

"I hope you keep in touch," he said.

Dad assumed I'd be writing, calling, and coming home for holidays. But I really didn't know what to expect, what kind of rules awaited me.

Failing my expectations, the goodbye of my life vanished in an instant. It seemed that it was gone before it even began. Dad rushed to get to work; I rushed to see him leave. We hugged hurriedly and each confessed, "I love you." Yet, the embrace seemed foreign and I didn't feel love. Some kind of magnetic repulsion frustrated a genuine emotional connection.

Dad turned away, opened the door, and walked out. I felt the goodbye hanging indefinitely. The door clicked shut behind him. I stepped back staring, with a strange sense of emptiness, loneliness, and oddly, freedom.

Bereaving a pleasant future that might have been, Dad headed off to work. Yet, it wasn't work that prompted him to break away so abruptly, but the desire to hide his inner sorrow and the tears in his eyes.

He made his way to a faded blue Toyota mini-truck, climbed inside, and slowly pulled out of the driveway. He clicked on the radio for traffic updates and soon merged with the flow of ants off to work. The morning commute from El Cajon to San Diego Pipe & Supply would take twenty-five minutes.

Dad left tongue tied, but the family room walls echoed how he really felt. My baseball trophies twinkled from their perch. The varsity soccer letter of my first year of high school dangled on the south wall, directly above the bust of John F. Kennedy. Most embarrassing, near the front door so that visitors would notice, Dad had framed and mounted the straight "A" report card of my senior year at El Cajon Valley High School. As Dad had dropped out of high school early to join the army, the exemplary completion of my studies evidently impressed him.

Even though I was the fifth of twelve children, I'd be the son Dad would miss the most. I was an athletic one hundred and sixty-five-pound bundle of energy. I bounced around the house with an agreeable laugh and smile on my face. When he came home from fishing trips, Dad knew he could count on me to clean the fish. Nobody could massage his right foot like I could. I helped around the house without complaining, even washing dishes. He knew he could depend on me to cut up the vegetables for his favorite army-sized soups. Having studied violin for seven years with a master of the San Diego symphony, Dad enjoyed showing me off to visitors. Besides, I knew the art of keeping the garage, his hideaway tree house, neat and clean.

No doubt, Dad already felt the loss of a smart and talented son that morning, and the passing loss of a cheerful and helpful hand. It hurt him to see me throw away so much, motivated thoroughly by piety.

Shortly after Dad drove down Poinciana Street, Fred and Paul eased to a stop and parked at the Sullivan residence. Miles Jesu recruiters. They arrived from Arizona in a dust layered compact car with worn tires and an insect pelted windshield. Gung ho members, these soldiers had driven six hours to escort me to Phoenix. They made the trip together because Miles Jesu didn't permit its members to travel alone, not even take a stroll around a street block without another's presence. I had no idea.

Fred Bach was a tall and handsome young man in his mid-twenties. With baby blue eyes, a playful grin, curly red hair, and politeness running through his veins, he made delightful company. Endowed with graciousness and stocked with an endless repertoire of jokes told with contagious laughter, Fred made friends with anyone.

He'd lived in Miles Jesu for a few years. Before joining, Fred had worked in his family's mortuary business in Chicago. His worldly experience amounted to clipping down Chicago's beautiful Lake Shore Drive in a Cadillac hearse and dealing with embalmed cadavers in a cold basement. No doubt, the business missed Fred's smooth manner with clients. He'd been recruited into Miles Jesu while studying in a seminary.

At twenty-three, Paul Vota was a skinny guy with a protruding nose, an ostrich neck, and no chin whatsoever. But he made up for his looks with an attractive personality. People felt drawn to confide in Paul because of his patient listening, intelligence, and compassion. With a rosary around his neck, nobody doubted where Paul stood religiously.

A handful of years ago, spinning out of the crazy Berkley campus of the 1970s, Paul had been a Californian follower of Guru Maharaji. Mingled with thousands of cult members, he'd submitted himself to a stringent lifestyle in exchange for the knowledge designed to open the third eye of inner awareness, the supposed doorway to perpetual peace. But Paul's sincere quest ended when he realized the deception. Guru Maharaji was not an incarnate god and the Lord of the Universe, but a chubby teenager from India who munched stoically on vegetables and Baskin Robbins ice cream. Disillusioned, Paul left the cult and soon afterwards bumped into Miles Jesu recruiters.

Fred and Paul appeared on my family's doorstep two weeks after I finished high school. Miles Jesu had first wanted to fly me to Washington D.C. almost immediately after graduating. The superiors then realized their mistake. It was better to pick me up at home. I didn't think this was necessary, but Miles Jesu had its reason for the change in plans. Getting such a nice fish so close to the boat, they didn't want to risk losing me. I really didn't see what all the fuss was about.

I didn't realize it at the time, but there had been a protracted strategy to recruit me. After meeting some members of Miles Jesu a year ago, Fred Bach had written or called me every Saturday. He'd been assigned to pursue me with religious tenacity. Because of my good family upbringing, youthful innocence and malleability, and zealous temperament, I was earmarked as a special catch. Miles Jesu at that time represented misfits with nowhere else to go. I had choices of whatever future I wanted. I ardently believed in Miles Jesu and intended to make it great.

Everything about Fred and Paul attracted me. Oversized and outdated clothes testified against worldly interests. Cheap watches reflected a simple and poor life style. Yellow papal leaflets bulging from their pockets declared an apostolic mission to spread the message of orthodoxy. Their speedy arrival regardless of distances beckoned me to a life of adventure. "Join Miles Jesu and see the world," they said.

I believed in everything and wanted it all. Blinded by idealism and determined to make my mark in the world, I couldn't see anything wrong. Fred and Paul towered like spiritual giants pointing the way to great achievements. Their iconic presence alone excited me to follow my dream to become a saint.

While I stuffed my scruffy suitcase in the trunk, Mom lingered on the sidelines, observing. At four feet, nine inches short, she waited with the latest baby slumped over her right arm. Mom was an energetic and slightly graying brunette, smart, pious, orthodox, resourceful and, after a dozen children, a virtual taxi driver by default. She loved a good laugh. Years ago, the surest way to escape a deserved punishment was to make her burst out laughing. Worked every time.

As Fred and Paul finished arranging things in the car, I said goodbye to Mom. "Don't worry about me. They promised I'll enter the seminary within a year or two. It's better to delay studies a bit and become an orthodox priest, rather than study now in a liberal seminary," I summarized and blurted out the important things Miles Jesu had told me. "Miles Jesu needs priests very much and I am an excellent candidate. If God wants me to be a priest nothing can stand in the way of that."

"Yea, right. I hope it all works out that way," she said.

Mom tried to remain calm, but she worried about my life's gamble. Upset, she thought Miles Jesu was a rag-tag group, untested, too small to promise security for me. Over the past few days Mom had expressed her concerns to me and lost every battle. She stood there now, defeated and silent. Her friends thought I was nuts for joining such an unconventional group.

I gave her a distracted hug, waved goodbye to my brothers and sisters, and jumped into the back seat of the car. Only eight siblings lingered that morning. Wasting no time, we pulled out and sped away. I turned to look out the back window for a last memory. Mom stood with a baby in her right arm, waving goodbye with the left. She stood in the midst of a bunch of kids running around. Anthony and Jim waved, innocent lambs who'd follow me and join Miles Jesu years later. I wouldn't suffer homesickness nor experience the blessed feeling of missing someone.

California's Interstate 8 East slid from heaven into hell. Leaving behind a Pacific paradise of palm trees and refreshing ocean breezes, the highway ventured boldly into one of the largest and hottest wastelands of North America. The Sonora was a monster of a desert, eating large chunks of California, Arizona and Mexico, spanning one hundred and twenty thousand square miles.

Four-thousand-foot-high mountains, looking more like enormous piles of blown up rocks, marked the desert's western entrance. We navigated through a curvy passageway and then descended into long distances of flat nothingness that offered little more than sun baked sand, scattered rock, and hot gusts of wind. Creosote bush and hedgehog cactus peppered the terrain at times. Occasional ocotillo cactus sprang from the desert floor like sporadic patches of unkempt whiskers gone wild. I spotted a roadrunner and wondered how it survived.

By the third hour of monotonous driving, the rosary finished and the ebb and flow of conversations settled down. Paul kept his hands on the steering wheel and eyes on the horizon. He pushed onward in a straight shot, barely moving his arms. Fred struggled to stay awake. Finally, he lost the battle. His chin sank into his chest and he fell into a deep sleep. From a comfortable pigeonhole in the back seat I stared out the window and let the wilderness hypnotize me.

I romanticized about what kind of life awaited me: a university degree, a priestly collar, the power to forgive sins with the compassionate wave of a hand. Free at last, it all seemed like a fairy tale about to come true.

But the relentless stream of road lines and pulsating blur of the desert eventually had their way with me. As the car charged toward the future, my mind drifted inward. Unable to hold onto the present moment any longer, my unleashed spirit fled to the past. Without my prompting, the spirit inside knew exactly where it wanted to go. The bittersweet memory of Linda Hughes flooded my unguarded mind.

Linda had been caressing my arm. It felt so good! Her soft touch ran through me like electricity. I had never felt so bodily pampered. How I yearned for more! Her wavy blond hair, her laughing face, her perfume, her admiring presence filled me with pleasure. At fifteen, I had felt the fire of passion for the first time, and it enraptured me.

That same summer evening, Mom had been peeling potatoes in the kitchen when I arrived home. My feelings had burst forth so intensely that I dared to talk about Linda. In a purple flowered apron, Mom leaned against the counter and listened patiently, as she dug the eyes out of a few potatoes.

Following my partial and cautious sharing, Mom's response implied her role as the moral compass of the family.

"Andy, you can't see her anymore. That kind of love is for marriage." My whole world came crashing down. My head started to spin. "You'll have to wait for marriage for that." I didn't know what to say.

"Are you ready to get married?" she asked.

Absorbed in the shock that I couldn't see Linda again, I didn't answer. Mom then tried to soften things a bit by encouraging me about the future.

"There are a lot more fish in the stream."

"But I want to have Linda as my friend now."

I walked away stunned. Mom's "no" was absolute. She had tried to help me, but it was more than my emotions could bear.

For three nights I curled up in a fetal position and cried myself to sleep. It felt like my soul had turned inside out. Torrents of uncontrollable sobs shook me. Fortunately, my bed sat in the family room where nobody could hear me. Protected by darkness, I repeatedly begged Jesus to let me marry Linda and have my own family. I didn't know how else to cope with the death of a precious relationship, the death of love for me. I lay there crying, beneath a National Geographic photo of a pigmy with a bamboo shoot piercing his nose.

Suddenly, the abrupt cackle of the radio snapped me to attention. Paul turned on the radio and started a hunt for classical music. Rock and roll wasn't allowed. Fred adjusted slightly and kept on snoozing. Zooming to the present, I felt relieved that nobody discovered my dreamy distraction. Just to be safe, I sank casually to the left corner of the back seat and closed my eyes, pretending to sleep.

But haunting memories of Linda kept me engaged. The momentary shuffle of images opened old wounds. The passing scenes reminded me that I had buried alive a profound yearning of my soul. I really wanted to marry and have a family. Journeying toward the priesthood now, I never understood how to handle that desire. It seemed I was called to the priesthood, but I didn't see how I could last without married life. Finding no solution to my dilemma, I made an act of faith in Jesus. I would pursue the priesthood, trusting that Miles Jesu would help sort out and resolve my interior conflict.

The mysterious seeds of self-destruction were already at work within me. A lack of paternal bonding, a drive to achieve great things for the sake of acceptance, a frustration of intimacy signaled psychological and emotional foreboding.

Several days later, I entered the front door of the Miles Jesu headquarters in Triangle, Virginia. Situated thirty-five miles south of Washington, D.C.

and just north of the Quantico Marine Corps Base, it was little more than a small house wedged between too many trees. With laundry hanging from a makeshift line in the backyard and overgrowth delineating the border of the property, the headquarters blended with other cheap houses in the neighborhood. Miles Jesu had suggested an image of something bigger in their literature, something institutional, not a shoebox lit up by fireflies.

Within the hour, I met all the members of Miles Jesu, all nine. Anticipating my arrival, a group of happy faces greeted me with gusto. With strapping hugs, everybody tried to make me feel at home. I learned that Fred and Paul were not the only members with colorful backgrounds. Tony had risked his life as an ex-gang knifer from East Los Angeles. Tom had rejected his Beverly Hills upbringing in favor of hitchhiking across the world. Omar had entered America as a Mexican immigrant. Steve had been a genuine atheist. Mary joined as a widow. Patricia, Mary's daughter, had worked as a legal secretary. Everyone had a unique story.

My first impressions of Miles Jesu doubled as first attractions. I felt especially drawn to the members. Each person seemed content. I sensed sincerity and generous heartedness from everyone. Equally impressive, the atmosphere imparted seriousness about high spiritual ideals. A simple and tough life style reflected this. Everything felt perfect. I could see myself pursuing the challenge of sainthood alongside these like-minded friends.

Running with superficial perceptions, I didn't subject Miles Jesu to a thorough evaluation. Had I done so, basic facts would have raised a red flag.

The Miles Jesu men's community had existed for fifteen years and now totaled three professed members and four recruits. The founding members had inexplicably fled. The headquarters had transferred recently to a third new diocese. The constitutions remained unfinished and experimental. By-laws still needed to be determined and written. A single college degree existed among the group, except for the sole priest who temporarily served as a member of another religious order. With no official seminarians, there were only three first year philosophy students. Although Miles Jesu promoted itself as an institute for lay professionals, nobody had a job. The most recent vocation entered a few years ago. Everything operated by begging. In short, underneath the surface of an enthusiastic facade, Miles Jesu barely survived in a radically undeveloped condition.

I knew some of the facts; others escaped my attention. The obvious concerns were adorned in positive terms. "Yes, of course we are small," the superiors would say. "That's because we're elite. We're more demanding than your normal wishy-washy seminary."

Regardless of the embryonic state of Miles Jesu, the stunted growth, reservations about joining didn't register. Had indoctrination already taken hold in my brain? I wanted a Mount Everest sized challenge in life. Yes, silly me. It never crossed my mind that Miles Jesu lacked the competence to recognize and cure my emotional immaturity. I assumed the group had the know-how to discern a vocation.

# CHAPTER THREE

By fall, Miles Jesu had packed up a U-Haul moving van and abandoned Triangle, Virginia. It now operated out of two closely situated properties at the foot of Virginia's beautiful Blue Ridge Mountains. The superiors wanted to sink roots near Christendom College, a conservative Catholic college near Front Royal, Virginia. Members could then study and cherry-pick vocations on campus.

Autumn crept around the newly purchased properties with an awesome show of color. Accustomed to unvarying palm trees all year around, I'd never experienced a conspicuous season change. Rusty brown oaks, red maples, orange birches, and green-needled evergreens flaunted their foliage. Lush hues of gold, purple, and pale yellow added superfluous detail. The cool crisp air, yelping dogs, and distant woodpeckers finished the job. I felt that a colorful jungle had swallowed me, far too claustrophobic for my open spaced tastes. But absolutely beautiful.

The women's property consisted of four separate red buildings tucked away behind tightly packed trees. Any passer-by had to squint to see the residence from the road. Three single-story wood constructions sat there in the midst of a sea of foliage. A fourth building had a little more substance; it included a mildewed basement. Under the open air, a frayed wooden walkway weaved around the buildings, creating the sense that the structures belonged together.

A ten-minute walk away, panting up a steep incline, the men's house roosted high on a hill with a breathtaking view of Virginia's treetops. Other than that, every imaginable headache explained the property's dirt-cheap price. Encircled by waist-high brush, the two-story camouflage-green house festered as a forsaken empty shell. The building lacked plumbing, running water, insulation, drywall, flooring, a heating system, a kitchen, and bathrooms. The basement still needed digging, a lot of digging. A well still needed sinking. Fortunately, the unfinished building had electricity and naked light bulbs hanging from rafters.

After a few hours of mind-numbing wood chopping, I whacked the block resolutely with the ax and left the long handle frozen in the air. That ought to be enough. While calculating the woodpile at my feet, I dug into my back pocket and pulled out the list of things to do. Scanning the day's priorities, I mentally checked off each completed item. I'd finished the envelope-stuffing job for a fund appeal mailing, the lifeblood of any struggling non-profit. The pipes, sinks, tiles, and bags of grout had been moved to the imagined bathroom area. I'd re-stacked the two by fours, correctly this time. The chainsaw now rested in its place, refilled, cleaned, and sharpened. So far so good. I'd pass the scrutiny of tomorrow's business meeting and the corrections for unsatisfactory work. I just needed to stack some firewood and get to the women's house for a formation meeting with Paul.

The stroll down the hill gave me time to think about my situation in life. An assigned companion and an impossible load of work usually checked my freedom to reflect. I now had a rare moment to myself.

A couple weeks past, a freak October storm dumped ten inches of snow on the Blue Ridge and left behind broken branches everywhere. Surveying the damage, I now questioned my life as though hit by an unexpected storm. Miles Jesu was not what I had imagined. I felt like the prided work-horse on a poor farm. While three lucky guys left home every day to study, I stayed behind washing their dishes. What was I doing with my life? How long would this situation last? I didn't come to Miles Jesu to lay cement and dig plumbing lines. The temptation of leaving Miles Jesu replayed in my brain.

As I walked down the hill, my unwatched mind gained momentum and wondered. The delay of studies rubbed me the wrong way. And there were other things that didn't feel right. The superior assigned Fred as my spiritual director. Although I liked the guy, I preferred to choose someone capable of giving educated advice. But my wish challenged community customs. All incoming and outgoing mail passed through the hands of the superior. Receiving two-week-old mail, already opened and examined, didn't seem right either. Strange. I practically corresponded only with my mother. And why the insistence on tucking the T-shirt in the underwear? What was that all about? Couldn't I decide how to tuck in my own shirt? Who really cares if your T-shirt was inside or outside your underwear? Turning to the right, the women's driveway stretched ahead. The sight of Paul in the distance made my thoughts run away inside of me.

Zipped up for the chill of an outdoor class, Paul sat at the broken picnic table in the front yard of the women's house. Whenever I sat there, I'd leave with curled red paint chips clinging to my butt. Motionless and focused, Paul's eyes flitted about as he skimmed class material. Gently swaying trees allowed sunshine to frolic on the tattered book in his hands, a tome falling to pieces from scrupulous usage. As instructed by the superior, class consisted of reading and applying a few pages of *The Practice of Perfection and Christian Virtue*.

This three-volume work stood out as the "Bible" of Miles Jesu formation. Indeed, evening prayers allowed for one sentence from a Gospel, but a standard chapter from Father Rodriguez, the highly esteemed Spanish Jesuit. Published in 1609, followed by twenty-five editions in Spain, the work aimed at teaching the basics of virtue to Jesuit neophytes.

After a quick greeting and some small talk about the woodpile up the hill, we brushed away the leaves on the table and parked opposite each other on cold benches. Wasting no time, Paul handed me the book and indicated where to begin reading. As required by formality, I started by announcing the name of the book and its author: "A reading from *The Practice of Perfection and Christian Virtue*, by Alphonsus Rodriguez." Today's class covered a few ideas on family relations and obedience.

Perceiving the family as a threat to the religious vocation, I read that Father Rodriguez advocated a strict separation, physically and emotionally, from parents, siblings, and relatives. He taught that the religious should "break off all communication" with the family. He viewed visits home as "dangerous for our salvation." Logically then, "no visits" should be permitted. Father Rodriguez even urged that the religious "reduce natural sentiments" toward the family.

After reading aloud a few pages, Paul asked me to restate Rodriguez's main points in my own words. Easy. Rodriguez laid down everything in black and white. Seeing that I grasped things well enough, Paul then reached over the table and closed the book. He then proceeded to apply the principles at hand to Miles Jesu's rules on family relations.

It didn't take long to summarize the fundamental practice of the community: Miles Jesu categorically prohibited family visits. Members could not visit home for weddings, family reunions, vacations, illnesses, or holidays. Exceptions allowed for rare fundraising trips if they promised good money, and the deaths of parents. Only parents. In this later case, a member visited home for the shortest amount of time possible, accompanied by an assigned travel companion. Miles Jesu wanted its members to live in affection without parents, even without the desire to visit them.

These regulations and ideals applied to everyone in the house.

Admittedly, Paul did his best to soften the blow of the rules. He made the effort to present everything with scriptural grounding and examples from the lives of the saints, relying upon Rodriguez to tie everything together as the practical authority. Yet, regardless of all the couching and garnishing, explanations and warnings, the unbending rules still seemed unnecessarily strict. Nonetheless, hearing that the customs reflected the best traditions of the Catholic Church for consecrated life, I accepted everything with little reservation.

Once we finished the material on the family, we continued with Father Rodriguez's nuts and bolts explanation of obedience. Better than chopping wood, I was eager to sit there and keep learning. Paul found his prearranged bookmark in volume III and parted the pages. Short on time, he suggested we cover a few essential paragraphs.

This reading targeted the preeminent practice of religious obedience. Father Rodriquez held that the religious must obey with an indifferent and compliant disposition, "with no will or judgment," with "no eyes to observe curiously superiors' actions." The religious must obey as if he had "no feeling," like a "dead body," like a "staff in the hands of the superior."

But even this high degree of submission to commands still fell short of the goal. The religious must submit "both will and understanding to that of the superior." He must "let his discretion be to have none at all whilst he obeys; and let his wisdom and prudence never appear in matters of obedience." As such, Rodriguez advocated not only prompt and resistance-free obedience, but intellectual conformity to the superior's personal reasoning and judgments. Blind obedience.

From the corner of my eye, I noticed Paul checking his watch. He had five minutes to wrap up class and dash to another meeting. Paul asked me to stop reading and straightforwardly applied things to obedience in Miles Jesu. As our legitimate Church authority, Father Alphonsus Maria Duran sat in the place of God. He therefore must be obeyed in all things but sin, in the exact manner Father Rodriguez outlined. Cut and dried, no additional context, no further distinctions followed.

The sun had passed and time had run out. After a closing prayer, Paul scurried for the mildewed basement and I skipped up the hill to work on dinner, happy to understand obedience.

That autumn of my first year in Miles Jesu, I experienced a dozen similar classes. Since Miles Jesu lacked structured formation programs, my picnic readings served as an improvised solution. Class themes emerged from Father Duran, whenever he thought a principle or custom indispensable to me. This slipshod arrangement resulted in spontaneous classes designed to heighten conformity to Miles Jesu. Yet, even this short-lived education abruptly terminated when Father Duran's attention turned to other matters of importance. The hand in mouth urgencies of work inundated my time and classes disappeared.

I popped out of bed on a chilled morning in late autumn and monotonous routines took over. While most of the guys stripped their beds, I grabbed a stuffed, fluffy black sock in Fred's underwear drawer. Finding a semi-private corner and pulling off my shirt, I extracted the knotted whip and stung twenty obligatory lashes on my back. The scourging of Christ flashed and faded in my mind. A rushed shave with a borrowed razor followed. After looping my tie and poking my arms through an out of style coat, I stepped outside the men's front door with a cup of water and a toothbrush loaded with baking soda and salt. Father Duran had banned toothpaste, aftershave, shampoo, perfume, and underarm deodorant, preaching with fire on the prohibitions a few days ago. Such commercial and non-essential niceties opened the doorway to the devil.

Daily Mass usually took place down the hill in the women's living room, transformed into a homey chapel. Two little white pigs frenzied near the front door, at least that's what I called the pathetic dogs, and got corrected for it. Everybody carefully avoided them while entering the house because the affection-starved creatures rolled over and peed when caressed. The more excited sprayer somehow had earned the name *Dulcinea*, Don Quixote's imagined princess. Ironically, the name signified a sweetheart hopelessly loved.

As morning prayers erupted in the chapel, properly in Latin, Father Duran appeared in the adjacent dining room. Underneath the eclipse of an economy bulb, vestments spread the extent of a chipped secondhand table. Latin echoed in the background as Father began vesting for his sacred duties.

Forty-eight at the time, Father Duran stood at five feet, ten inches tall. An action man, he maintained an outwardly fit body, not due to an exercise regimen, but attributed to a high-strung metabolism. The priest carried a full head of almost black hair, vainly free of the tiniest thread of grey, but needing a trim. His well-proportioned face included slightly protruding lips and dead-pan black eyes that devoured all color. Loud black rim glasses didn't help. Oddly enough, his fingers stood out, long and elegant, like portrayed on the hands of the saints in Eastern icons.

Unwinding a black rosary worn on his left hand, Duran took hold of the top vestment. Stretching out the amice, an oblong of white linen with long apes sewn on the corners, Father Duran ceremoniously touched it upon his head, kissed it, mumbled something in Latin, and wrapped it over his shoulders. It symbolized the helmet of salvation to guard against the attacks of Satan. Many priests no longer bothered with the amice. Not Duran. He scrupulously observed the rubrics of Holy Mass, unless a housefly hovered around the altar. Then, he'd pull out all stops and order an altar boy to hunt down the menace and kill it, regardless of all unorthodox appearances.

The smell of boiling pinto beans and a donated, freezer-burned ham hock floated through the house. A nice break from oatmeal. Father bent and tugged at the hem of his alb, a flowing white robe signifying purity of heart. A magnetic charm had attracted me to Father Duran. Was it his apparent self-assurance that lured me? Perhaps the magnetism sprang from his enthusiasm, and my idealism and father hunger. The dream of marching through the world saving vast numbers of souls united us. But our raw impulses differed. He seemed to be pushed forward by fearing hell, I by wanting to belong. The priest yanked the cincture tight about his waist, the cord of braided wool expressing the restraint of sensual desire.

Removing the crumpled handkerchief inconspicuously stuffed up his sleeve, Father Duran waded through the chapel's swinging door. He approached the altar, an old drafting table, bent over and kissed it, and stepped back to blow his nose. I idolized the man as a knight in shining armor. He radiated the air of a hardened Spanish warrior who had proven himself in distant battles long ago.

The passionate blood of Spain charged proudly through the veins of Father Alphonsus Duran, the compelling leader of Miles Jesu. Breathing the ragtag tenacity of Pelayo and bravado of Cortez, the heroes of Spain's illustrious past colored his intense temperament and radical governing style. A true underdog, Pelayo stubbornly resisted the climatic onslaught of the Moors at Covadonga in 718. The seven-hundred-year war to reconquer Spain began from Pelayo's impenetrable rocky foxhole. Eight-hundred years later, Cortez launched his offensive against the Aztec Empire by burning his eleven ships at Vera Cruz. This left his five hundred men with no other option than to conquer tens of thousands of man-eating fighters or die trying. Imbued with such marvels of Spanish glory, Father Duran lived in an atmosphere of unconditional drive, no matter the wounds.

As the shockwaves of Pope John Paul II's recent visit to D.C. still reverberated, Father Duran preached on unconditional loyalty to the Pope this morning. Shunning notes and comfortably wearing his authority, he offhandedly insulted, praised, challenged, and frightened all in the same breath. Outwardly, sparkling like a saint, he aptly persuaded fidelity. Everyone welcomed the general's call to arms.

The sermon kept going and going. With fire in his eyes, like a knight riding the wave of a righteous fight, Duran beat back the Pope's enemies. That was the image of Duran. But what personal mystery hid behind appearances? What made the man tick? I had no idea of the deep undercurrents of his lengthy haranguing, how life's blows had gradually chiseled Duran into a warrior. The untold story lay buried beneath the subtle influence of Spanish culture.

From different angles, the Spanish Civil War had pounded and shaped Father Duran into a soldier-priest long before Miles Jesu existed. The brutalities of war had stretched their tentacles over his young life and impressed their indelible character in his psyche.

From July 1936 to April 1939, little Alphonso experienced the Spanish Civil War as a five to eight-year-old. The chaos of the war, the bombings, the creeping encirclement of Madrid, the dreadful presence of the communists lead to Alphonso's placement with his grandparents in Avila, Spain, tragically estranged from his own father and mother. Ninety kilometers northwest of Madrid, Avila fell within the Nationalist zone by the fall of 1936, making it a relatively safe place. Once the insanity of the war had subsided, including the execution of his grandfather by the communists, Alphonso's parents returned to pick up their child. So traumatized, the boy didn't even remember his own father and mother. At a critical moment of life, parental bonding had been sacrificed for physical safety, leaving Alphonso a living casualty of the war.

As he grew into adulthood, the socio-cultural environment of post war Spain apparently militarized the meaning of Catholicism for Alphonso Duran. In 1937, the country's bishops had denounced the Spanish Civil War as an attack "to eliminate the Catholic religion in Spain." The war's rage had martyred almost seven thousand priests, religious, nuns, and seminarians. By 1939, General Francisco Franco, a savior-figure for many Catholics at that time, had violently seized power to end the madness. He then ruled with authoritarian style. Alphonso developed in this post war environmental classroom, where conservative Catholicism emphasized strength, perseverance, loyalty, and unconditional commitment. Assertive qualities rose to the top of Alphonso's list of values, along with the conviction that authoritarian governing worked best.

Duran fiddled with the rosary on his hand. A rush of dismay swept through him and the sermon took an amazing twist.

He paused and surveyed the chapel. "There's Andy!" Duran suddenly locked on to me. Wild digression seized him. With a firm voice and icy stare straight at me, Duran aimed to impress.

"Andy, do you think you'll be saved?"

My heart jumped. Everybody stared at me. Dead silence. He repeated himself, "Do you honestly think that you'll avoid hell?" "I think so," I said.

"You think so?"

"Yes." Trained to think and respond properly, I correctly acknowledged the doubt of my salvation, and said very little.

"Andy, you are close to losing your soul! You can't hide your thoughts before God, maybe before men, but not God. Not before me either! When the Blessed Mother shakes her mantle you'd better be holding on tightly."

My mind raced to the conversation I had with Fred yesterday. Seeing the dream of the priesthood slipping through my fingers, I'd finally decided to quietly leave Miles Jesu and let Fred know my thoughts. From that moment of disclosure, I'd been searching for a way back home. How much did Father Duran know? Was he drilling me by coincidence or did Fred tell him I was planning to leave? Duran and Fred spent long hours together.

He kept pressing, "Andy, watch out! The devil is playing with you." I looked down, grasping my violin, trying to protect myself with it. Duran recounted how his superior had called him a "dog," and warned me not to allow anyone to destroy my vocation. Abandoning his ideas about papal loyalty, an aroused bulldog now, Duran pounded away at the heaven or hell consequences of leaving the family and following the vocation and persevering unto death.

As he preached, publicly exposing the risks to my salvation, Duran didn't relate the story of his own vocation. Family blood convulsed incessantly when Alphonso left home at eighteen to enter the Claretian seminary. The Congregation had idolized the rugged missionary detached from family ties, sent to wherever, never to visit father and mother again. The Duran household never recovered from Alphonso's vocation. His mother stopped singing in the house. Lamenting the boy's existence, his father recklessly snapped at Alphonso, "I wish you had never been born!"

From a pious viewpoint, seminary life deepened the imprint of war upon Alphonso. Awash with anecdotes, heroic stories, and survivors who had escaped death, the seminary radiated the spirit and memory of the martyrs. The rooms, books, conversations, and excursions bathed in the spiritual presence of Spain's latest heroes, including two-hundred and seventy-one Claretian martyrs. The seminarians assimilated a martyr-copy spirituality characterized by austerity, unyielding discipline, enduring enthusiasm, and radical availability in the face of death, values that Miles Jesu would inherit and stress years later. Young Alphonso lived his seminary days with the martyr's death song ever on his lips: "Jesus, you know well, I am your soldier: ever at your side I will fight."

Duran relaxed his grip on the podium and the barrage abated. His holy fit exhausted itself and an awkward pause ensued. The priest made the sign of the cross and ended the sermon. Father took a few steps to the altar. I distractedly announced the offertory song, feeling like Judas.

By the time I'd climbed out of my embarrassment, Mass was almost over and Father Duran stood at the drafting table cleaning the sacred vessels. In the flat of his hand he drew the gold-plated paten six inches from his eyes. Light reflected in his face as Duran squinted from multiple angles, moving around the elegant plate and examining it, trying to make sure that no Eucharistic particle remained. After licking a spot and rubbing with a corporal in another area, Father set the paten on the chalice, placed the pall, and covered everything with a veil and burse. He then knelt down, closed his eyes, and lead thanksgiving prayers. He petitioned God for the grace "to fight and not to heed the wounds," quoting the Spanish soldier saint, Ignatius of Loyola.

If the Spanish Civil War forged the soldier at the altar, ten exhausting Cursillo years seasoned Duran's methods of influencing people. Spiritual guerrilla warfare.

By 1958, the toddler soldier-priest arrived in the Claretian's recently organized Western province in the United States. Itching with a dissatisfied goad to establish the Spanish Congregation globally, moving their pawn forward, superiors placed the newly ordained priest in the desert of Phoenix, Arizona.

Gifted with the art of rhetorical persuasion, Father Duran soon gravitated to preaching Cursillos. The Cursillo was a new retreat movement within the Church designed to bolster faith and stir apostolic zeal among mediocre Catholics. Father Duran's Patton-like rallying infused exactly what a proficient Cursillo required, an intense and swaying personality. Thousands of conversions followed. This was something Duran was good at: moving listeners to repent and turn to God.

Chiefly sketched by a Spanish psychologist, the Cursillo advanced a leadership instruction shrewdly designed to orchestrate conversion from behind the scenes. Before long, Father Duran had mastered the tricks of the trade.

Cursillo thinking preferred men to women and leadership types to simple souls with commonplace capacities. Father Duran assimilated the inclination of targeting natural leaders and pounding them into apostles. He learned how to hide informants and instigators in a crowd to report on retreat participants and artificially shape group dynamics. By teasing and embarrassing, Father Duran perfected the technique of constraining personal commitments. Late at night with his inner core of loyalists, he discovered how to spot and encircle key persons, hand tailor plans of subtle manipulation, and assign leaders to induce changes of heart. Duran's Cursillos included spying and reporting on whoever went to confession. The vital end of spiritual conversion justified his propriety of method.

Mass was just about over now. Father Duran stood up, extended his arms, and imparted the final blessing. At this point, the Catholic faithful of the world usually make a sign of the cross, genuflect, and exit the church. Father Duran's unbending piety promoted an exception. He charged ahead praying for strength and protection in battle, "Holy Michael the Archangel defend us in battle. Be our protection against the wickedness and snares of the devil." He kept going, asking God to cast Satan into hell.

Poor Alphonso. He championed high spiritual ideas but life had weighed him down with excessive baggage. He wanted to do worlds of good in his subjectively saintly way but could only jump forward and backward, bound by twisted human roots. Throughout his life, tragedies and boot camps had choked off sensual feelings of softness and tender love. Instead, deliberate force came to characterize nearly everything he did, against himself and for the presumed benefit of others. Beneath his conquering flag of religious salvation, free choice lay bleeding as collateral damage upon a battlefield.

Father Duran's life experiences saturated the Miles Jesu formative environment. I therefore swam in a milieu where love meant achieving and not receiving; willing regardless of feeling. Duran's kind of love invariably resulted in forcing any kind of good on someone, regardless of that person's disposition to receive it.

After Mass the community filed into the dining room for coffee, bread, and a bowl of beans. Due to an urgent begging trip to Front Royal, nine miles away, Steve Purcell and I were excused from the morning business meeting that followed breakfast. We hoped to return with a carload of flawed produce and expired packages of anything. Meat would be nice.

The prided twenty-three-year-old convert from atheism, Steve somehow supported enormous glasses on a miniature nose, making him look like a cartoon character. I jumped into the car as he slowly revved the engine, simultaneously raising his brows, bulging his eyes, and unrolling a mischievous grin. Then he slowly turned to me and snorted like a pig. No matter how often he did that, I always cracked up laughing. I appreciated Steve's attempt to make me laugh after my shake up in the chapel. He itched for a breather, too. No surprise, he practically lived in the basement, pitted against a rickety printing press that chewed up more paper than it printed.

I looked forward to the errand. A light rain added an extra blessing. The "dust bomb," an old Dodge Dart, tended to fill up with a cloud of dust whenever driven on a dry dirt road. Patching the gaping hole in the trunk was frowned upon as an unnecessary expense. This morning's drizzle and damp soil promised a dust-free ride.

The second we rolled, Tony Barrios flew out of the women's office building, whistling and yelling. Still able to sprint when necessary, his short ex-knifer legs whisked him to the car. With curly black hair and a banana nose, his eyes permanently drooped between open and shut. He bent down and with a half-awake stare found my face through the window.

"You guys aren't going anywhere. Father Duran wants to talk to Andy right now."

Tony smiled at me and my stomach turned. As I stepped out of the car, he laughed.

"Andy, just think of it like going to the dentist."

Father Duran waited in his mildewed basement office. He hated waiting. I already knew that. I hurried. An elongated figurine of Don Quixote stood gallantly upon his desk, hovering over the latest matters of importance. A letter from a bishop sat dead center; a new yellow card design lay to the right. He wanted its message printed immediately and distributed on the streets, as soon as possible. Two things stood out on the wall. There hung an elegantly framed photo of Claretian seminarian martyrs. To the right of the photo shouted a conspicuous sign written in fine chirography. It read, "God is first. My neighbor is second. I am third."

I knocked on the door and Father Duran answered, "Yes?"

"It's Andy."

"Come in."

Upon entering, he motioned for me to sit near Omar Salido, the

Mexican immigrant, currently Father Duran's right hand man. A witness meant a serious meeting. I felt like a troublemaker entering the principal's office, nervous as hell and expecting the worst.

Adept at navigating hundreds of similar meetings, Father Duran opened with a bolt from the blue.

"Andy, this meeting is to help you. We should never trust ourselves. We need others to help us understand ourselves and see clearly. I understand that you want to leave your vocation and go home. You should go home today. You can pack your bags right away and Omar will take you to the airport."

Did he really mean that? I squirmed in my wobbly chair and a creak pierced the numbing silence. Dazed by the bombshell, freedom passed before my eyes. The situation required a mere "yes" for everything to change. But my agreement was choked by something inside of me that resisted self-assertion. I didn't want to displease Father. Respecting him, too much, I floundered. A "yes" couldn't find its way through my lips.

Gripped by an appeasing movement within, I impulsively asked about studies. Skirting around my desire to leave, I politely complained,

"I came to study. I think God wants me to be a priest and I don't see how this is possible if I don't study."

I didn't mention I had entered Miles Jesu under the clear impression I would study for the priesthood. He knew that. "But who said that you will not study?" "Nobody." I didn't want an argument.

Duran softened and urged me to think things through.

"Andy, what good will studies do when you die and appear before God's judgment? He will only ask if you had loved him and did his will. Without love, you can go to hell with your diploma. The Blessed Mother went to heaven without a diploma." I was silent.

"Do you want to go to hell with a diploma?"

"No."

He began again.

"You will make a fine priest. Miles Jesu needs priests. If we had the money, everyone would study. You just need to wait your turn. Don't make a serious mistake with your life. Be careful! Think about what you are doing."

Sweating now, I objected.

"It doesn't seem that Miles Jesu is my vocation. I think it's time for me to leave and start my studies somewhere else."

I'd wished to find a non-confrontational way to leave, but the unexpected meeting made a mess of things.

Omar came to life. "Ah, starting studies somewhere else may not be as easy as you think. If you can't make it here, you probably won't make it in a seminary, or even be accepted."

"Saint John Bosco began his vocation with the Franciscans and later left to become a diocesan priest," I replied. I'd read a lot about Saint Bosco, my favorite saint.

Father Duran was skeptical. "I don't know about that. I'd like to read about that," he said, insinuating that I was wrong. He then recounted the signs of my Miles Jesu vocation, how I had felt called, how I'd already received an abundance of graces through the community.

He added, "But you're not John Bosco."

Admittedly, some of his words seemed to make sense. My weak persistence incited him. With stalemate in sight, a torrent of zeal flooded Duran's face. He wasn't about to lose me. He shifted restlessly and warned me about hell. Duran then plunged into a diatribe on the frightening, eternal risks of abandoning my vocation.

The meeting's reasonable start up now yielded to deliberate emotional and psychological blows. Alarmed, Duran emphasized Christ's admonition not to look back after following the vocation. He pummeled me with Saint Paul's exhortation to continue in the original calling. He warned that Saint Jerome linked salvation to persevering in the vocation. Examples gushed from Alphonsus Rodriguez.

Stories underlined the dangers of turning away from my vocation. Duran stressed how the rich young man of the Gospel probably lost his soul, precisely because the man didn't accept his vocation. He told the story of Robespierre, who'd abandoned his pursuit of monastic life by visiting home at Christmas time, against the advice of the superior. Subsequently, Robespierre, whoever he was, became the rebel responsible for the French Revolution's bloody reign of terror. Duran spouted this loudly, waving his finger in the air.

Fire leaped when the priest spoke of a member who'd left Miles Jesu three years ago. Shortly after forsaking his vocation, Patrick Walsh had suffered a diving accident that left him paralyzed from the waist down. Now the wild Spaniard cautioned that a similar fate awaited me if I should reject God.

"Is that what you want Andy? Do you want to leave your vocation and become paralyzed?"

"If I leave Miles Jesu to study for the priesthood it doesn't mean that I'd become paralyzed."

"Don't be too sure of it!"

The meeting carried on for a long time, most of it a relentless exhortation by Duran. Little by little, the hour-long meeting had sown enough guilt, fear, and doubt to wear me down. Father Duran fought like a matador, jabbing and weakening my resolve. I was no match for his expertise with the cape and sword. By the end, I felt uncertain about what to do and lacked the emotional backbone to charge. Then I thought up a silly resolution to my dilemma. No, not silly, tragic:

"Father, in Miles Jesu I've learned that God speaks through the superior and blesses obedience. So, if you command me to remain in Miles Jesu, the will of God would be clear and I could please God by obeying."

I don't know how this came out of my mouth, but felt it was a virtuous approach to resolve my uncertainty. I had no idea of the immaturity and ignorance that fed into my appeasing sincerity.

Welcoming my childish theology, my mistaken view of obedience, Father Duran accepted the suggestion and without the slightest scruple acted upon it. Proceeding as if everything was normal, without hesitation, he said, "Andy, then I command you under obedience to remain in Miles Jesu. That's right. God blesses obedience. God will bless your openness and generosity with him."

At that moment, I felt heaven intervening and coming to my rescue.

"Fine, then it's clear. I will obey and stay," I said.

What had I done? The matador stood aside and watched me plunge the sword in my heart.

Peace appeared in my soul. With a renewed trust in the wisdom and judgment of Father Duran, I believed I'd experienced the voice of God regarding my vocation. We hugged each other and he encouraged me to be faithful. While his warm body welcomed me, the gaze of the martyrs upon the wall congratulated me for dying to myself. Father was happy with the meeting's outcome, just as I was relieved. Reassured of my vocation, I folded my chair and left the room. Now unburdened, I bounced up the stairs, looking forward to a day of begging.

A few days later, in a chapel clouded with sweet smelling incense, evening prayers lingered with a round of self-accusations and penances.

The public confessions revealed nothing out of the ordinary. Steve Purcell accused himself of daydreaming during the evening reading of Rodriguez. For a penance, he had to lie at the doorway of the chapel and let people walk over him. Tom Cahill, the bushy head from Beverly Hills, accused himself of wearing a tattered shirt. Father Duran lost his patience, reprimanded him, stated that poverty doesn't mean dressing like a bum, and ordered that he sew the shirt before wearing it again. It was a recurring annoyance. Other accusations included allowing a candle to burn out, not keeping custody of the eyes, and breaking a coffee cup. Each penitent received an admonition and humiliating penance from a voice veiled in fog.

I held my breath and jumped into the pool: "I accuse myself before almighty God, the Blessed Virgin Mary, all the angels and saints, and you my brothers and sisters, of irresponsibility." With a contrite tone, the correct formula had to precede the self-accusation.

"Irresponsibility? That could mean anything. How were you irresponsible?" Duran asked.

"I didn't feed the dogs on time," I answered.

As if he'd heard something entirely different, Father Duran stared at the tabernacle, shook his head, and began to philosophize about old women and their cats. He couldn't stomach the inordinate affections women lavished upon their cats, complaining that the pampered animals got more love than human beings. Father Duran stressed that animals were created to help man save his soul, and should serve that purpose alone.

The digression landed with a warning about the dogs. "Andy, if dogs eat late, it's not going to kill them. Be careful about replacing human beings with dogs. God wants you to love your brothers and sisters here in this chapel, not the dogs outside."

He then gave what he thought an appropriate penance, an expression of love, "For your penance, you can kiss the feet of Paul, Tom, and Pat." As they sat and slid their feet forward, I crouched down and pecked the first shoe.

The instant I finished, Father Duran asked everyone to stand up. He had something important to announce. Coughing and clearing his throat, he said, "It was unanimously decided today to appoint Andy as the vocation director. He has the experience of organizing the best youth group in the country."

Actually, I had merely tried to make a Miles Jesu youth group back in El Cajon and it miserably failed. Father Duran continued. "After organizing everybody's possible vocation list, Andy will use his experience and enthusiasm to coordinate a letter writing campaign for vocations."

As Duran proceeded to buoy up the plan, I stood there dumbfounded. Duran asked, "Omar, what do you think of Andy's appointment?"

"I think it's a very good idea. Miles Jesu needs vocations."

Duran turned next to another supporter, "Fred, what do you think?"

"I'm sure Andy's going to do a great job. He has the enthusiasm to make things work."

Duran's inquiries received the expected answers from docile faces. Then he turned to me with a blessing. Lightly resting his hand upon mine, looking me in the eyes, he said, "Andy, God wants to use you for great things. The Blessed Mother wants to bring many vocations to Miles Jesu. God will bless your faithfulness. Andy, believe me when I tell you that thousands of souls are waiting for you."

Feeling God's pleasure, I believed that the appointment blessed my decision to remain in Miles Jesu. A wave of gratitude swept over me and I smiled. I finally could do something important. The goodnight hymn to the Blessed Mother resounded in the air; my mind fantasized about the upcoming work.

Although I didn't realize it at the time, the appointment was intended to stabilize my vocation. Father Duran knew the Jesuit stratagem for squeezing out a commitment. As a teenage recruit of a Jesuit run youth group in Madrid, Duran had learned long ago how to seize the interest and dedication of youth group members. Waning attraction demanded a prompt appointment of importance, a coveted title, a call to arms. This technique of human management replaced personal reflection with the meaningful distraction of a critical project. Throughout the years, I would see this method of retaining members used repeatedly whenever someone wanted out of Miles Jesu. At the moment, I had no idea.

It worked. The manipulation produced its anticipated effect. From that day forward, I became more firm in my vocation and a steadfast apprentice.

Less than two months later, exactly six months and sixteen days after leaving my family in El Cajon, I sealed my future in Miles Jesu. With a formal and perpetual intention, I declared my resolve to "remain in the Institute for the rest of my life."

Virtually immediate and permanently binding commitments were the norm in Miles Jesu. Father Duran wanted to advance reliable membership without delay. Upon resolving my doubt, I saw no reason to hit the brakes.

The ceremony took place in the men's freshly painted chapel. Two cans of Navaho White and a cheap throw rug on particleboard dressed up the room for the serious event. Before Mass, Father Duran asked me to come to his vesting area. After placing a gold laced stole over his shoulders, the symbol of priestly authority, he warned me of the serious nature of my self-offering. Oral and written declarations, multiple witnesses, and signatures upon the altar suggested that there was no turning back, unless I'd risk the fires of hell.

The ritual required us to hold hands, signifying the bonding of my life into Miles Jesu through obedience to the superior. I knelt down at Father Duran's feet; the eyes of the faith family fell upon me. We gripped each other's right hands and I pronounced the formula that would profoundly define the next twenty-eight years of my life.

Our interlocking of hands made me feel good all over, happy to give my life to God, happy for acceptance, happy to experience fatherly closeness. The clasp of unity expressed my faith in God, and concretely, in Father Duran. By the time I reached the "Amen" I'd surrendered to his unwavering assumption that I had a vocation to Miles Jesu. At that irrevocable moment, I buried the discernment of my vocation beneath layers of trust in Father Duran.

# CHAPTER FOUR

Sixteen years later, exhausted, I tried to relax in row fifteen of a Boeing 737 en route from Warsaw to Rome. Perfectly fit for medium range European city hopping, the blue-tinted tunnel plane clipped to Fiumicino, Italy at 700 km/h.

I ordinarily liked a window seat to enjoy the terrain inching by, but on this flight a massive wing blocked my view and I couldn't care less. Lost in my own world, obsessing about escaping, I contemplated breaking free from Miles Jesu.

The frequent flyer across the aisle gave me a dirty look, probably for not showering for days. Apathy swept over me. Who cared what the bald tourist thought? With a rumpled Eastern orthodox style beard, approved by Duran, uncut hair and an oversized shirt, I shot him the evil eye back.

Father Duran wanted me in Rome, but I dreamed of somewhere beyond, Christmas with my family in California. In the hidden recesses of my mind I secretly devised a way back to America, using Rome as a stepping-stone.

A few years ago, during a supposed two-week trip to Eastern Europe, simply as Marcus Gelson's travel companion, I was unexpectedly ordered to live in Ukraine to help recruit vocations. I had no provisions and no appropriate visa. I feared foreign languages like the plague. A hospital in Czech Republic had just discovered my second stomach ulcer. But I knew how to recruit vocations and would stay.

After the fall of communism, Ukraine sparkled as the Promised Land of vocations, where pious young men flowed like milk and honey. Not far from the Polish border, in the Archeparchy of L'viv, the Rudno seminary burst at the seams with vocations. Each year more than a hundred seminarian applicants got turned away because of an over-packed seminary building.

This off-the-beaten-path vocation goldmine of Ukraine had a

hypnotizing effect on Father Duran. Shortly after the Berlin wall crumbled, he rushed to situate vocation recruiters in Ukraine before the boom would inevitably dissipate. I had developed into a resourceful vocation recruiter and ended up in a shabby house in a Ukrainian village for three years. Surrounded by collapsed floors, leaking ceilings, no heating system, and no running water, I lived the heroic dream of a vocation hunter.

The early morning flight back to Rome felt like a nerve-racking dash through the eye of a hurricane, fleeing from one disaster, anticipating another.

How would I confront Father Duran and explain my reason for leaving Miles Jesu? How could I avoid that? Where would I find the money for a plane ticket? The anticipated encounter with Father Duran filled me with anxiety and sapped my energy.

With the first half of the flight behind me, sleep deprivation caught up with my racing imagination and I stared at the rising bubbles of the Seven Up on the fold-out flap. Soaring somewhere over Northern Italy, cradled by the aircraft's powerful twin engines, the monotony of the flight finally lulled me into a zombie-like trance. The aircraft's dull whirr and subtle vibration stirred up vivid daydreams and I nose-dived into fresh memories.

The pristine interview room had been dressed to impress. New leather furniture and fresh white paint threw off beckoning scents. Expensive Eastern icons of Christ and the Mother of God hung with care, draped on the sides with yellow and soft blue ceremonial hand towels. An ornate Persian throw rug, never before subject to a foot, warmed a polished-oak parquet floor. It seemed that God had blessed the day with a breathtaking final touch; upon the centered coffee table, which appeared more like a mini-altar, an unfurled Bible basked underneath the kiss of morning sunshine.

Behind the walls of this carefully arranged room, chaos ruled. Bricks, pipes, cement bags, paint cans and chunks of clawed walls lay everywhere. Stubble faced men danced around tangled veins of power cords slithering across the floor. Drilling, scraping, and pounding filled the air. The clock was ticking to transform a former communist propaganda center into the Miles Jesu "Monastery," as we called it, for recruitment attraction purposes.

I brushed the dust off my clerical suit, wiped my shoes, and entered the recruiting room, the stage, ready to play my role as a big shot. Nobody would suspect that neither education nor ordination supported the priestly collar I wore around my neck. David Regan and the first two guests were already waiting.

Dave parted wild hair down the middle of his head. He maintained a sharp athletic alertness about him, not consistent with his graying beard. Sanguine to the core, he radiated an impetuous spirit, a refined and dry wit, a winning smile for everyone. The Irishman customarily played everything by ear.

A former NSA communications man and hip-shooting cowboy from New Mexico, and now the director of Miles Jesu in L'viv, Ukaine, Dave introduced me in flawless Ukrainian. "Mister Danaluk, this is Andrew Sullivan, our provincial from Rome." I shook hands with Danaluk and his son, and everybody sat down.

Accustomed to playing the angles on the basketball court, Dave and I understood the power play we weaved; the pressure was on to net thirty vocations. This was the first interview. You'd have to do really bad to flunk.

Volodia Danaluk sank in the claret red couch. The first name on the seminary rejection list enjoyed the protective touch of his father's arm. The teenager's dangling feet underlined his innocence. With wavy blond hair, a perfectly shaped face, and big blue eyes, Volodia looked more like a surfer from California than a mountain boy from the Carpathians. Definitely a keeper.

"So, there's no room for you in the inn?" David Regan translated my launching point. The boy's Father smiled at my allusion to scripture. Reeking of sausage, tobacco and garlic, Mister Basil Danaluk stuck out as a stout farmer with nicked and calloused hands. He wore an ugly scar on his left cheek and a mafia style black leather coat. Appearances misleading, Basil represented a man of genuine faith who knew his scriptures thoroughly.

"That's right," he said, "and somebody better help out Joseph and Mary." Acknowledging our shared understanding, we smiled at each other.

The subtle plea was clear: Dad and Mom wanted their boy in the seminary. After the chitchat subsided, Volodia wasted no time.

"The seminary rejected my application; but told me to apply again next year. Then your invitation letter came."

The boy's face glowed with sincerity and expectation. After hearing the translation, I asked Dave to telegraph my response, at least, that's what it felt like.

"If the seminary said that, there's good news, too. You still have the possibility of getting into the seminary and becoming a priest."

Father Duran had given instructions to assume each young man's Miles Jesu vocation and give each recruit the hope of reaching the priesthood.

"This is why we answered your invitation letter," said Mister Danaluk. He stroked his enormous mustache and underneath the shadow of his bushy eyebrows gave me an intense glare.

"My son still wants to be a priest. I believe the good Lord brought us here to find a way for Volodia to enter the seminary."

"I believe the same, Mister Danaluk." I didn't. I just wanted to please Duran. "Nothing could better dispose the seminary authorities to accept Volodia's application next year than to live in our monastery this year."

Dave's back and forth translating felt like slow motion talk, but my authoritative voice worked its magic. We both knew that uneducated villagers had a god-like reverence for monastic heads with Roman collars. We sweated no scruples playing our advantage.

"For a full year? But what would he do here?"

Dave conveyed Basil's questions with a spin and pass toward the net. I grabbed the ball and responded.

"He would live our way of life and learn virtue. He would study in the monastery to learn the basics of the spiritual life and acquire a fundamental understanding of philosophy and theology."

Mister Danaluk assumed Miles Jesu was capable of teaching such things. The Americans directing the Miles Jesu Ukrainian recruiting post had high school educations.

"So, if Volodia lived in the monastery for a year, he would be free to apply at the seminary next year?"

Deeply concerned for his son, this was the father's vital question. Begging for God's help during the entire three-hour journey, he'd made the burdensome trip to L'viv to personally hear the answer to this specific question.

"Absolutely!"

I confidently asserted a lie, half-believing it myself.

"And it's almost certain that our good relationship with the rector will help Volodia get accepted into the seminary next year."

Winning parental approval was vital to our overall plan. The goal was to get Volodia into the house with the support of his parents, where we'd have a year to change the boy's mind about the priesthood and persuade him to remain permanently in Miles Jesu.

"Glory to God!" said the father.

The father squeezed his son's arm and they looked at each other with smiles of renewed hope.

"This is wonderful. See Volodia! God always finds a way." Dave and I smiled and rejoiced with them.

A roar of laughter erupted from behind my seat and made me jump. My eyes blinked open. Bothered to no end, I fought the desire to glare behind the seat to make my annoyance felt. The laughter kept burbling, only gradually fading away. It sounded like the burly smoker I saw when cramming my luggage overhead.

Dog-tired, I repositioned myself for a little more rest. Turning to the right, a beautiful and scantily dressed blonde flashed on a magazine cover. The split second image released an eruption of feelings within me. A barrage of raw memories exploded.

Natalia's soft hands warmed and massaged my chest, her lush lips, her intense gaze; her giggling whirled around and tickled my ears. Playful, sensual eyes memorized me. Leaning over my body, Natalia teased me with her thick, sweet-smelling, black hair dancing in my face. Wild kisses gushed uncontrollably, caressing my hopeless soul. Starving for the touch of a woman, I grabbed hold of her breasts and felt a world of shapely softness hidden behind a pink furry sweater. The woman's tenderness intoxicated me and stripped away every resistance.

Overworked and drowned with the chaotic care of thirty new Miles Jesu recruits, my spirit bucked against unworkable responsibilities. I felt that the God of work had crushed me, until there was nothing left to give.

As usual, Father Duran had clamored for the impossible. Always more. He expected me to teach and "father" the new recruits, fundraise, feed and clothe them, repair the property, attend to its complicated legal status, and oversee the rest of Europe. But I could barely stutter enough Ukrainian to buy a loaf of bread. Deprived of training for anything, I only knew the life of obedience. After months of intense pressure from Rome and nightmare phone calls, I finally collapsed, barely able to walk and breathe. Both my body and soul revolted. Desperate, searching for someone's, anyone's empathy and comfort, I disappeared from the "monastery."

Just before Natalia entered the bedroom I'd crossed over the forbidden barrier of despair. My soul had never been there. I lay naked, encircled by family pictures, happy faces, and defiantly cried out to God.

"I don't care what happens to me anymore! I don't care if I go to Hell forever! You abandoned me; I'll abandon you."

While shaking my fist at God, the lyrics of "I'd rather be a hammer than a nail" floated throughout the house. Lost in a Ukrainian nowhere land, where did those words come from? A forgotten radio played classic rock, and the rebellious catchphrase taunted me.

"Ladies and Gentlemen, we should be arriving at Fiumicino Airport in twenty minutes. Please return your seat to its upright position and make sure your seatbelts are securely fastened."

The P.A. system broke the silence and slapped me with reality. Why did the pilot have to speak so loudly? Wiping my eyes and stroking my beard,

I realized that I actually understood the announcement. It was nice to hear a few words in English.

A confusing explosion of rambling Italian followed. Everybody seemed to know Italian now, except for me. No surprise. My anxiety level definitely jumped up a notch. Tightening my seatbelt, I tried to ignore the budding headache.

Average build and height, neat and clean, Marcus Gelson stood out as a handsome gentleman. His eyes reflected intelligence and gleamed with enthusiasm. A well-proportioned and tanned face enjoyed the complement of perfectly trimmed thin brown hair. With a slightly pointed nose, barely noticeable cheek bulges added a brush of character. Gelson's congenial personality lit up front and center.

The thirty-one-year-old man had long ago absorbed the warm hospitality of the Deep South. The Gelson family, Fred and Lynette and their nine children, grew up near Eden Isle in Tammany Parish. Situated on the Northeast shore of Lake Poncetrain, the sea-breezed town enjoyed a little distance from New Orleans. Eden Isle knew the scenic bayous, the lush willows, pig frogs and swamp lilies. It breathed the cultural life of the meandering but adventurous Mississippi swirling in the souls of each citizen.

Marcus Gelson's dad had served with honor on a submarine during World War II. A fisherman and part time barber, Fred had the magic of making friends. Everybody loved the guy. His happy mug and colorful wit radiated a contagious good feeling. Marcus inherited a generous portion of his father's hard working values, common sense, and sociability, growing up no stranger to good belly laughs and Southern comfort foods.

After high school, Marcus ventured to land a job as a dredge boat chef on the Mississippi. He believed a steady flow of income would reward his hope of eventually studying medicine to become a doctor. Dreams postponed, he plunged into the wild and wet world of dredging.

Non-stop, the dredge boat, oil-rig, hotel platform, whatever it was scraped and sucked the river bottom of sand and sludge and logs. While thirty men rode the back of the sea monster and vacuumed day and night to maintain navigable waterways, Marcus kept the rugged crew satisfied with the best of Cajun cuisine.

A natural cook and gracious mate, the crew appreciated Marc's company. Every few hours Gelson's hectic galley teased the ship with varieties of beloved Southern aromas. He'd rustle up a stream of chicory coffee, fried grits, eggs, bacon and cornbread before the break of dawn. For the rest of the day, knowing the secrets of every dish, Marcus kept a ravenous bunch of men happy, as far as stomachs go. The job depended on Marc's ability to clockwork crawfish boils, chicken gumbo, etouffee, and jambalaya.

Whenever things slowed down, he waded through the hanging pots and pans and surfaced on the ship's deck. An avid lover of nature, the young cook loved to stand there with his hands on a rail and inhale the sweet Mississippi sunrises. A smoke and a coffee, an injection of nature's beauty would energize him to tackle the next meal.

Miles Jesu entered Marc's routine life the morning he haphazardly stumbled across an article in a Catholic newspaper. Fred Bach and I had hitchhiked from Virginia to North Dakota to beseech a respected Catholic journalist to write a promotion piece about Miles Jesu. The gamble paid off. Our brazen grit moved the heart and pen of Father Robert Fox, resulting in a praiseworthy description of the Miles Jesu way of life published in the *National Catholic Register.* Along with his breakfast, Marc devoured that article.

The Catholic faith had steadily grown important to Marc until he wondered about the possibility of studying for the priesthood. The vocation exposé tickled his noble spirit; Marcus soon packed his bags, bid farewell to his family, and joined Miles Jesu in Front Royal, Virginia. Excited to play a role in his recruitment, I enthusiastically embraced the greenhorn.

As years passed, Father Duran noticed Marcus Gelson's finer qualities, his pleasant appearance, good mind, courteous disposition, his natural sense of diplomacy. Duran then drew Marcus to himself and groomed him as the Miles Jesu protégé. Before long, an unbreakable bond of soldiery formed between the two of them.

Call it fate or destiny, my autumn trip from Warsaw to Rome occasioned a pivotal conversation with Marcus Gelson, now Father Duran's personal secretary and an ordained deacon moving toward the priesthood. That encounter kicked off a series of events that would radically alter the course of my life.

The flight from Warsaw ended at the doorstep of Miles Jesu's nondescript apartment in Rome. Upon arriving, I asked Father Duran if we could talk and he agreed that we should, "a little later."

Whenever. After two days of worrying, I couldn't play the waiting game any longer. I had to talk; I was about to explode. Although I knew I should leave the community, guilt about abandoning my vocation gnawed at my soul. Fear of Father Duran paralyzed me.

Elegantly dressed in shiny black suit coats, Duran and Gelson had just returned from visiting a bishop in the Vatican. Father Duran went to his bedroom; Marcus sidetracked to the narrow kitchen to offer some hands-on instructions about peeling artichokes. Joe Kenney, a pious Kentucky vocation had no idea. Exiting, Marcus found me waiting in the hallway where I dug up the courage to ask for a talk.

Marcus let his innate compassion take over. Perhaps he read the desperation on my face, or heard the anxiety in my voice. Whatever the reason, he jumped at the chance to get out of the apartment.

He looked at his watch and noted the time: just past three o'clock. Asking me to wait a minute, Marcus disappeared into Father Duran's bedroom for five minutes, making me nervous as hell. No doubt, he let Duran know where he was going and probably received instructions about how to deal with me. He exited wearing a brownish coat with stitched patches on the elbows and holding a compact black umbrella. His life was so intertwined with Father Duran that Marc seized the opportunity to separate himself for a short hour.

We raced down the long and narrow hallway as if our departure might suddenly change for whatever reason, often the reality in Miles Jesu. At last, securing the apartment door behind us, we descended the worn marble stairs, hit the entrance door of the apartment building, and broke into the crisp November air.

We immediately turned to the right and assumed a leisurely walk along the wide and wet sidewalk of Lorenzo Magnifico. The street honored the despot who'd ruled Florence by threats and payoffs.

The name was less menacing, I suppose, than Via Machiavelli, where Miles Jesu had recently lived. He was the devil who advocated the methodical exercise of deceit, manipulation, brute force, and expediency for political and personal advantage. Rome packed an abundance of crooked streets to indiscriminately flaunt any saint or demon they wanted. Strange. Why had Miles Jesu landed on the avenues of the renaissance weasels?

Piazza Bologna hid a few football fields distance away, down and ahead. Deacon Gelson led a standard Hail Mary and asked Jesus for help. "....

Pray for us sinners, now and at the hour of death. Amen." Studying his cheap Timex watch, calculating the limits of his time, he then invoked the aid of the Blessed Virgin Mary and St. Joseph. Having completed the rituals, Marc was finally ready to listen. Since arriving in Rome it felt like an eternity to reach this point.

My pent up energy and Marc's time constraint aroused a visceral reflex of conflicting feelings deep within me. Up until this moment I'd felt determined about what I wanted to say, what I planned to do with my life. I felt the urge of letting loose and saying exactly what I thought. Yet, in the presence of authority, my backbone seemed to melt away.

Guilt and fear gagged me. A shrinking of courage seemed to emerge from something deep within my psyche, something mysterious that muzzled my behavior in the face of authority. The bold stance, the defiance that had stirred within me, now barely made it through my lips. Only a few abrupt statements broke loose, padded in soft tones.

Immediately passing a bar, dodging a batch of miniature tables, an irresistible aroma of fresh coffee blind-sided us. With Gelson a few steps ahead, I nodded to a couple of American tourists as I passed by, momentarily envying them.

Breaking through the obstacle course and reestablishing our stride again, Deacon Gelson broke the silence.

"So, how's it going Andy? We haven't had a chance to talk since you arrived from Ukraine."

I looked down and swallowed.

"Things are not going well. As of now, I'm planning to leave Miles Jesu." Bombs away.

Marc squinted and shot me a serious look.

"Why? What's wrong?"

"I've come to realize that something must have been seriously wrong about my vocation from the very beginning."

I thought of my yearning to marry and my nagging inability to experience intimacy with another human being. From the first day I'd entered Miles Jesu, sixteen years hadn't changed anything. Nothing had been sorted out.

"I don't understand."

"You know my history Marc. You know about my sexual encounter with Candy Harmon only a couple years after I'd joined."

She was a cute thirty-five-year-old widow with five children. Marc didn't know of my other infatuations throughout the years. I was thirty-three years old now, with a vow of chastity, addicted to porno and masturbation.

Not far from Hotel Laura, we passed by the three-story concave facade of the post office on Piazza Bologna. Tall marbled window frames and light shaded bricks hinted at Roman dignity, spoiled by vulgar graffiti. A light sprinkle stood still in the air; a heavy silence descended. As we wandered forward, Deacon Gelson waited for more bad news.

"I never had the chance to discern my vocation. My vocation was always presumed. No time or attention was given to see what was really best for my life, what I was really cut out for."

Gelson seemed disinterested. Maybe he wanted to change the subject or he just wanted to cut to the chase.

"So what happened in Ukraine to make you think of all these things?"

"What do you mean?"

"It just seems that something happened there."

"I was so overworked in Ukraine that I couldn't function anymore." Fine. He wanted the details; he'd get them.

"The work repulsed me. I worked twelve hours a day. I could barely speak the language or understand what was going on with the guys around me. Taking care of thirty teenagers was an impossible situation. I kept asking for help, and no help came."

"Andy, the plan was to send someone out there to help you, but we couldn't do it right away."

It didn't matter to me anymore. Ascending the curb, we felt a few heavy droplets hit. Gelson toyed with his umbrella but decided not to open it. Rain swept over us and we dashed for cover under the colorful awning of a fancy pastry shop. Safely tucked away, we watched the traffic and last-ditch pedestrians fumble with their umbrellas.

"I couldn't take the pressure from Rome anymore and kept escaping to the homes of women I knew. Sometimes I'd be gone for days at a time."

Gelson looked a little shocked.

"But how were you able to go out like that without being noticed? What about going in twos?"

"Community members were either busy in L'viv or distracted with fundraising trips. I was alone with thirty new guys. I'd just appoint some-one in charge and give the appearance of leaving with another guy on an apostolic trip."

A faint sound of thunder rolled in the distance and a wave of heavy rain danced in the streets. The downpour upon the blue awning hanging overhead and the flowing run-off made me feel safe.

"Marc, I ended up living with a woman for a week, while her husband was out of town. It was like pretending I was married. I couldn't take living in the community any longer. In my heart, I've already left Miles Jesu. I just want to go home."

Surrounded by pelting and splashing, Deacon Gelson stared ahead, not saying a word.

I kept going.

"My health broke down and I couldn't function anymore. I couldn't even walk. My worst sin was that I despaired and gave up on God. I realized that I'd never overcome my desires for intimacy with a woman, never even understand those things inside of me. Everything in my vocation was wrong from the very beginning."

Wanting the details, he asked a few specific questions about the woman and I divulged some abbreviated answers. Gelson wanted to bandage the situation and get back to the apartment.

"Andy, does anybody know about this woman and what you did?"

"No, not that I know of."

Though Marcus Gelson seemed empathetic about my ordeal, Miles Jesu formation only allowed him to focus upon the absolute issue of faithfulness to the vocation.

"Andy, we all make mistakes in life. I don't think your encounter with this woman is a good enough reason to leave your vocation. Don't do something rash, something that you'll regret later. Especially in your state of mind, you're not thinking straight. Let some time pass and decide later."

His approach only knew one side; hang on to the vocation at all costs. My point of missing an unbiased vocation discernment went over his head. As the rain started to subside people dawdled in the streets and I stood there staring into my past. Our sinking conversation ran aground. Gelson could only reiterate the standard moral absolute.

"You have a commitment now, and your salvation depends upon it."

I'd heard it a thousand times. By the time we made it back to the apartment I felt uncertain about my future and increasingly vulnerable. I second guessed the useless attempt to talk. Why talk at all? I didn't see any good coming from it. Why didn't I just find a way to get a ticket and leave? Unusually, I still had my passport. The superior had not yet fulfilled his obligation to confiscate it and lock it in the safe.

The apartment door clicked shut and Gelson started down the hall toward Duran's bedroom door. I'd wandered into the chapel and sat down. Filled with indecision, I struggled to pray, but Natalia's smiling face wouldn't permit it.

A few hours later, lying on my back, staring at the ceiling and seeing nothing, the conversation with Gelson still echoed and bothered me to no end. It lodged in my head and laughed at my cowardice.

Thoughts and feelings drifted from one extreme to another. I stewed in self-pity and doubt. Guilt burrowed into my spirit. I teetered on the edge of packing my bags and fleeing beneath the cover of night. Cut off from anyone who could rescue me, floating in limbo, I no longer knew what to do. Although I lived in an Institute designed to foster spiritual development, there was nobody I could trust to give common sense advice.

The community bell pierced the silence; an announcement clambered from one end of the apartment to the other.

"Father General would like everyone to come to a meeting in the living room!"

Duran wanted to be called Father General now and addressed in writing as Very Reverend. As the ringing grew stronger, Joe Kenney's hillbilly mug protruded into the bedroom crammed with three bunk beds. He dutifully shook the bell one last time and repeated the announcement.

I sprang off a top bunk, hit the floor, and grabbed my shoes. Tying them, looking up, Joe disappeared before I had the chance to fish for the meeting's purpose. Showing up late would provoke a stern correction. Taught by years of experience, I rushed.

My soul dreaded moving at all. The bell implied an emergency and probably meant a public thrashing. The vigorous clanging set off an alarm in my brain.

From a hodgepodge of eclectic throwaway chairs donated by charity stores or pulled from neighborhood garbage bins, everyone found a seat in the drab living room. The two most comfortable chairs, and most clean, were reserved for Father General and Deacon Gelson. They entered and everybody respectfully stood up. Duran indicated where he wanted me to sit: out in the open and surrounded by judgmental eyes. He sat down and the household amenably followed. The General opened straightaway with a Hail Mary and invoked Saint Anthony Mary Claret. Everyone responded with a "pray for us" and the wild ride of an unpredictable "formation meeting" took off.

Pumped with holy fury, as he saw it, Duran cast aside all sense of restraint. With a measured and clear voice, he opened the can of worms.

"This meeting is to help our brother, Andy." I squirmed and braced for the worst.

"Andy fucked a woman in Ukraine."

He paused and surveyed every face, effecting a dramatic numbing.

"What do you all think about that?"

The room froze in silence as Duran connected with his devotees. His abrasive rhetoric hung in the air. My head spun. I broke out in a sweat and started picking at my fingernails.

A tenacious bulldog, once Duran clamped onto something he didn't easily let go. The latching and tearing could go on for hours, days, years. He shot Marcus Gelson a glance.

"What do you think, Marc?"

Given the context of the moment, Marc wore a compassionless face in public. He had to parrot the General's condemnations or be cuffed with the victim and cast away altogether. The meeting followed the standard cave man protocol. Father Duran clobbered someone on the head and every other cave dweller backed him up. Any dissenter would be hit on the head too and beaten down by the mob.

An environment of fear prevented anyone from speaking freely and made it impossible to know if people really believed in what they said. Gutless silence, if allowed, was usually the best course of participation. Gelson gave his response.

"Andy has no control over his feelings."

Duran couldn't wait for Gelson to say more. Any compliant statement served his purpose. He grabbed hold of it, twisted it if required, and repeated it to demonstrate objective support of his position.

"That's right. He has absolutely no control over his feelings. Look how fat he is."

Duran's brutality was expected, but the pain of Marc's betrayal hurt. I thought our conversation had been confidential, that he actually cared for me.

"Nobody is scandalized here, Andy. You are playing with your life. What is the woman's name?"

I reluctantly coughed up her name. "Natalia," I said.

He continued raging as if he hadn't heard me.

"You're so naïve. Do you think her husband doesn't know? He knows already and wants to hunt you down and kill you. Look at your face, like an impenetrable rock."

My expressionless glassy stare infuriated him. My psyche recoiled into a primitive state of self-protection. Duran pointed his finger at me and tried to rally everyone in the room.

"Look at his face! It's as hard as a stone. He has no heart. Andy is not capable of loving anyone."

With a confrontational posture Duran turned on me and raised his voice. "I'm saving your life if I don't send you back to the Ukraine. I can't send you back to the Ukraine. You don't appreciate what I'm doing for you. I'm saving your life! And it's not the first time. Do you understand?"

He was yelling now, feeding on his own agitation.

Everybody sat motionless in that shadowy and cold room, evading eye contact with Duran. I sat there staring down and feeling dizzy. Thumping away upon the awnings, a downpour reverberated throughout the apartment.

The odor of unseasoned and overcooked chicken carcasses filled the apartment. Joe Kenney had packed two donated birds into a crockpot, turned the knob to high, and abandoned the kitchen hours ago. They were old hens on the verge of tossing into the garbage. The unpalatable smell of dinner permeated everywhere. Gelson noticed it and frowned, but Duran remained focused.

The frantic General decided to widen the target. He directed his attention slightly to my right and focused on David Regan.

"David, don't tell me anymore lies. Satan is the father of lies. How can you know what's going on in Ukraine if you didn't know about this? You and Andy have made a mess out of everything."

Nothing was mentioned about the thirty new vocations we'd just recruited.

"We should be much bigger in Ukraine, but you guys waste your time going to night clubs, drinking beer and smoking."

Although the consumption of alcohol was not permitted by the customs of Miles Jesu, we had one beer in a bar once, because we were totally stressed out. That was over a year ago. We never smoked. But the slightest objection would only make things worse. Duran continued with David.

"Did you know this woman?"

"I don't know."

The satisfaction of proving his point flashed on Duran's face; David's answer clearly provoked the priest.

"You don't know? That's right! You don't know!"

Dave discreetly turned to me and whispered a private question, hoping he wouldn't be called on the carpet for showing disrespect. "Andy, was she the mother of the three children I met in Khodoriv?"

"Yes."

Dave then blurted out some information.

"Father, I did meet her. She's a professor in L'viv."

"Is she a fat, ugly mama like the other women Andy played with?"

Duran couldn't hold back his loathing, but he did want Dave's judgment of her looks.

"No. She looked okay. When I met her, she was wearing a low cut blouse with her breasts hanging out. She looked like a prostitute."

At meetings like this, veteran participants tended to say whatever earned points and deflected attention away from themselves. No, there was no such thing as true friendship.

With my tail between my legs, I recoiled in the chair. Duran stood up. Nothing could contain his impatience. Thoroughly disgusted, he paced up and down the room, speaking from wherever he walked.

"And what else, David?"

"With such a good job, I wouldn't be surprised if she was a member of the KGB."

*Did you have to say that?* David wouldn't look at me.

Duran shook his head in disbelief, eyed me over, and raised his voice. "I saved your life. Do you know what her husband would do if he found you?"

"I don't know." *You tell me.*

"He would kill you! And you just sit there with a stone face. You have no control of your feelings. You stuff yourself like a pig and pick at your fingers." Suddenly, he saw my fingers and discovered a new way to humiliate me. "Get up. Show everyone what you are doing to your fingers."

For many years, I'd developed the mad habit of biting and tearing away the skin around my fingernails. It had a lot to do with hundreds of meetings like this one. At the moment, a few of my fingers were a bloody mess and I was trying to hide the fact. Reluctantly, I stood up and took a couple steps to my left, avoiding the David Regan direction. Joe Kenney, with his big nose and wide open eyes, surveyed my fingers as I held them out for scrutiny. Duran pressed again. "What do you think, Joe?" "They're bloody," he admitted.

"They're bloody! Why?"

Politely, Joe simply gave the surface reason. "He picks at them and tears away the cuticle around his fingers."

"Why do you think he does that?"

"I guess because he's nervous." Joe knew more than he chose to say.

But the answer enraged Duran. He wanted no mercy shown to me. "Nervous? We're the ones who are nervous — about what Andy is doing to us!" Duran then looked at me directly and erupted.

"You play the martyr, but we're the real martyrs here. Sit down."

I retreated, relieved that I didn't have to show my fingers to anyone else.

No meeting was complete without Father Duran publicly recounting my history of failures. Everyone had been through it before, many times over, but it made no difference to him. He checked through a long list of my faults and sins, analyzing the causes of my downfalls. As if I didn't exist, Duran elaborated on my pride, stupidity, gluttony, blind ambition, and whatever else, while salt and peppering the meeting with comments fed from the crowd. Nothing was sacred.

I clasped my hands together in my lap, holding back from picking my fingers. The never-ending meeting sapped my energy. My eyelids drooped; I sagged a little to the right, emotionally battered.

After wearing me down, Father Duran sat down and took off in a new direction.

"You told Marc that Miles Jesu is not your vocation and that you want to leave."

He paused and a few members turned their heads.

"This is just another grand manipulation of yours. You want sympathy? None of us feel sorry for you."

After I'd been made to feel guilty about Natalia and dragged through the embarrassment of my life, Father Duran turned down the heat and softly scolded me for wanting to forsake my vocation. Trading the stick for the carrot, his face changed and he assumed a civil tone.

Duran could never comprehend my discovery of the dubious nature of my vocation. From the beginning, it had been built on deception, ignorance and manipulation. It was presumed that Miles Jesu was my vocation. Such a conclusion was utterly foreign to Duran's way of thinking.

Friendly now, Father Duran pursued a paternal path to reach me. "Andy, my son, was this the first time you had sex with a woman?"

I didn't know where he was going with this question, but welcomed the unexpected softening of his attitude.

Cautiously, I responded, "Yes."

"So you're shaken up. You'll be shaken up for a while. You need to talk about what you've been through. You can talk with Marc whenever you need to."

This really meant that I'd better talk to Marc and nobody else about the matter. Marc was wrapped around his finger and Duran wanted to prevent my negativity from influencing other members. I didn't want to talk with Marc again. Whatever I'd say would be heard and twisted by Duran. I ended up talking with somebody else.

Noticing my bloody fingers, Duran chose to ignore them.

"You don't really want to leave Miles Jesu, you're just disturbed. You're shaken up from that woman."

Blind to the internal workings of my mind and heart, he attributed my vocational instability to the emotional intensity of first time sex.

The meeting grinded away as Father Duran described the tricky nature of women. He discoursed on men's gullibility and women's sensual duplicity, rashly lobbing darts of insults right and left. Every woman was fair game. At length, after recounting the ruses and charms of Cleopatra and condemning Eve for the world's evils, Father Duran concluded his long-winded digression by placing the blame of my mess on Natalia, prejudicially branding her as a malicious seducer.

After two hours of mental anguish the meeting terminated, and I corkscrewed down the hall like a drunken sailor. Closing the chapel door behind me, I found refuge in darkness.

Enclosed by red crystal, the flicker of the altar candle cast a morphing rosy glow and dancing silhouettes of bargain statues upon the walls. I sat there recovering, wavering between a drugged stupor and confused tears. Life had turned out very different than I'd planned.

Thirty-five minutes passed. The faint outline of the tabernacle came into view, goading my weary spirit to start picking up the pieces of my life, and reminding me to pray. By habit I swooped up an old devotional book and knelt down. Hoping for any kind of inspiration, I shuffled the pages at random and took a look.

"You can be a saint, if you want to be."

I closed the book. That was enough. These words rushed through my veins and revived my soul with a glimmer of hope. Darkness and light hit at the same time. While every cell within me begged to leave, a resurrection of idealism and trust in God rekindled. Warring against my feelings, I vowed to pick myself up and try again. Somehow, I'd find the meaning of love and learn how to love others.

Although my intentions were good, I didn't realize the serious flaws that hid within my budding determination. I'd just abandoned the sound judgment that my vocation had been defective from the beginning. I'd just set out to achieve love, like any other project. I'd just receded from a necessary confrontation against tyranny.

Perhaps the most powerful internal force that kept me in Miles Jesu at that time was the same kind of emotional tangle that hopelessly binds battered wives to abusive husbands. Brainwashed with a flawed understanding of moral obligation, I believed that Duran's beatings were his way of loving me, God's way of loving me. I needed Duran's tough love. I needed Duran.

The chapel door swung open and startled me. A voice called me back to the living room. Round two. Father Duran wanted to show the community the movie *Body Heat*. Although R rated for its strong sexual content and nudity, Duran intended to dramatically underline the seditious nature of women and gullibility of men. He couldn't stop. Knowing that the movie would invariably turn into a "formation meeting," I dreaded the next round of corrections.

I didn't make it back to Ukraine. Two months later, a cold blast of wind stung my clean shaven face and I felt the pre-dawn crackle of frozen snow beneath borrowed boots. Duran had decided to chaperon me to Chicago and safely tuck me away in Miles Jesu's Lincoln Park residence. Supposedly, underneath a thick blanket of snow I'd be unable to cause problems. I pried open the passenger side of the steel-blue Ford Transit, grabbed the University of Chicago pamphlet, slammed the door shut and hurried back into the chapel.

Upon leaving Rome, Father General had somehow brewed up the idea that I'd make a good lawyer. From his perspective, Miles Jesu needed lawyers and I needed a new ideal, a vital blood transfusion for my vocation. He kept asking if I'd like to study to be a lawyer. I kept answering "yes," not really believing his words. Regardless of my moods, I collected information on the University of Chicago Law School and started to feel attracted to the possibility of studying.

The chapel smelled like bleached lime with a twist of sweet Roman incense. Window frames sat straightjacketed with taut cellophane to keep the warmth from escaping. A yellowish hue blurred the room, still and silent, except for Mary Hudock's snoring. Half asleep and half meditating, I sat there with the pamphlet in my hand, hoping, praying, dreaming of rubbing elbows with fellow students. Although the thought of becoming a lawyer disgusted me, it didn't matter. At least I'd finally get an education.

Just as I closed my eyes and rested my forehead on the pew, a hand tapped me on the shoulder. Robed as a black and white altar boy, Jerry Kroll had slipped through the glass door and approached me. He bowed slightly and whispered into my left ear.

"Andy, Father Duran wants to see us in the sacristy."

I heard him and nodded. My heart skipped a beat, adrenaline rushing helter-skelter through my arteries. Following Jerry out the door, I tried to appear calm.

Jerry Kroll stood five feet, five inches tall. Though twenty-six years old, his youthful appearance didn't show it. He sported a baby face, green eyes, and short brown hair that liked to spring off his head. Although he had a serious spot hidden somewhere inside, Jerry was a natural comedian. He had the Michael J. Fox look. An expert with facial elasticity and tweaked accents, he loved making funny faces and imitating quirky characters. With a thick Chicago attitude, he indulged in colorful name calling and sarcastic wisecracking. Years of rough and tumble work in a lumber yard had branded him with an in your face realism and a passionate loyalty to the Chicago White Sox.

Kroll had entered Miles Jesu in Chicago four years ago. His entrance resulted from a vocation recruiting experiment blazed by Father Paul Vota and myself. At his Homewood, Illinois family house, Jerry received a letter from Father Vota, inviting him to join a pilgrimage to Medjugorje, Yugoslavia. Mysteriously, the letter arrived emitting the scent of roses. Nobody knew how. Really. Believing that divine intervention was at work, accustomed to a Mary Poppins kind of spirituality, Jerry readily joined the pilgrimage. The recruiting lure worked; Father Vota befriended him, one thing led to another, and eventually Jerry Kroll joined the community.

Jerry and I stood there in the dinky twelve by eight-foot sacristy, waiting for Father Duran to tighten his cincture and gather his thoughts. Gelson moved to the background and let the General do what he wanted.

Father Duran turned around and faced us, paternally holding his left hand with his right, caressing his rosary ring.

"What I'm going to say is important. Miles Jesu needs more priests. God is giving me an inspiration. Both of you could make good priests for Miles Jesu. The second semester of the school year is just starting in Rome. Are you both interested in studying for the priesthood? You should think and pray about this."

What? What did he say? We stood there flabbergasted, each for different reasons. For the past couple months Jerry had been repeatedly scolded for his superficiality and lack of responsibility. He was specifically told that priestly studies were impossible for him. I'd been whisked away from Europe and warned that I couldn't be trusted. Quietly tucking the law school pamphlet into my back pocket, I waited for anything to be said about studying law. Nothing came. Obviously, God had changed the General Director's mind. Still ruminating over my recent vocation crisis, I couldn't comprehend an invitation to study for the priesthood.

Duran looked at me and continued.

"Andy, Jesus wants you to be a loving priest. But the decision is yours. You can go or stay. Whatever decision you make would be fine."

Unusually, his face seemed to convey the sincerity of offering a genuine choice in the matter. I didn't need time to think about it.

"Yes, Father, I'm ready to go. If it will help the Institute, I'm ready."

My timeworn dream to be a priest roused from slumber.

"Andy, are you ready to be a loving priest?"

"Yes."

Duran turned his attention to Jerry.

"What about you Jerry? What do you think?"

Jerry shifted his weight, crunched his shoulders and raised his eyebrows.

"It sounds good to me. I'm still in shock about it," said Jerry. He cracked a big smile and giggled.

Before sending us away, Duran gave a quick summary of his plan.

"You should both pray about this and ask if God wants it. If you say 'yes' we'll need to rush you to Rome."

He finished by nodding to Deacon Gelson, who stepped forward to fill in the details. Gelson particularized about possible flight dates, only two days away, and the essential documents required for school registration. After the run down, pleasantly confused, Jerry and I scrambled back to the chapel, bumping into each other on the way.

Within a couple of days, Jerry and I scurried overseas and zigzagged through heavy traffic from Leonardo Da Vinci airport to the university. My life boomeranged back to Rome, coming to rest in the Pontifical University of the Santa Croce, the jewel of Opus Dei.

As far as superiors go, any project or person could move faster. Duran wanted you to run before learning how to crawl. Just when I thought the dizzying pace more than enough, it accelerated the moment I landed in the back row of a medieval theology class that lurched ahead in unbroken Italian. Adrift at sea, I clung to the life preserver. I didn't speak Italian. Although the speed of events should have raised a warning flag, I interpreted the opening doors of a new life as a gift from God.

Mesmerized with Roman culture and classrooms brimming with

cosmopolitan seminarians from far and wide, I barely noticed the foreboding perspective of my situation. During the past few months, I'd experienced emotional and psychological burnout, physical collapse, spiritual shipwreck, despair, adultery, a harrowing abandonment of my vocation, a humiliation that would haunt me for a decade, and an impromptu resolution to become a lawyer. And now the priesthood?

A good part of my instant decision to study for the priesthood stemmed from the desire to escape my past and Father Duran. My choice didn't result from a gradual internal awakening and mature discernment. Rather, it gushed from within, springing from sixteen years of educational hunger.

From another perspective, my choice yielded to Father Duran's calculated enticement dangled before me at a moment of weakness and perplexity in life. Wanting me re-committed to Miles Jesu, Father Duran simply offered me heaven. Entering the seminary therefore set me on an inevitable path of personal crisis all over again somewhere down the road.

Meanwhile, by the sixth month of Miles Jesu seminary life I learned that I was six thousand dollars in debt. Surprise! Duran wanted responsible seminarians. I had to pay off the debt and raise a thousand dollars a month thereafter if I'd continue the next year of studies.

# CHAPTER FIVE

The nineteen subdivisions of Rome sprawled out in every direction, claiming the beautiful and lush countryside that maternally cradled the city. The thirteenth municipality demarked the southwestern corridor toward Ostia and the Tyrrhenian, a marginal sea of the Mediterranean.

Before Benito Mussolini seized and inaugurated the development of this municipality, a chunk of this area had languished as malaria laden swampland. Now, it flourished as a blooming landscape with modern roads and finely manicured pine trees soaring like colossal umbrellas.

A congenial township named Axa, occasionally tagged the Beverly Hills of Italy, sat in the middle of this administrative box. It acknowledged Rome by hanging on the thread of the Lido di Ostia nearby, a suburban rail line creeping from the convoluted Roman transportation system. Axa signaled the midpoint between Rome and the dark sanded beaches of Ostia, a twenty-minute dash in either direction.

Via Tespi, a street named after the ancient father of Greek Tragedy, sliced through the upper edge of Axa. With spacious two-story apartments lining both sides, the kilometer-long street stretched from a hardware shop uphill to a modern grocery center. Free of the clutter and pollution and timeworn stones of the claustrophobic neighborhoods of Rome, Tespi reflected an open and clean appearance, complemented with smartly cut hedges and carefully pruned trees. Authorities pampered its public areas, probably due to the high rate of international renters working at places like the United Nations.

Six months after I'd arrived in Rome for priestly studies, Miles Jesu had packed up and relocated from Lorenzo Magnifico to a red brick apartment on Via Tespi. Jerry Kroll and I had organized the whole drawn-out affair, one small van load at a time. It had taken thirteen trips under a hot sun and a nineteen-hour day.

A Miles Jesu women's community soon followed, settling into the contiguous apartment within the same complex. At street level, the residences appeared as two distinct dwellings, each with their own entrances, porches, and miniscule front yards. But superiors wasted no time cutting into the basement wall to construct a subterranean door.

Obedient to Father Duran's plan, a new Miles Jesu international headquarters rose practically overnight. Duran, Gelson, and their Chicago entourage invaded in full force, and the two united apartments assumed the character of a battleship at war. Planes came in from every direction. Airport pick-ups, wordy meals and heated meetings vacuumed away time and energy vital for studies.

In the midst of a relentless heaven versus hell military operation, the Miles Jesu seminary hardly resembled a seminary at all. Although there was an officially appointed rector, this was misinformation for ecclesiastical authorities, documented merely for seminary program approval. The paper rector actually lived overseas and the seminary floundered without a head. Nobody could really report this tricky arrangement to Church authorities because the rector would have miraculously appeared before any concerned bishop to pooh-pooh away any discrepancy. Nobody saw a problem anyway. Duran was the real head.

The naïvely approved three-page seminary program represented an abbreviated rehashing of generic Miles Jesu customs, some quotes from the constitutions, and a short list of the rector's duties. It was a provisional sketch speedily contrived for an inquiring bishop. Although it suggested orthodoxy in print, the document lacked the canonical meat and potatoes of actually preparing someone for priestly ordination.

The seminary operated simply as a Miles Jesu community, void of unbiased vocation discernment, psychological evaluation, objective assessment of priestly suitability, and competent spiritual direction: the building blocks of sifting souls and nurturing mature priests.

Six years had passed since I'd entered the men's community in Rome, and the summer season for priestly ordinations threatened in the fast approaching distance. Believing myself morally and emotionally deficient to be a priest, I searched for a way to let Father Duran know where I stood. I no longer believed that a normal conversation could exist between us.

Around three in the morning, while everyone slept, I snuck down into the basement. Stealthy floating across the floor, stopping at the deep freezer, I knelt and reached. My hand fumbled in the dark until it fingered the hidden bottle wedged between the freezer and the wall. I yanked it out, held it close to my eyes, and mentally noted the bottle's ebbing contents.

Walking to the dining room table, I set down a glass and poured just enough vodka for the job at hand, and a little glop more. Since I didn't trust my ability to personally voice my panic with relation to the prospect of the upcoming priestly ordination, I planned to draft an important letter to Father Duran. I had to do something. An early morning swig might help the ideas flow, so I told myself.

I sat at a dull brown table, a piece of furniture Jerry and I had begged for from the Legionaries of Christ years ago. After a few sips, I stared at the blank paper and set out to tame the thoughts that had haunted me for the past few weeks. An hour later, an opening paragraph emerged from three false starts, a sea of scratches, and a dozen word replacements:

*Dear Father General, with this letter I ask if I may indefinitely postpone taking the immediate steps to be ordained a deacon. It is clear to me that I am not prepared to be ordained. I lack the maturity to serve Miles Jesu well either as a priest or as a layman. I want to be a Miles Jesu priest and prepare for it, but I do not want to become a priest who creates problems.*

"That should do it," I whispered to myself. Father Duran liked to harp on priests who create problems.

Swallowing another mouthful of vodka, squinting my eyes, a wave of tiredness swept over me and I leaned back in the chair. A dwarf black cabinet hugged the wall to my left, supporting a white board leaning against it. My gaze drifted to the theology freehanded upon it, and my fresh memories rocketed to the class I'd survived only eight hours ago.

"What?" With indignation on his face, Father Duran shook his head in disbelief. "You have no idea what you are writing! Read it again."

I felt everyone's eyes burrowing into me as I looked at the board and repeated the sentence.

"Sacramental character is an instrumental power of the soul, left permanently impressed as an effect of the sacrament."

"Stop! Do you have any idea what you are saying? You have no idea what you are writing. It's ambiguous. Which Sacrament? What is a sacrament?"

Duran waited as I turned around and started to sweat and hyperventilate.

"It's an outward sign instituted by Christ that gives the grace it signifies," I said, knowing it was the correct definition in a no win situation.

"Bah, you only memorize things. You don't understand them. Anyone could say that. A ten-year-old could say that. You have no idea of the meaning behind your words. What is a sacrament?"

"I'm not sure."

I'd given the standard catechism answer. *What the hell did he want?*

My surrender intensified Duran's anger. He turned to his right and complained to Gelson, as if I didn't exist.

"He's not sure. What do you think of that Marc? How can I ordain him when he has no understanding of theology?"

"You can't ordain him. He'd do a lot of damage if he doesn't know his theology."

Father Marcus Gelson looked annoyed too. Everyone in the room looked annoyed.

Duran kept pressing.

"Andy, how many times have you presented this paper?"

"This is the third time."

"It's a piece of trash. It's like the Latin sheet you got back from Professor Foster. He wasn't fooled. You try to fool us, but the Latin professor wasn't fooled. Marc, tell everybody what Foster wrote on Andy's Latin homework."

"Foster wrote 'shit' three times with exclamation points," Marc said.

Suddenly, Duran shot a fuming look at me and raised his voice.

"Do you think this is funny Andy? There's no reason to smile. This is serious and you're laughing at us." Perceiving that I'd smiled, he went ballistic. "Get down on your knees and say a Hail Mary. I am going out of my way to help you and you're taking the whole thing as a joke."

After I'd knelt and finished the penance, Gelson spoke up.

"He wastes his time reading about the Masons, and after six years he doesn't know theology or Latin. It would be a disaster to ordain him."

Duran ordered me to get up and pressed again.

"You don't understand what you're writing. You can't even write a coherent sentence." He paused and looked around. "Or am I not seeing things correctly?"

That was his way of inviting everyone to jump on the bandwagon. With overlapping voices, almost everyone expressed his or her assurance of Father Duran's accurate judgment. Some remained silent, hiding in the crowd.

For twenty minutes, an eternity, I stood there in silence as Duran's public rebukes and humiliations flew by. My theology presentation, as usual, provoked his hypercritical attitude and turned the reading of my labored paper into another veritable torture session. After years of penetrating criticism and a thousand heated accusations of my stupidity, I doubted my ability to write anything that made sense.

Distracted by the wounding memory, my pen rolled across the table, dropped to the floor, and brought me back to the present moment. Picking it up, I slowly shifted my gaze from the sentence on the white board back to the raw paragraph scribbled beneath my right hand. Extreme tiredness blurred my mind. The early hour, the stress, and the alcohol converged in my gut, just as the community started to rouse upstairs.

I gathered my papers and scrambled to hide the vodka bottle. It was time to lock myself in the basement bathroom and gargle with Listerine.

Three early mornings later, my confidential letter would be handed to Father Duran. He'd shamelessly have it read at a public meeting for everyone to scrutinize. The request would be literally held up as a proof of my egocentricity, laughed at, filed away, and forgotten. Except for the impromptu public embarrassment, no further response would be forthcoming.

Five thousand miles away, Puerto Rico danced on the waters of the Western Atlantic rim. Clear blue skies yielded to a blistering sun that cooked the tiny island. Endowed with palm trees, guava, avocado, mango, and a plethora of tropical plants, this dot on the map absorbed the salty breeze of the Caribbean. Beautiful beaches, colorful jungle fowls, cockatoos, and translucent coquis with their high pitched whistles suggested a paradise, if not for the drenching sweat, mosquitoes and rampant crime.

Opposite San Juan, directly north, the midget city of Ponce hung on the underbelly of the island, brazenly strutting itself as the "Pearl of the South." San Juan claimed roughly 450,000 of almost four million inhabitants of the U.S. Territory; Ponce boasted a population of 185,000.

Puerto Rico soaked in an ocean of eighty-five percent Catholicism and the natives breathed the faith. The Church, bishops and priests still enjoyed a genuine respect. This reverence extended to the newly installed Bishop of Ponce, His Excellency, Most Reverend Ricardo Surinach, who inherited a large flock of believers, including a hundred and twenty-three priests.

At seventy-one, Bishop Surinach's big and strong appearance hid a frail and sickly condition. Except for the bushy eyebrows and white nubs circling his ears, most of his hair had perished years ago. Thick lips stretched wide, unsmiling. Hovering over sagging cheeks, thick rimmed and tinted glasses blanketed his eyes with shade.

A shooting but fading star, the bishop's passing reign wouldn't last long. After twenty-five years of hard work as an auxiliary bishop and now racing toward mandatory retirement, his installment came as a brief interim reward for years of subservience. Rumors spread that higher authorities had wanted to by-pass his appointment, but Surinach raised a fit and complained. He deserved it. He won the argument.

A mini-Lord protected by guards and a six-foot fence crowned with razor wire, he resided on a secluded hill at the edge of Ponce. Like many Puerto Rican homes, prison bars safeguarded the doors and windows of the residence. A ruthless drug scourge had transformed every home into a fortress.

Though his residence looked drab and purely functional on the outside, the inside dazzled with good taste. Underneath the mercy of a superbly carved crucifix, the Bishop relaxed at a polished mahogany desk and dictated a letter to Father Alphonsus Maria Duran in Rome.

Linked together by mutual interests, the two had known each other for many years. Fifteen years ago, after failing to find a favorable bishop in the United States, Miles Jesu took refuge in the diocese of Ponce, Puerto Rico.

According to canon law, Miles Jesu required a primary sponsoring bishop and a principle house for the Institute. After fleeing four dioceses, the Institute couldn't find the welcoming arms of any bishop left in the United States. Father Duran contemplated moving the entire operation to Europe until he met Most Reverend Juan Fremiot Torres Oliver, Surinach's predecessor bishop. Juan Torres was the Bishop of Ponce at that time. Call it a virtue or vice, he characteristically sanctioned any cat or dog that professed an orthodox creed and loyalty to the Holy Father. Unsurprisingly, a bond of affinity formed between Torres and Duran, and Miles Jesu moved its center of operations for the fifth time. Ponce surfaced as the next headquarters.

Once Bishop Torres stepped out of the picture, Bishop Surinach inherited the magic wand of episcopal power over Miles Jesu, making him accountable for monitoring the group and incardinating its priests. He sat as the arbiter of a prearranged and mutually beneficial pact. Surinach got a couple of Miles Jesu priests out of the deal, legally bound to his own diocese and working at a parish. Miles Jesu won a provisional but anchored position in the Church, permission to spread worldwide, and a green light to operate a Ponce-backed seminary program in Rome.

With the morning nearly spent and the irresistible whiff of bacalaitos and asopao beckoning, Bishop Surinach looked at his secretary and verbally underlined the main point of his letter. A well-proportioned, docile, pretty blonde wrote in shorthand. He wanted Miles Jesu more involved in the diocese and he needed to know if Father Duran had seminarians ready for the big ordination planned in August. The unwritten supposition was that Miles Jesu functioned as a self-serving island on the island. The Institute's lack of interest in the activities of the diocese needed to change.

Pleased with his own clarifications, Surinach massaged his bulky episcopal ring with his big fingers and promised to return in a few hours. He scooted back his chair, stood up, and headed toward the aroma.

Accustomed to his own self-importance, attracted to pomp and bravo, Bishop Surinach planned to make a memorable splash before retiring his miter. The ostentatious ordination of five seminarians fired his imagination: three young men from the island and two more seminarians from Rome. The ceremony would surely leave a resounding clang of proficiency with vocations.

The Bishop's confident voice ended up in print and the competent secretary had the letter signed, sealed and in the mail before the day finished.

A few weeks after my letter to dodge ordination sank to the bottom of the general government files, Surinach's letter found its way to the nicked and bruised desk of Father Duran. Tucked away somewhere between household bills and correspondence from India and Poland the unopened letter slept in darkness on the desktop. Meanwhile, a late night meeting concluded in the basement at Via Tespi.

His black cane clutched the table end. Father Duran sat bored, listening to everybody's comments. Pain killers kept him subdued. Attempting to humiliate a person to change, Duran often liked to stir waves of laughter by making fun of somebody, contorting his face and exaggerating a targeted victim's mannerisms. Adept at nailing characterizations and capturing audiences, he lacked the stamina and agility to perform tonight.

A dozen members huddled around a long table, the women on Duran's left, the men on the right. It didn't matter if someone had lived in Miles Jesu for twenty years or two weeks. Veterans and neophytes, young and old, everyone participated. Reserving his own judgment, Duran neared the end of his investigation: should we ordain Andy as a priest or not? Jerry Kroll had quickly passed through the group's scrutiny. The inquisition focused upon me.

He started with the row of women, Marie, Jeni, Annemarie, and Patricia. These were women of authority, blindly loyal to Father Duran. They echoed Duran's surmised opinion and built a momentum of disfavor against me. Establishing the proper negative tone, the subtle manipulation worked.

One by one, each participant said, "no." Each "no" required a reason or two, or three. Unabashedly, the meeting forged a long list of faults and expounded upon my unpreparedness at length.

"He's too immature."

"Andy's way too independent; he'd cause a lot of problems. You can hardly control him as it is, Father."

"There's something strange about the way he relates with women."

"He's a tricky manipulator."

"He doesn't know theology and his Latin is terrible."

Each member reworked Duran's well known judgments.

Eleven sour verdicts later, a lonely note of discord reverberated from the last member of the jury.

Sean Brennan was mister personality: outgoing, jovial, respectful, spontaneous, tall and good looking. He embodied the swashbuckler type, swinging on a rope with a dagger clenched in his teeth, boldly dashing into the fray of things. Everybody liked Sean.

He kept his brown hair trimmed like course sandpaper on the sides and long enough on top to neatly slick back with gel. As the comments looped around the table and inched toward him, Sean's carefree countenance and instinctive eyes assumed a watchful bearing.

His maverick tendency was about to buck loose, just for a minute.

Twelve years ago, Brennan had savored the simple sensualities of life. He loved his outside job fussing over the greens of his father's golf course while drinking in the beauty of crisp nature and Budweiser beer. Surfing the fairways in a beat up golf cart, he relished the unsophisticated pleasure of a good smoke with the wind blowing in his face. Trimming greens, flushing out gophers or raking bunkers, Bob Seger blasted away on a worn cassette player.

Apart from his dawn job, Brennan improvised the wild life of a rock star. He dreamed of fame and partied hard as the gifted lead singer of two home grown bands in the rolling hills of Southern Michigan. Savoring hardcore tastes, Sean's second band, "Down and Out," indulged in classic rock and heavy metal.

Life had been a big adventure until tragedy blindsided Sean and forced him to think of God. One titanic night, somewhere in the sticks, his band banged away and spirited a midnight drinking binge. The cops got wind of the unruly party and raced to the scene. Before they arrived, many of the motley crew dove into their cars and scattered. But one stray car never made it home. Two brothers and a sister, Sean's close friends, couldn't escape the fate of a train burrowing through the darkness. It smashed into the side of the car and killed everybody instantly.

Life was never the same again. The band fell apart from internal bickering and Sean wandered away to make a retreat. His guilt and conversion to God had found a beginning.

That's when he bumped into the ever-ready Father Paul Vota, the good natured priest who never missed a chance to recruit a promising youth to join Miles Jesu. With encouraging words, Vota handed him a vocation recruiting booklet written by me. Soon enough, a few months later, Sean entered the Miles Jesu residence in Chicago.

When Sean had first entered, Father Vota wanted him to make an Orientation Week, a week long instruction I'd developed to help new recruits understand the kind of life they were joining, as if I knew. Father Duran heard of the plan and immediately took control. He didn't want a week long instruction, seeing it as a recruiting obstacle. The lad should just join without delay.

Duran and Brennan's first encounter set the tone for an inevitable working relationship. Impressed by Sean, Duran lavished compliments and praise. Sean represented everything Duran wasn't, and the General soon absorbed the young man into an inner sanctum of friendship and governing. With Father Marcus Gelson, the three gradually formed a veritable trinity of dominion over Miles Jesu. Sean assumed the role of Duran's sounding board, familiar valet and surreptitious smoking buddy.

Sean Brennan broke the basement's stillness with his true opinion.

"I don't see why we couldn't ordain Andy. I think he's prepared. Nobody's ever perfectly ready to be ordained a priest, but he's ready enough."

Anathema! Sean's reckless opinion challenged everything.

Sean was tired of Duran's meetings to get in my face. Relying on his privileged status as Duran's favorite, Sean dared to say what he really thought. He alone could get away unscathed with a discordant remark unsupportive of the meeting's unspoken purpose. Anyone else would have been chided for defending me, and everybody knew it.

After a moment of awkward silence, contrary opinions burbled up again, drowning out Sean's impropriety. Following an unalterable script, the pack felt the need to rescue Duran's sentiments.

After a few comments, Father Duran adjusted his chair and cleared his voice. Things had brewed long enough. Something must be said if the footing of the meeting should not be lost.

Addressing himself to me, his concise summary ignored Sean's deviation. "Andy, the consensus is that you're not ready to be ordained. It's clear to everyone."

Duran then lost interest in the whole affair, pushed his seat back, and formally ended the gathering. His pain level needed attention. Marc and Sean helped him exit and shuffle upstairs. Sean would share a smoke, give Duran an enema, and inject him with a Demerol fix.

After a stern rebuke, Sean's misdemeanor would be forgiven.

Down in the basement, everybody scattered. I sat there in limbo, lost, knowing nothing of my future. My written request to postpone ordination remained unanswered. The meeting ended abruptly with no final decision about my fate. I only hoped that Duran would side with the crowd and declare not to ordain me.

Everything was silent at the Miles Jesu apartments on Via Tespi. Rain beat upon the windows and everybody slept dry and snug inside, except for me. Hidden in the chapel's shadows, I slumped, trembling, with my elbows planted upon my knees and my head cradled in my hands. Sometimes I cried; sometimes terror gripped me so completely I froze wide-eyed as my tear ducts dried up altogether.

Upon the eve of ordination to the deaconate any normal seminarian enjoyed feelings of hopes fulfilled and anticipated a warm celebration with family and friends. It was different for me. I stared into a black abyss of ordination the next day and agonized over the darkest hours of my life.

A couple weeks earlier, immediately after the inquisition that probed my inadequacies, Father Duran had sliced open Bishop Surinach's letter. He read it and concocted a threatening situation for the survival of Miles Jesu. Either let Jerry and Andy be ordained or suffer Surinach's consequences. Persistent rumors of religious orders fleeing from Ponce and priests called back to the island captivated Duran's imagination. Such a recall would derail Miles Jesu's latest appeal for a higher approval. An innate fear of superiors and propensity for paranoia grabbed hold of his mind and Duran succumbed to panic.

Kroll and I were called to a meeting in Duran's office. He and Gelson explained how Miles Jesu would benefit by ordaining us. Sweeping my unpreparedness under the rug, Duran focused on the urgency to provide more priests for a rapidly expanding Institute and underlined Miles Jesu's interest in appeasing Bishop Surinach. Duran pitched to ordain us as soon as possible.

After consenting to the plan, God knows how, we wobbled out of Duran's office with our heads spinning, deputized to make all preparations for hyper speed ordinations as deacons within seventeen days. The deadline for the deaconate ordinations related to August 15, 2001, the date set for Surinach's big priestly ordination splash in Puerto Rico six months away. Canon law mandated a six month waiting period as a deacon before ordination as a priest.

It took two weeks for Jerry and I to piece together two dossiers of documents, plan the ceremony, collect books, candlesticks, vestments, and recruit two bishops. We needed two because the first bishop refused to skip the waiting period between the lector and acolyte ceremony and the deaconate ordination. Canon law required a six month wait as a lector and acolyte before ordination as a deacon. So, leaving the first contracted bishop in the dark, we secretly recruited a naïve second bishop for the deaconate ceremony. Every corner was cut to hit the deaconate ordination deadline. The first bishop would make us lectors and acolytes; the following weekend, the second bishop would make us deacons.

Though the responsibility for ordination preparations rested on the shoulders of the General Director, Father Duran was incapable of such duties. He lived day by day riveted on the emergencies of his own health.

A raging roller coaster, Duran's health had absorbed relentless ups and downs, twists and turns. During the past year, he'd pulled through a giant hernia operation with mesh sewed through the hip bone, a life threatening bowel obstruction, and crushed vertebrae disks. Trying to manage his pain, he'd transfigured into an inadvertent drug addict.

Time dwindled away, tranquilized by profusions of Demerol, valium, fentanyl patches, and vodka. Duran fought to govern from his bed, whenever lucid moments allowed. Yet, these precious pieces of time gravitated to criticisms of the thankless souls surrounding him and discussions regarding the next procurement of drugs. Who, which donkey would cross which border? When would he arrive? How much Demerol? The persistent preoccupation of every waking hour invariably focused upon Duran's next bowel movement.

The night before my ordination to the deaconate I sat in the dark. Exhausted from the insane rush of the past two weeks and filled with anxiety,

I cried. Trapped at two in the morning, my mind labored to understand how I'd ended up at this crux in life. I'd said "yes" to everything. What the hell was wrong with me?

Dressed in black from head to toe with an uncomfortable plastic white square on my neck, I felt constricted, clothed forever in a clerical straight-jacket. Now obligated to pray the entire sacred office every day, in Latin, I felt lost, no longer even recognizing my prayers. Skipping the Church's official daily prayers for priests and religious implied new paths of sin for me. The slightest deviation from the Latin guaranteed fresh humiliations from Duran. I couldn't take the weight of these abrupt moral duties already suffocating me.

Suddenly, welling up from within, a vivid image appeared before my eyes and I burst out sobbing, begging God for help.

"Jesus, please! Help me. I can't do this!"

I imagined myself on a slippery muddy slope, facing a gigantic wall. The thickness and height of the wall, besides my lack of footing, made it impossible to pass. I intuitively sensed the meaning of the image. The wall symbolized the priesthood itself, impassable and insurmountable. Placing my head upon the wall and kneeling in the mud, I slipped into despair. That imaginary wall seemed more real to me than anything in the room.

I knew I wasn't ready for this commitment. How could I be a priest if I couldn't even hold up in the presence of my superior, couldn't even stop masturbating? How could I take on the responsibilities of the priesthood when pornography and alcohol enslaved me? I lacked the maturity to make a real friend and the freedom to share my true feelings. I felt alienated in a desert without a drop of understanding from others, without the smallest relief of good advice. Somewhere down the road I knew ordination would end in disaster. Paralyzed by fear, I felt helpless to change the course of the bishop's fateful seal the next day.

Sitting there, lost in miseries, I was hardly aware of the wider context of my predicament. I'd lived for twenty-two years in an environment that had profoundly shaped my thoughts and feelings. The beliefs and attitudes and patterns of judging things, the perspectives and prejudices of Father Duran and Miles Jesu had penetrated into the deepest corners of my spirit. I approached ordination permeated with a Miles Jesu paradigm.

Countless sermons, corrections, humiliations, meditations, self-accusations had conditioned me to live by an unalterable set of perverted moral presumptions. The advancement of Miles Jesu came before the good of any member. Blind obedience to Father Duran represented the sum of generosity to God and service to the Church. In the last analysis, salvation grew from conformity of thoughts, desires and opinions to the divinely appointed head of Miles Jesu, the Very Reverend Father Alphonsus Maria Duran.

My "yes" to ordination did not flow from a calling to the good of the priesthood in itself. I didn't even know if I really wanted to be a priest any more. Miles Jesu formation had conditioned me to view the priesthood as a threat to my lay vocation. My path to ordination issued from surrendering to God's Will, manifested by the concrete needs of Miles Jesu and the preferences of Father Duran. In that isolated chapel, during that critical moment, I surrendered to ordination as a result of the subtle manipulation of cult indoctrination.

The altar candle flickered and threw a laughing glow on the elongated Eastern icons hanging from the ceiling. The rain finished, followed by a howling wind. Nature's wail pushed through the crack of a rattling door and reminded me of my profound loneliness.

Duran's bed rested directly above the chapel. The bounce of the springs and the creak of the bedframe intensified the feverish biting of the bloody skin hanging loosely around my fingernails. I mindlessly stared at the Byzantine rendition of Christ the King on his heavenly throne, as my teeth did their work. The tasteful art didn't matter; I stared but didn't see.

Boom!! "Aaoow!" I jerked my head upward toward the ceiling. A dying thud gave way to indiscernible conversation seeping through the floor of Duran's bedroom. *What the hell's going on up there?*

The shock angered me and unexpectedly drew curses escaping from my lips. "Stupid Duran! Leave me alone."

The commotion made me look at the time and decide to go to bed, even if sleep wouldn't come for a while. I stood up, stepped forward a few steps, and knelt before the altar.

Locked onto a fresh distraction, I shook my head in disbelief. Staring at the tabernacle, I openly complained.

"I waited sixteen years to study and then wasted six more writing fundraising letters. Why did I have to study theology in Italian? Why did I have to raise so much money?"

I'd collected over five-thousand donations and raised almost $200,000.00.

"And for what?" I wagged my head, disgusted at myself.

Dog-tired and defeated, I whispered an act of faith in Jesus, sealed the prayer with an absentminded sign of the cross, and left the chapel. Eight hours later, a bishop placed his hands upon my head and turned me into a deacon.

Exactly six months later, on the south side of Ponce, Puerto Rico, I drifted in a crowd outside the church of Santa Maria Reina. One of five deacons stuck in a surge of believers, I shuffled toward the building, toward ordination as a Catholic priest.

A few palm trees loosely marked the parameter of a huge parking lot of baking cars. The massive church structure looked like a giant capsized ship with its rounded white hull looming skyward. On each side of the elongated shell five arched windows had been cut into the roof, designed to spice the spacious interior with stained glass colors. The temperature hovered around ninety degrees, with a seventy-five percent humidity that cranked up the heat and made every thread of clothing crawl upon my skin. Layers of garments, T-shirt, shirt, cassock, amice, alb, and a thick deaconate cloak, akin to a knight's chain mail, draped me from head to toe in discomfort. A packed church with a broken air conditioning system promised no solace.

The wait vibrated with a chaotic spark. No civilized line filed into the church. A Latino mob flowed toward the entrance door, pushing through the narrow entry like sand in an hourglass. Giggling, restless children ran about. Spanish chatter filled the air. A sheep dog at work, a nervous priest worked the outer rim of the crowd. Trying to avert a flare of episcopal temper, the frantic sacristan searched everywhere for Bishop Surinach's missing vestment.

Father Duran and Father Gelson appeared out of nowhere. Duran hadn't shaved well and stood there strangely subdued. With the sun beating upon them, making them squint a bit, both looked tired. Tired from what? I had no idea. It was none of my business I childishly believed.

I hadn't seen Duran for about three months, when he'd disappeared from the Miles Jesu map. Superiors had merely announced that the General Director was sick and needed a rest.

I'd last glimpsed Duran's face in June, as I hurried down the stairs of the Miles Jesu apartment in Rome. Carrying a quickly-packed shoulder bag, I caught sight of his face through the crack of a door as I descended the second floor landing.

That strange morning, along with seven other guys in bunk beds on the top floor, I'd been rudely shaken awake. A loud voice boomed clear instructions to eight half-awake zombies:

"Everyone needs to get up and get dressed, pack one piece of luggage and meet outside in twenty minutes. We're going to Terracina for a vacation." Terracina was a seaside tourist town, sixty kilometers southeast of Rome.

After the initial shock of the announcement, obedient activity erupted. Everybody scrambled to abandon Via Tespi. Happily confused, I'd barely found the chance to grab a book on the Illuminati, some hidden euros, and my secret stash of licorice liquor.

Surprise! Here he stood now. Duran's left hand touched his forehead, trying to block the spell of a merciless sun. Duran moved closer to wrap his arms around me. With words of encouragement he wanted me to feel his paternal support. Without offering details, Duran let me know that it had been difficult to find a way to attend my priestly ordination, nonetheless he made it.

"I came to show my fatherly love for you," he said, aware of my own father's decision not to attend the ordination.

Duran, Gelson, Kroll and I crammed into a sardine stuffed church, overflowing with people standing in the aisles. Since the air conditioning didn't work, the doors remained open. Even so, a faint outside breeze refused to enter, making it feel like a sauna inside. The bells rang and Mass began.

I didn't know it then, but Gelson and Duran had kept the bishop in the dark regarding the details of their unexpected appearance. Bishop Surinach only knew that Duran had been in Chicago, presumably tending to the needs of the Miles Jesu community. A convenient perception.

Actually, Gelson had just wrestled with the authorities of a drug rehab clinic in the States to let Alphonsus Duran take a trip to attend the ordination. At the last moment, the clinical director reluctantly gave permission, making it clear that Duran was still a patient in treatment. This patient had to be continuously chaperoned and had to return directly to the Guest House clinic in Minnesota after the trip to Puerto Rico. Prior to admittance to rehab, Father Duran had been temporarily, unofficially removed from governing Miles Jesu. Only a few members of Miles Jesu knew.

Bishop Surinach would have freaked had he known the truth.

An incompetent and authority-stripped General Superior and the omission of properly prepared seminarians would have set off alarm bells. It was just enough negligence to postpone the ordinations of the Miles Jesu seminarians, me included. Nothing was said, and the long awaited ordinations proceeded with unbridled solemnity.

A multitude of happy faces, the lingering scent of incense, and exquisite music created an atmosphere of content respect. Swimming in glory, Surinach enunciated an elegant sermon. Comfortably lodged in the sanctuary's priestly niche of honor, Duran observed from a mini-throne.

Although the ceremony looked picture perfect, nobody knew the underlying mess beneath the surface. Duran's life had spun out of control. My life had fallen through ecclesial cracks. Leading up to ordination, I was not permitted to consult anyone outside of Miles Jesu. Fidgeting with his rosary ring, waiting for Surinach's sermon to wind down, Father Duran sat there dreamily. Only a few months ago the evacuation of the Miles Jesu apartment in Rome had paved the way for a face-off that left him barely functional. With every possible witness sidelined to Terracina, the confrontations at Via Tespi began.

Lead by Gelson and a few other Miles Jesu top dogs, Duran was surrounded and challenged in his bedroom. The group respectfully accused him of sexual abuse and drug addiction, and urged him to resign, at least temporarily to help himself. They had a document ready for him to sign. After a lengthy denial he uncharacteristically admitted the abuse.

"Fine! I did it. So what? I can go through treatment, but I'll never sign anything!"

In the same breath, Duran vehemently denied drug addiction. Needing time to evaluate his position and its logical consequences, Father Duran fled to the balcony to smoke and think. Ten minutes later, he stepped back inside. Everyone hushed as he pried open the sliding glass door. Carefully closing it, he turned around, faced his accusers, and stated his new stance.

"Nothing ever happened. There will be no treatment. I will not sign anything." His line drawn in the sand complicated everything. It took twenty-four harrowing hours to remove Duran from the apartment. He went through yelling fits, crying spells, and a failed ambulance attempt to take him away. He burst into the chapel and threw himself at the foot of the altar, pounding the floor and wailing, "They're destroying the Institute!"

Nearby, the house dog pawed its eyes and moaned in unison. Duran jumped up, ran out the front door, broke through the gate of the property and fled into the street. Escaping into the neighborhood, he lapped water from front yard hoses and victoriously exclaimed his freedom.

"I'm not a prisoner anymore! I'm not a prisoner anymore!"

Neighbors and by-passers stood in shock as the scene of madness unfolded. Brennan tried to follow, but Duran kept moving away, yelling. "Get back! Get back!" With the help of a sympathetic driver picking up a priest in need, Duran strayed all the way to Ostia. He carried a piece of Styrofoam he'd found on the street and repeated the mantra, "This is my bed. Here is my bed. Nobody understands the founders." The guys went through hell getting the General Director back to his bedroom.

The next day, it took two burly paramedics from a second ambulance to finally overpower Duran. They grabbed hold of him with a flashing needle waving in the air. With terror in his eyes, Duran kept shouting, "What's happening? What's happening?" He struggled in vain, twisting and kicking, sending Gelson flying down the stairs. A swinging arm plunged the syringe into Duran's leg, emptying a strong sedative into the wild man. At that instant, Alphonso's rebellion peaked and rapidly ebbed to a manageable calm.

After passing through a couple of hospitals on the edges of Rome, Father Duran was whisked away to Rochester, Minnesota and admitted to drug rehab. After months of cold turkey Duran looked improved but still disoriented.

Bishop Surinach finished his sermon and walked to the sanctuary. The seminarians knelt in a line, waiting for the imposition of hands. Tracking the Bishop from the corner of my eye, I prayed. Robed in a gold-trimmed chasuble, Surinach stepped before me, stretched out his arms, and placed his hands upon my head. He mumbled a prayer, backed away, and scooted to the next guy. I was now a Catholic priest.

Instantly transformed, I felt no change, no new power, no renewal of life. I felt nothing but a river of sweat rolling down my entire body.

Literally following Surinach's footsteps, Father Duran moved in and laid his unsteady hands upon my head. He held the honor of buttressing Surinach's consecrations. I knelt with my head meekly bowed and hands pressed together in prayer. Father Duran bestowed his blessing.

By the time I rose, my imagination raced ahead toward distant horizons. As Miles Jesu had hammered, the roman collar should be used to recruit vocations and raise money. This is what I could expect in life. Soon, the church emptied into the night. I exited, muddled with the hope of productivity and haunted by the dread of inevitable failure.

# CHAPTER SIX

Following my priestly ordination, life bounded ahead at hyperspeed. Father Duran now wanted an eye-catching general house and seminary in Rome. My fundraising experience and fresh Roman collar suggested a way to materialize his fixation. Money. Depositing over a quarter million dollars of nickel and dime donations in the Vatican bank, my methodic flow of income showed no signs of slowing.

By the end of my first year as a Catholic priest I'd mutated into a fundraising brute. Aspiring to quench Duran's insatiable thirst for deposits, I ran a weekly community meeting aimed at rearing guerrilla fundraisers. Analyzing appeal letters in the basement at Via Tespi, I cracked the whip on the sluggish and inept. Duran loved it.

He kept driving to hit the same potential benefactors over the head with a stubborn flow of letters until they'd break down and start donating. Equally important, he kept spanking members until they produced. His persistence worked and small sized checks dribbled into Rome, mostly from America.

Duran attributed his successes in life to hard headedness. "I pounded my head against walls until I'd get whatever I wanted," he'd repeat in sermons every now and then. Applying his mode of operating to fundraising seemed a given. He'd certainly applied it to spirituality.

When it came to bringing in the bucks, Duran often turned the spotlight in my direction and lavished me with public praise. This favor toward me reflected Duran's carrot and stick governing style. During an after dinner session, he'd typically point his finger at the irresponsible leeches seated to his right and left. He'd then humiliate the loafers by comparing their sterility with my productivity.

"Look at Andy. You should all produce income like him."

At each mandatory meeting, every participant felt the pressure of accountability. The express purpose of double checking each member's five letters a week quota and reading through each appeal was to provide hands-on instructions. But underneath appearances everyone knew the real objective. Using me as his hatchet man, Duran wanted to increase monthly donations by embarrassment. He didn't want to appear as the only person dishing out shame. Every Thursday evening, I obediently mopped the floor with the low producers.

After an endless repetition of meetings, Father Duran finally had enough "small shits" or small ideas with little results. Now he wanted real money. Swayed by the pursuit of prestige, Duran postponed a pastoral assignment for me and appointed me instead to spearhead a five-million-dollar capital campaign.

Hoping I'd scrounge the money for a decent property, he wanted Miles Jesu to assume its respected place among the revered religious institutes of Rome. With Gelson doing the footwork, Duran checked the price tags of huge properties and consulted a few Vatican friends. Persuaded by the irresistible advice of a big shot cardinal, he realized his miscalculation and enlarged the goal to twenty million dollars. Then he assigned Jerry as my sidekick and placed his bet on me. It felt like I had no choice in the matter.

*Deja vu.* The recurrent twisted interchange between Duran and me would end badly. It happened when I joined, decided to leave, accepted ordination. Each time, his manipulative, domineering authority seduced me and exploited my inability to resist. A familiar inescapable pattern took charge of my life again.

This whole fundraising thing stretched way back to early seminary days. It sprang from the same old dysfunctional, disparate attempt at communication between Duran and me.

About five months into seminary life, Duran and Gelson had called a meeting to secure the financial footing of the Miles Jesu residence in Rome. Pounding the table, Duran had raised his voice.

"It's a disgrace that we produce irresponsible priests in debt to Miles Jesu. How much in debt are they, Father Gelson?"

Although Duran already knew the numbers, he wanted to hear the shameful figures again. Just the idea of sheltering parasite priests bothered him to no end.

"They're each in debt thousands of dollars, with no plans to pay for their educations. Father Nicoletti is about five thousand dollars in debt and Father Dietrich much more than that."

Gelson referenced the financial summary at his fingertips.

Duran reacted. "We should call Dietrich and Nicoletti back to Rome and make them pay their debts."

Such a rash command wouldn't have been unusual, but the General's mind cut in a different direction.

"We're not going to allow this to happen again. What kind of lazy priests are we producing? It's the priests who are causing us problems!"

Without air conditioning or a fan, the dining room felt hot. Only Duran had water. He took a big gulp and carefully placed a half empty glass upon the table. Refreshed, Duran waved his finger and warned Jerry and me.

"Be careful. Are you two going to cause us problems, too? We need to make some changes about how we do things. Everyone should be responsible for raising monthly income."

Gelson added a pre-determined calculation.

"A thousand dollars a month would cover everyone's expenses and schooling."

It would actually cover far more than the house bills and the surprisingly low twelve-hundred-dollar annual tuition. Duran turned to us with a prodding stare.

"Do you two have any suggestions?"

"Why don't we just make the rule that each seminarian and priest must raise a thousand dollars a month? If Jerry and I can't raise the money, we can't study."

My statement pleased Duran; he knew I could raise the money. I made the proposal to avoid years of public accusations of irresponsibility. Unaware at that time, my spontaneity sprang from an inner need to please and feel accepted.

Pleasure danced on Duran's face. A faint smile and barely noticeable nod of his head spoke of satisfaction.

"That's an excellent idea. And it came from you. I'm not imposing this. This is a rule you are making for yourselves. What do you think of the plan, Father Gelson?"

"I think it's a sign of responsibility. But it should apply from the day Andy and Jerry first arrived in Rome to study. We're at the end of June now, so they're each five thousand dollars in debt. In a few days it will be six thousand. By the time the school year begins in October they'll need to pay off their debts and be raising a thousand dollars a month."

His face projected a cold, administrative indifference. Just the facts.

I didn't expect to walk out of that meeting with a debt arbitrarily assessed at nine thousand dollars by the first day of the approaching academic year. With an attitude of 'joyful acceptance,' as idealized by the constitutions of Miles Jesu, I enthusiastically agreed with the plan.

"I'm sure we can hit our mark by the fall," I said with a smile.

Sheepishly embracing the plan, Kroll sat there silently with incredulity stamped on his forehead.

The twenty-million-dollar fundraising venture seemed promising at first. I found a professional who coached me each step of the way. I was "extraordinarily good at nudging the ships," he said. The 'ships' were the potential millionaire donors. I wrote a dazzling project presentation, solicited thirty-five thousand dollars to fund a top notch DVD production, and made my first million-dollar donation pitch. The targeted benefactor laughed and denied he had that kind of money. But the research on him was accurate. He ended up donating a hundred and fifty thousand bucks.

After a year and three months of exploring the personal passions and social networks of eighty-six carefully selected California millionaires, uncovering contribution histories, estimating donation capacities and evaluating approach strategies, my foray as a big time fundraiser abruptly terminated. Just as I started to squeak through the doors of a few financial empires and the Vatican bank account climbed, life imploded. Though I possessed the aptitude for the work, I lacked the emotional stability indispensable for such a colossal undertaking.

To the degree that my feverish labor remained isolated from the realm of adult relationships it flourished; to the degree that it progressively depended upon mature emotional rapport it unraveled and fell apart.

Two extended six-month fundraising trips to Los Angeles landed me back in the Miles Jesu dog house. Free in California, more than six thousand miles from Rome, the dread of dealing with Father Duran controlled me. I found it easier to stride into a power office with a cardinal's letter in hand, drafted by me, and propose a million-dollar gift than to converse for ten minutes with Duran.

The Los Angeles-Rome weekly phone call with Duran barely lasted an hour, but brewed a depression for three days. My tattered nerves begged for the only habitual alleviation they knew: nail tearing, shots of vodka, pornography and masturbation. By day I masqueraded as a super-fundraiser; by night I shriveled into a human mess as opportunities allowed. Kroll and I practically lived co-joined at the hip.

Volcanic pressure surged within me, stemming from the inability to function under Duran's scrutiny. The plodding of capital campaigning ran counter to his instinctual grab, go, and spend without earmark mindset. Walking on egg shells, I knew that at the worst possible moment Father Duran would demand a face to face account. I would stand almost empty-handed before him. At that imagined encounter, a few pledged seven figure donations would mean nothing.

I felt trapped. Whopping donations required the slow nurturing of budding friendships and strategic persuasion. Duran's potentially explosive patience had a short fuse. At any minute, he might evaluate my entire effort based upon real cash in hand and scoff at promises. The situation demanded a race for significant financial backing before the winds changed.

At last, the doom of vain expectations, the futility of pleasing Father General, and the hurry for big money shattered my already fragile emotions. The overriding problem was that I couldn't communicate with Duran as an adult; he couldn't communicate with me as an equal. And any member partially involved in my fund raising project categorically agreed with his viewpoint, even if they didn't. Painfully alone, the pressures of life cast me headlong into a wild pursuit for intimacy. Overlooked pocket money and a donated silver Sable I'd procured provided opportunities for backstairs disappearances.

Under the cover of darkness, I yielded to my feelings and risked everything: cozy phone conversations, bar hopping, secret rendezvous with women, even a desperate proposal for sexual intercourse. She politely thanked me for asking, but said the timing was bad. Sometimes I'd just sit in the car and burst out crying, intensely wanting a woman companion, no matter the cost. I felt broken and alone, ravenous for love and true friendship.

My recklessness almost got me arrested once at two in the morning. Shaken by flashing lights in the rear view mirror, a Hispanic policeman pulled me over for swerving. My driver's license exposed me as a Catholic priest and I played dumb, explaining an urgent need for medicine. I had to find a pharmacy. The young cop had mercy and told me to return a few blocks to my residence and go back to bed. Did he see right through me? Probably. Tipsy, I just wanted to pick up more liquor and another porno magazine.

Father Duran somehow discovered a few of my escapades and went berserk. This resulted in years of relentless humiliations and admonitions.

The first series of blows fell in Phoenix, Arizona, where I was stripped away from the fundraising project. At that time, Duran and Gelson were visiting the Phoenix Miles Jesu community. They demanded that Kroll and I get there immediately. The dreaded encounter had arrived.

The initial meeting set the tone for a never-ending stigmatization. Father Duran sat at the head spot; Father Gelson at his right hand. Eight more community members filled out the table. A bounding tiger, Duran pounced upon me.

He recapped a long list of my faults, mistakes and sins since I'd joined Miles Jesu. Nothing was confidential.

"Look at Andy. Look at him!" He rallied everybody. "You're a fat pig. You're not a spiritual man. You're selfish, full of pride and a manipulator. There's no hope for you. You'll likely go to hell forever. It was a big mistake to ordain you a priest. I don't know what I was thinking. It was a disastrous mistake! You didn't learn anything in school."

The tirade kept going. By the end, Duran had ripped apart my life, piece by piece, example by example, and laid it bare to everyone. The crowd sat there in silence. Nobody dared say a word. With nowhere to run and hide, I retreated into a protective stone face.

My younger brother, Jim, happened to be seated at the table. He'd joined the community in Phoenix a few years ago. Duran suddenly widened the target and ripped into him too.

"Jim, you're a master manipulator like your hopeless brother, full of pride. You'll probably go to hell, too."

The exasperated priest shook his head in disgust.

"What's wrong with the Sullivans?" He wobbled his head and scanned the crowd, soliciting agreement. "You two, and Anthony, all three of you should go to a psychiatrist."

That never happened. Duran had no faith in psychology, unless it could be leveraged in a pragmatic way to buttress the principles and policies of Miles Jesu. He merely wanted to debase.

Jim was so disturbed and fed up by the meeting, a few days later he escaped the Miles Jesu house at two in the morning and fled back to California. Once Duran found out, he raced three members by air to greet Jim when he stepped off the Greyhound in San Diego. I was one of them. Our mission was to do everything possible to obstruct Jim from leaving, change his mind, and bring him back to Phoenix.

"Save his vocation and save his soul," Duran trumpeted.

The frantic mission to save Jim didn't produce a Miles Jesu happy ending. After waiting all day, boarding a twilight bus, and dashing through the desert he stepped off the Greyhound into the arms of three members. Jim had prearranged for a personal friend to pick him up; we had underhandedly thwarted that plan and replaced the guy. Late at night, without any means to continue his escape, his shock gave way to surrender.

I was assigned to isolate Jim and talk some sense into him. While the other two Miles Jesu members blended into the background, Jim and I had a long talk in a Chinese food joint. He was sick of Miles Jesu and wouldn't budge an inch.

Our threesome detained him in a cheap motel against his will and kept him separated from the family for three days. My family. We believed that if we could hang on to him and talk, Jim would eventually come to his senses and break down. But he held firm. When the talks stalemated, he defiantly left. Mom picked him up. It would take years for Jim to recover from the emotional trauma he suffered in Miles Jesu.

Returning to Phoenix, the meetings to help me resumed in full force. The next scolding focused on the appalling damage I'd supposedly inflicted upon Miles Jesu. Duran's fuming erupted from the beginning.

"Andy, you're the kind of person who could destroy Miles Jesu. To protect the Institute, you must renounce your passive and active voice in Miles Jesu."

As a professed member of an institute of consecrated life, canon law assures the right to participate in governance by voting. An active voice is the right to vote; a passive voice is the right to receive a vote. Free elections hardly existed in Miles Jesu anyway, but that was beside the point. Father Duran intended to neuter me from any kind of participation in leadership.

He instructed someone to get me a piece of paper and a pen and proceeded to dictate what to write. After I signed the document, Duran emphasized that my written statement was done "freely and voluntarily." I agreed. I would have agreed to anything.

The charade reminded me of my "voluntary" resignation as the General Secretary of Miles Jesu eight years ago. Here was history repeating itself all over again. He dictated, I wrote, he proclaimed my free choice in the matter.

After the collapse of the California fundraising venture, Duran, Gelson, Kroll and I returned to Rome. Almost immediately a new wave of meetings followed. Father Duran now emphasized my wasted education. Time and time again, he publicly made fun of me and slammed me for not learning philosophy and theology. His hounding climaxed with the snap decision to send me back to school, not for post-graduate studies but to re-study everything from scratch. The plan amounted to a six-year punitive education.

Repeating my first year of philosophy was humiliating. I felt like a dummy wedged in a third grader desk with children poking fun all around. As a forty-two-year-old Catholic priest, I sat there hedged in by kid dreamers. The astute professors with raised eyebrows couldn't figure it out.

Although another five years of studies had been chiseled in stone, after the first year of repeated studies Duran changed his mind. No surprise. He seemed to change his mind about everything. He second guessed, third guessed, stopped and re-started, and radically rethought everything he initiated. The General Director had stumbled upon a better way to deal with me and protect the Institute from my destructive behavior. Apparently, my repeated education was not sufficiently penal.

After finishing my first year of philosophy for the second time, in June 2004, Father Duran called me to his second floor office. He and Gelson sat there waiting. The duo wore unsmiling faces. I settled into an uncomfortable chair and braced myself for the worst. Anything was possible. My antennae sensed something bad. While I picked away at my fingernails underneath the marble tabletop, Father Duran related the story of the Birdman of Alcatraz, even if he couldn't recall the man's real name.

During the first half of the twentieth century, more or less, this Birdman was a prisoner of the U.S. federal penitentiary system. He had served a life sentence, confined for fifty-four years, the last twenty at Alcatraz. Duran underlined the creative intelligence of the prisoner, who employed his bottled up energies becoming an authority on birds. Derived from his care for sparrows and canaries, the prisoner wrote two respected books on bird diseases. Where was Duran going with this?

Then he got to the point.

"Andy, from now on, you're not allowed to leave the house. You can't control yourself. We can't place the Institute in jeopardy. The house will be your prison, although it is not. It depends on how you look at it, and what you do with yourself. If you must leave the house for an important reason, you must come to me and ask permission. Only me. I'll then appoint a specific person to accompany you and keep you always in his sight." He looked me in the eyes. "Do you understand what I'm saying?" "Yes," I answered.

Feeling a knot in my stomach, I thought the whole thing extremist and paranoid. But any reservations or questions would have provoked more rules.

Duran spun the positive side of the new arrangement.

"The Birdman of Alcatraz used his confinement to learn. He didn't brood about his imprisonment; he did something constructive. Whenever a person is put into such a situation you can often see his intellect develop. Your intelligence will come out. I'm sorry to have to do this, but you force me to treat you this way. See how much I love you? I discipline you because I love you."

Duran had no idea what to do with me. No idea how to care for a human being. Rising from his chair, pacing around, Duran babbled a few more things. Gelson looked neutered. The meeting leaped to its end. My clogged mind prevented me from paying attention. A vision of Andy behind bars gripped my imagination. Duran and Gelson concluded with a Hail Mary and dismissed me. They had other things to do.

I left Duran's office, slogged upstairs, and distractedly wandered over to my desk. Nobody was up there. Reeling in disbelief, I sat down and stared at a piece of the neighborhood through the narrow sliver of a small window.

I felt like a punching bag. After a lifetime of correction meetings, brutal assaults upon practically every aspect of my life, I felt beat up and useless. More than a thousand correction meetings had left me disillusioned, paranoid, and apathetic.

The constitutions of Miles Jesu promoted the ideals of 'brutal sincerity' and love by 'harsh corrections.' Despairing, I wished that some tragic turn of fate might end my hell on earth. I'd had just about enough Miles Jesu love.

Fifteen months into my house arrest, on a faraway beach, a solitary seagull floated effortlessly in a cloudless sky. Its shadow brushed over a few limp sun worshipers. Basking on the Island's underside, Bahia de la Ballena lay forty-five minutes west of Ponce, Puerto Rico.

The pristine beach retained the peaceful slumber of raw nature, undeveloped, overlooked, and off the beaten tourist path. Wild coconut palms, kapok trees, and prehistoric looking plants dabbled in clumps wherever they wanted. Here, where color and life took over, the arms of time hardly ticked. The natives loved the place. The pale blue hue of the Caribbean and the rhythmic waltz of lapping waves soothed the soul better than any sedative.

Father Michael Dietrich found a shaded fragment of sand and reclined in a tattered beach chair. He wore an old Cleveland Indians baseball cap, mostly to manage the scorching sun. He felt his forty-five years; the cap doubled as a cover for thin and rapidly receding hair. With a slight lowering of his book, Mike's weary hazel-green eyes scanned the infinite horizon. Stretching out his body, he allowed the seascape to penetrate his battered spirit. This was a new kind of experience for him: the passive reception of beauty.

He dog-eared the psychology book, tossed it on the bag containing a ham sandwich and thawing Gatorade, closed his eyes, and deeply inhaled. The smell of the ocean settled his nerves and spread healing throughout his body. Twenty-five yards away, precisely at the shoreline, two hotheaded seagulls scuffled over a small fish caught up in a wave. The squabble reminded the bathing-suited priest of Miles Jesu conflicts. Remembering them, the amusing dispute forced a smile on his wide-chinned face.

Although a revved motor kept him skinny, Dietrich packed a ferocious intellectual appetite. Had he not joined Miles Jesu in his youth, he would have made a decent scientist. With eclectic tastes, he loved diving into worlds of untapped knowledge. An affinity for Latin, metaphysics and symbolic logic barely scratched the surface of his existential curiosity.

Just by reading and dabbling Dietrich had forged himself into a brilliant pianist and adept piano tuner. In his spare time, he poured over the engineering blue prints of a vapor-carburetor that promised ninety miles a gallon. Actually, he had the thing halfway built before Miles Jesu superiors nipped the project in the bud. He moved on to new terrain and delved into Tesla's zero-point energy. Dietrich's latest, more practical interest touched upon the mystery of emotional healing.

The psychology book hit the lunch bag and sent an emerald anole, a little green lizard, scampering for safety. As the other members of the Miles Jesu community frolicked in the breakers, a soft breeze and merciful shade lulled the priest into a recurring childhood memory. He relaxed and slowly shut his eyes. The horrific scene invaded Mike's imagination.

That tragic Ohio day, Michael Dietrich's dad had rough handled the family's Saint Bernard back into the house. Jupitor had jumped the fence and ran away for the last time. Dad yanked Jupitor down the stairs into the basement. Michael saw the defiant spell on his father's face and feared for the dog. Sick with fear, Michael heard the wiz and wallop of the chain upon the dog's back. Awful yelps of pain pierced the air and got to the hearts of Mike's siblings huddled safely upstairs. As the dog cried, so did they.

Suddenly, Dad yelled out in pain and Jupitor growled between yelps. With the dog's walking chain still in hand, Dad ran upstairs, frenzy-eyed. His right forearm dripped with blood; the trapped dog had given him a severe bite. Dad quickly wrapped his wound. Furious, he threw down the gauze, the tape and scissors, went to the closet and grabbed the spiked snow chains, and descended back into the basement. Michael felt like throwing up.

The blows started again with heavy thuds and sickening high-pitched cries from the dog after every lash. The licks were much worse now and wails echoed throughout the entire house. The spikes ripped into the flesh of the failing dog. Regardless, Dad kept torturing the creature until he lacked the energy to inflict more wounds and the victim could no longer move. At last, the chain hit the floor and silence fell.

A few hours later, Dietrich tip toed to the basement to see the dog. The bloodied animal lay still, whimpering, with tears flowing down its face. The brutality sapped his energy and provoked dread within him. He stayed there with the dog, believing that his presence might comfort it, but nervous about showing compassion.

A graceful Bananaquit darted to a skeletal twig two yards to the left of Father Dietrich's head. Its sudden fly by and pinpoint landing forced the priest's attention. Disengaging from his memory, he twisted his head to the left and caught sight of the tropical 'sugar bird.' The black, yellow-chested nectivore perched just for a minute, scouting the terrain for signs of food. The bird prided a long and tapered bill, perfect for puncturing wild fruit and funneling out sweet nectar. Mike mentally noted the bird's elegance.

He skimmed the sparkling abyss, harboring its teaming populations of mullet and mackerel and barracuda, and reflected upon the persistence of his childhood trauma. That sickening event kept surfacing from the depths, as if it wanted to make itself present, as if it offered more meaning and begged for more healing. Again and again, the painful memory had ripped open old wounds and roused fresh tears.

But not today. The memory had been gradually transformed into a wellspring of meaning and love. Father Dietrich had experienced a decisive turning point in his life that had imbued his heart with the comfort of forgiveness. The Bananaquit catapulted into the wilderness and Mike whispered a prayer of gratitude. Feeling the freedom of that unfettered bird the priest enjoyed a swell of healing

After a childhood of cruel beatings by his own father and twenty-four years of calloused humiliations by Father Duran, Michael Dietrich had experienced a dazzling rescue of mercy. He'd encountered a radical kind of prayer that birthed profound emotional healing.

This dynamic prayer had zoomed past decades of static meditation. For many years, meditative humdrum had crawled along in a quagmire of intellectual exercises. It had languished in ancient Palestine, dryly analyzing the cultural nuances of gospel scenes, building knowledge, while leaving his emotions untouched. Miles Jesu had taught Dietrich to distrust his inner feelings. Sixteen months ago, Father Dietrich had embarked upon a new path in prayer that brushed the cobwebs from his heart and stimulated genuine feelings toward God and His creation.

This new prayer, for the most part, abandoned the standard patterns of meditation, the rational preludes and premises, the behavior oriented goals, the choking obsession of moral conformity to every inspiration. It took the Miles Jesu doggedness of fear out of the equation, too.

Instead, Dietrich had learned to simply close his eyes and enjoy paradise. Swept away with his imagination, He'd feel the touch of a comfortable beach, see the rays of sunshine shooting through the branches of tall pine trees, and hear a waterfall in the distance. A friendly Jesus would appear in this scene of bliss. This contemporary figure would approach him and convey unconditional love. After sixteen months, this wild adventure in prayer had healed and love-filled Father Dietrich. He still had a long way to go, but he'd already experienced a fresh outlook on life.

The priest dug his heels into the warm sand and let comfort creep up his legs. Cracking open his eyes, they rested on a white sailboat in the distance. The memory of the bleeding dog flashed in his mind. But it was an altered memory now. Jesus knelt before the dog, resting his compassionate and healing hand upon the poor creature. Then it hit Dietrich. He was that dog!

The memory suddenly doubled as a symbol of a newborn truth. He lay beaten and bleeding at the hands of his own father and Father Duran; Jesus knelt before him with compassion. He really cared. He rested his healing hand upon him. Dietrich saw a tear stream down the face of Jesus. The Miles Jesu priest stared ahead. A tear of happiness rolled down his face.

By the fifteenth month of house confinement, the continuous stream of menial chores, the monotony, the peering out at the street, the loss of any future killed my spirit. Everything life could have been no longer existed. I desired only to escape or survive the next round of harsh corrections.

The walls of the apartment, the passport locked away in the house safe, the inaccessibility of money, the isolation of Italy, the vast Atlantic Ocean confined me at Via Tespi.

A visceral terror of Father Duran hardened the barriers that entrapped me. Anxiety shot through me for daring to take out the garbage. Just the mere perception of my walking outside unaccompanied provoked a fresh wave of Duran's rebukes. For months thereafter he mocked my alleged rebellion at the dinner table.

More than anything else, my beliefs and conscience determined the extent of every movement and choice left to me. Indoctrination. My mind entangled me more than any physical impediment. Ultimately, I yielded to captivity and disgrace because God wanted me to stick to my vocation, no matter the cost. That's what I thought. I believed that my salvation depended upon it. Although my vocation proved impossible to live, this moral conviction made the idea of fleeing unthinkable.

Isolated from friendship, meaning, love, my faith slowly rotted. My relationship with God had been severed long ago. An unbridgeable gulf kept us apart. I believed that He had abandoned me and broken me for years with no help or explanation why. Prayers were never answered. Life descended to deeper and deeper levels of despair.

Lacking a trusting relationship with God, religion had devolved into a formal, hollow, heartless check-marking of daily duties. Devotion was nothing more than a dry calculation to avoid hell. Yet, a barely flickering light of faith persevered, telling me to hang on for some kind of impossible happy ending. This last hope was eventually extinguished by an endless stream of pointless days. Father Duran never mentioned even a remote possibility of when and how my confinement might end.

By the fifteenth month of confinement my decay reached a breaking point. An entrenched, conditioned fear of Duran gave way to obsession. I felt that there was no place of refuge or safety. At any moment he might call a meeting to mop the floor with me. Sometimes he even awakened me from sleep and brought my exhausted body to his office for fuming tirades. These encounters began and ended with accusations of laziness for going to bed early. The mere announcement of a meeting made me a nervous wreck. And such announcements were absolutely unpredictable.

I didn't want my involvement in anything to be known by him because my connection to a project invariably roused Duran's criticisms and reservations. So I lived and died in the shadows of the apartment as hushed and removed as possible.

Signs of advanced emotional and psychological deterioration appeared.

New kinds of dreams, daydreams and wishes inundated my thoughts and feelings. I suppose my inner powers searched for an escape.

My alienated spirit grasped at feminine intimacy. I daydreamed of freedom as a sexy woman. While cooking or cleaning or praying, I suddenly discovered myself lost in a make believe world. A thousand times over, my heart drifted to the same strange fixation.

I recurrently imagined an expansive and plush hotel lobby, somewhere near Rome's Piazza Republica. On the other side of a huge window, beneath the summer heat, tourists strolled along an open and shaded walkway. I sank in a comfortable recliner within a smoke filled lobby, waiting for the man I'd like to seduce.

A beautiful and erotic brunette, I barely wore anything. Perfectly comfortable with my body and not caring what anyone might think, I enjoyed exposing my legs and breasts. I shut my eyes and with a circular motion slowly caressed my nipples. Opening up and stretching out my entire body, I unreservedly fondled my genitals and imagined the sensation of receiving sexual intercourse from a man.

I increasingly experienced an irresistible urge to wear woman's underclothing. Sneaking through the door in the basement that connected the women's and men's apartments, I'd find something on the drying racks that suited me. I had no idea how this bizarre compulsion overpowered me. Perhaps the alcohol, indulgent masturbations, and pornography had lost their power to anesthetize me adequately. My whole inner world was falling apart and I couldn't care less.

Besides these sexual fantasies and their copious variations, I could no longer fall asleep without imagining the possession of a handgun. The instant my head hit the pillow I'd imagine the touch of a cold and smooth revolver in my right hand. This image forced itself into my mind, leaving me unable to break away to other possible visualizations. I learned to surrender to the obsession. The power of a loaded gun somehow made me feel secure, and lullabied me to sleep. Then I'd dream of shooting off guns in the wilderness.

# CHAPTER SEVEN

The kiss of autumn descended upon Chicago and high temperatures tumbled downward. A stifling humidity surrendered its oppression. By mid-October, 2005, welcomed splotches of bright fall foliage emerged. Maples with pale and vibrant oranges, oaks with lobed leaves afire with shades of pulsating reds dressed up a proud city.

Hugging Lake Michigan due east, on the northern edge of Chicago, Rogers Park wore the season change with style. Vintage apartments and quiet, tree-lined streets, exceedingly stroll-friendly streets, embraced the pleasant smell of fall. The relief of a light lake breeze blessed the vicinity with serenity.

Sandwiched between two towering universities, Northwestern on the north border and the Jesuit's Loyola on the south, Rogers Park flourished as a college village. A diverse blend of students, professionals, and professors from faraway places converged and coalesced into a singular independent spirit. The Rogers Park melting pot embraced close to eighty languages and welcomed a hundred culturally distinct restaurants. One of the bloggiest neighborhoods of the country, it flaunted trendy shops, fraternities, art cliques and theaters. The village harbored a vast variety of non-profits, including Miles Jesu.

Ten years ago, Miles Jesu had purchased a nicely located property five blocks north of Loyola University and a football field's length from the Lake Michigan shoreline. Father Duran and his inner circle had smacked down $415,000.00 for a three story, 11,592 sq. ft. six flat building located at 1126 W. Morse Avenue.

Built in 1912, the handsome structure retained its original character. Contrasted with tightly packed red brick, cumbersome white stones capped the windows and front door. White trimmed frames, outdoor balconies and a concave front entrance distinguished the place. A scanty front yard allowed for a modest patch of lawn and row of hedges. The neighborhood nursed a peaceful atmosphere where elms and ashes shaded the surroundings, offering respite to pigeons and squirrels, and pugs on leashes.

Duran and crew planned to occupy the bare minimum of space for the men's and women's communities, while continuing to rent out the other four apartments to supplement income. The men grabbed the basement, knocked down a wall and established a common dormitory. They invaded the first floor apartment on the building's west side, while the women took the opposite apartment on the east. Throughout the years, tenants came and left depending on the needs of Miles Jesu to inhabit more or less space.

By 2005, the once intense Miles Jesu hub on Morse had declined, numerically and operationally. After sending a good chunk of members to Europe and assigning almost half of the women to Rome, Father Duran also disappeared from Chicago. Bishop Torres of Ponce, Puerto Rico, and later Bishop Surinach, had allowed Father Duran to live wherever he wanted, letting the Founder travel far and wide to spread Miles Jesu throughout the world. That was a nice perk for the Institute.

Throughout the 1990's, the dismantling of the Chicago hub steadily resulted in crippling the community's ability to recruit vocations and grow. Without Duran's unmanageable presence, a mad plate spinner at a circus, Miles Jesu on Morse slowed to a snail's pace, relatively speaking. A sane pace. With a drastic cut of personnel, the chaotic and unofficial headquarters lapsed into a fund gathering and administrative shell.

Father Duran had relocated to Rome because he wanted to establish a prestigious foothold in the Eternal City. Like so many other religious orders, he'd wanted Miles Jesu to plant its roots in Rome. He sometimes repeated this aspiration in sermons, underlining the political expedience of running a general house near the Vatican. With his eye on the future, it was no surprise that Duran inevitably packed up his bags and headed for Via Tespi near Rome.

But there was another reason for the General Director's chess move from Chicago to Rome. In Miles Jesu the whole truth was often concealed, known only by Duran and his carefully composed government.

In 1992, Father Alphonsus Duran was accused of years of sexual abuse by an ex-member of Miles Jesu, a former personal secretary. Fred Bach! The accuser was the conscientious, curly redhead who'd recruited me into Miles Jesu many years ago. He fled Miles Jesu a few years after I'd joined.

The accusations were formally submitted to the Archdiocese of Chicago. Under Joseph Cardinal Bernadine, an investigative case was opened and managed by the newly appointed chancellor of the archdiocese, Father Thomas Paprocki. The investigation involved the suspension of Father

Duran's faculties to hear confessions and say Mass publicly in the Archdiocese of Chicago.

The members and candidates of Miles Jesu in Chicago knew nothing. Duran continued to govern and perform the sacraments in the community, as if no problem existed.

While this case and its disabling effect dragged on, another young man left Miles Jesu in 1994. I'd recruited Tom Jackson into Miles Jesu ten years earlier in Long Island, New York. He'd been so traumatized by his ten-year membership that he'd attempted suicide. Tom had been sexually abused by Father Duran for years.

By the mid 1990's the priest sex-scandal in the United States had mushroomed to thousands and thousands of pedophiles, predators, and angry victims. An avalanche of articles and books and financial settlement cases approaching hundreds of millions of dollars buried the Catholic Church.

By the time Miles Jesu purchased the Morse property, the accusatory environment in the states and Father Duran's sexually abusive history suggested a defensive maneuver. Both Fred Bach and Tom Jackson lived in Chicago and the national culture begged victims to boldly come forth and seek justice.

It was time to move on. By 1996, after a series of international trips far away from Chicago, Father Duran officially transferred his residence to Via Tespi, a hop, skip and jump to the Vatican.

Before long back in Chicago, Father Paprocki received notice from someone in the Vatican to abandon the investigation of Father Duran. The General Director of Miles Jesu was not to be touched, though the suspension of the priest's faculties in Chicago would remain in place. While a raging exposure of sexually perverted priests swept from Boston to Los Angeles, Duran had fled to a place of safety five thousand miles away.

Though the menace of Duran's public exposure momentarily receded, it surfaced again following Francis Cardinal George's installment as the new head of the Archdiocese of Chicago.

In 2002, Fred Bach returned to the diocesan offices and failed again to obtain justice. Beaten down by the futility of challenging a guarded bureaucracy, Fred went to Chuck Goudie and taped a lengthy interview. Chuck was a television newscaster for Channel Seven in Chicago. Standing up for the downtrodden, Chuck championed lost causes.

Tom Jackson chose a different path to expose Father Duran. In 2004, he wrote an alarming letter that unmasked the priest's sexual propensities and exposed an abusive pattern. The letter was sent to four cardinals close to Miles Jesu and Archbishop Stanislaw Dziwisz, the personal secretary of Pope John Paul II. Tom had lunged at the jugular veins of the Institute.

From his perch of safety, the General Director orchestrated his defense. Fred received an intimidating letter from a famous trial lawyer in Chicago, David Schippers, the indomitable lawyer who tried to impeach President Clinton in 1998. Chuck Goudie was approached by the same lawyer and persuaded to abandon the Fred Bach story. Schippers and Goudie were friends. Duran then sent his henchmen, Gelson and Brennan to the appropriate authorities to discredit Tom Jackson. The General Director had danced through the rain drops once again.

Duran's quest for prestige and bolt for safety worked. The Morse property survived. A few recruits dribbled in; hardly any stayed. The brick structure, wearied by the saga of Miles Jesu, welcomed and bid farewell to fair-minded young souls.

By the end of my fifteenth month of house arrest in Rome, an unexpected circumstance whisked me away to the Miles Jesu six-flat in Rogers Park, Illinois. A crazy inspiration, a fit of charity, whatever it was, had throttled Father Duran. He felt compelled to send a priest to the Rogers Park women's community to help Mary Hudock get to the sacraments more easily.

Winter threatened. Mary was a warm-hearted widow, greying, hard of hearing, and barely able to walk. Cheerfulness, prayerfulness, and sweet kitchen aromas indelibly identified her. No matter the discomfort, her clear eyes and inclination to smile marked genuine piety. Many years earlier, Mary had helped Father Duran found the women's branch of Miles Jesu. She lived in the women's community at Morse, and I happened to be the only Miles Jesu priest available to drop everything and fly to Chicago.

Duran didn't want to send me, but his concern for Mary dominated the decision. He probably figured that he could manage me from Rome with a moral leash. So, I arrived in Chicago tethered with the same rules that had controlled my daily routine back in Rome. Regardless of the beauty surrounding the Morse property, I couldn't leave the house. And just in case I felt tempted, an ominous letter threatening hell lined my pocket, signed by Father Marcus Gelson. It really didn't matter, even without the intimidating menace in my pocket and overseas phone calls my despair bound me enough.

Then it happened. A miracle! After a few weeks of pecking theology in the basement at Morse, the heavens opened and God reached down to touch my withering life. Duran had no idea that he'd inadvertently sent me to the pivotal meeting of my existence. God had finally set out to rescue me.

The most important and far reaching meeting of my life took place October 24, 2005 in the Miles Jesu men's apartment at Rogers Park. I experienced a conversation that immediately penetrated me and gradually transformed me and my world.

Father Michael Dietrich had arrived a few days prior to that memorable Monday morning. He and another member had just closed down the Miles Jesu residence in Puerto Rico. After a few days' layover in Chicago they'd head off to their new assignment in Phoenix, Arizona. The diocese of Ponce sparkled no more. Rome had become the newly erected ecclesial seat of the Institute. The island that once secured the canonical footing and global dissemination of the Institute was no longer needed.

That lazy morning, Father Dietrich and I met in the parlor adjacent to the chapel. How the heaven did our path's cross? He'd resolved months ago to share his prayer experience with me whenever the opportunity allowed. Dietrich was amazed to find me in Chicago. The time had come. He believed that I too could be changed into a soul brimming over with love.

I closed the door and we situated ourselves across from each other, separated by a stylish coffee table. A ceramic vase with fresh daises sat on a crocheted white doily. Father Dietrich relaxed on a comfortable couch, while I pulled up a wicker-worked chair. Our feet rested on an old parquet floor, shamelessly dulled by the ravages of bleach. As the world roared by, our words froze in time, marking the dramatic ending and beginning of my history. If there was a key turning point in my life, this was it.

We asked how each other were doing, first chit chatting about the shutting down of Puerto Rico. Dietrich lamented the loss of the peace and quiet he had enjoyed on the island. I then related the weird way I'd ended up in Chicago. Past the preliminaries, Father Dietrich launched into the depths.

"Andy, I've wanted to have this meeting with you for a long time, for about six months. Nobody asked me to meet with you. This is just between us. I had no idea when we'd be able to sit down and talk." Now he looked serious.

I felt relieved that the meeting was Dietrich's initiative. Assured that Duran was not behind it, I lowered my guard and became open to what Mike wanted to say. Duran often spoke through puppets and employed them to gather evidence against his targets. I'd often played the role.

"It hurts me to know how cruelly you've been treated. I cried when I heard of Duran's harsh dealing with you," he said. Mike put it politely. "I know the despair that comes from such treatment. I've been treated the same way for years."

Suddenly, spontaneously, Father Dietrich broke down in front of me. Emotion flooded into his face and tears ran down his cheeks. He cried at the injustice and cruelty of it all. Shaking his head in disbelief, Mike let his heart go.

"How useless it is to help anyone by humiliations, insults, and intimidations. It's useless! Totally useless! Now, I'm assigned to recruit vocations. For what? I don't want candidates to experience what I wouldn't wish on my worst enemies."

It felt awkward to hear a member of Miles Jesu speak this way. I tried to appear non-committal, but inside I agreed wholeheartedly.

After Mike wiped the tears from his eyes and blew his nose, he gathered his composure and introduced the substance of our conversation.

"Andy, I know what is wrong with you." He paused and looked directly at me.

"I believe that you have emotional deprivation disorder. I've known you for many years and I now understand this disorder. Maybe it's not full blown in you, but it's there. It's fully curable, and I know how to help."

Hanging on to every word, I had no idea what he was talking about.

He continued.

"Emotional deprivation disorder is a state of emotional retardation. It's experienced unsuspectingly by many adults. Of the two categories of human emotions, the heartfelt and softer emotions, such as desire, joy, tenderness, empathy, affection and love, are frozen in a non-developed state. Subsequently, lacking the support of these softer emotions, the other set of assertive or doing-oriented emotions take over. These emotions, such as hope, courage, audacity, anger, fear, anxiety, overdevelop. I know that's a mouthful to say, but the disorder boils down to a lopsided state of thinking and feeling. In a nutshell: the love-experiencing side of a person is stuck in infancy or childhood, the action side is jammed into high gear."

Wondering if this condition applied to me, I squirmed a little and asked the obvious question.

"Okay, so what's the cause of this disorder? How does a person end up lopsided?"

"It's caused by a deprivation of mature and affirming love during the early years of life. This mature love is characterized by its unconditional and unselfish quality. Naturally lavished by parents, it's expressive and experienced by the infant or child in a healthy sensual way. It's absorbed by the beloved through the mother's facial expressions, hugs, kisses, caresses, and various signs of acceptance. As this love is progressively soaked up by the developing child, a virtual emotional nursing and growing occurs. This inherent process strengthens and makes firm the emotional and later psychological dimensions of the person. As such, quality love passively received creates an emotionally complete adult."

The rain intensified outside the window. The white washed radiator clicked and another round of heating started up. Oblivious to the subtle sound of an old radiator, Dietrich barreled ahead. "A deprivation of such love results in the crimping of a natural developmental process. Without the freely flowing love I've described, a frustration or deprivation ensues, robbing the person of the indispensable emotional food he or she must receive to mature.

"A parent may have radiated no feelings of love or hatred for an infant and this would cause a deep deprivation. But it's enough that parental love is defective, lacking expression, weak or selfish for a less severe deprivation to occur. Or it may be enough that love is present but not subjectively experienced by the child, for the adult in later years to suffer the frustrating effects of deprivation."

He paused to inhale and I jumped in with a question.

"So, if a deprivation of love stops the softer emotions from developing, how is this related to the overdevelopment of the action-oriented emotions?"

Mike seemed to know the answer to every question.

"When love is withheld at the existential level, the person eventually experiences a difficulty establishing a genuinely felt emotional rapport with other adults. Deep seated feelings of non-acceptance, non-belonging, insecurity, and inadequacy prevail. As the emotionally unaffirmed adult feels misunderstood relationship fears grow and heartfelt friendships become elusive. The unaffirmed come to feel that they have no place in an emotionally tough adult world, where they feel like children. This internal disconnect then spills over into the external social life. Here, the assertive emotions either compensate by driven activity to win love and acceptance, or recoil in fear." Without skipping a beat, Dietrich scooped up a dog-eared softback near his right hand.

"In short, when the softer emotions stop growing, the assertive side of a person strives to fill the gap and survive."

Mike's volume of knowledge and precision of distinctions seemed encyclopedic, at least to me. The guy was a brain in a wheelbarrow, something I'd always admired about him. The heavens burst open and a downpour hit the streets. Father Dietrich next detailed the historic origins of emotional deprivation disorder and the story of the doctors who had pioneered its definition and therapy.

Doctor Anna Terruwe of the Netherlands and Doctor Conrad Baars, who had survived the Nazis' Buchenwald Concentration Camp, identified the symptomology of the condition and tweaked an original salutary approach. Pope Paul VI and Pope John Paul II had endorsed their breakthroughs.

As Dietrich rapid fired the particulars, I began to search within and suddenly realized the truth of it all. I had the symptoms he described: father hunger, a people pleasing disposition, workaholic tendencies, oversensitivity, difficulties in establishing and feeling adult friendships.

More than that, Mike was different, less controlled by fear, warm hearted, empathetic, loving. Something had changed him. I could see happiness in his eyes. His new demeanor convinced me; the long explanations hinted at a successful path he'd traveled.

"Mike," I interrupted him. "Can we go to the cure? How is emotional deprivation disorder cured?" It was a personal question now.

The once broken priest momentarily paused. A discernable gaze of satisfaction accented his face. My eyes must have said it all. I really wanted the answer.

Leaning forward, he began.

"Terruwe and Baars devised a psychotherapeutic treatment that proved remarkably successful in their clinical practice. It stemmed from a simple premise: a frustrated natural process resumes its development once the proper conditions of growth are restored. Accordingly, they allowed their patients to finally experience the mature, affirming, and expressive love they had missed during the early years of life. In such a generative environment, monitored by reason, the softer emotions grew and the assertive emotions mitigated until a state of emotional balance persisted. They called this treatment 'Affirmation Therapy.' By a loving presence, passively received, the therapy effected emotional maturity. This kind of therapy is distinct from the ordinary psychotherapies aimed at correcting repressive disorders."

The answer both encouraged and discouraged me. I frowned, dropped my eyes and shook my head. Nothing good ever happens. Yes, there was a real cure. It existed on a fairy-tale island a million miles away. My heart sank. How could I possibly go to psychotherapy? How could I find the right psychotherapist? And the money? Duran would never permit any of this nonsense.

Dietrich perceived my changing attitude as a sudden wave of pessimism and doubt swept over me.

"Andy, there's a way to replace clinical affirmation therapy with a therapeutic kind of meditation."

"Meditation?" I could hardly fathom this. I needed therapy, not prayer.

"Yes," Dietrich replied. "And who could better assume the role of a psychotherapist, then the Divine Physician himself, Jesus Christ?"

"Okay, I understand that." I grasped it in theory, not in practice. "I'm doubtful. I've been practicing meditation for twenty-six years with no therapeutic benefit. There's hardly any spiritual benefit."

I didn't explain the miserable state of my soul and the impossible gulf that separated God and me. Father Dietrich smiled and described the radical new direction of his prayer life.

"I replaced years of almost fruitless and dry intellectual considerations with vividly imagined encounters with Jesus Christ."

Wait a minute. Still pursuing the treatment for the disorder, I frowned and resisted the idea of meditation as a therapeutic substitute.

"I don't understand the connection between meditation and the healing of emotional deprivation disorder. Can a homemade remedy really replace professional therapy?"

"The essential element of a cure is the passive reception of mature love," Dietrich continued. "This love is experienced in the senses and emotions, and then makes its way to the mind. Through the power of the imagination, which is closely linked with the sensual and emotional powers, the loving presence of Jesus can be felt and absorbed into the psyche, producing therapeutic effects."

Though I was still skeptical, Dietrich's profound transformation made me think twice.

"Okay Mike, how do you do this?"

"The gains I've experienced in prayer were in spite of Miles Jesu. Discard Miles Jesu's malformation regarding meditation, its systemic obsessions of fear, exacting accountability, self-analysis, self-improvement, and intellectual cherry picking."

Dietrich had just jettisoned the pillars of Miles Jesu meditation. He was now a heretic.

"Andy, affirmation meditation is simply imagining Jesus loving you. You see and breathe and touch a comfortable setting, such as a seashore or forest, and find peace and relaxation there. Then, you imagine Jesus with you. You experience His loving gaze and touch. You witness His loving responses to your feelings, dreams, discouragements, likes, thoughts, memories, and daily occurrences. Everything is spontaneous. The emphasis is placed on the passive reception of love, not on what you can or should do, not even on understanding."

He explained more, encouraged me to read some books by Terruwe and Baars, and urged me to commit myself to trying this prayer. Seeing my hesitancy, Mike implored me to promise that I'd read the books and give the prayer a chance. I gave him my word and he visibly leaned backward in relief. Dietrich had accomplished his self-appointed mission.

The rain had come and gone. The room seemed brighter. The aged radiator had sputtered and clacked off a while ago. A couple of hours had vanished. The work day beckoned. White daises stretched upward in the foreground, a calm, happy-faced priest made his own promise.

"Andy, the meditation I've described is extremely powerful. It will tend to take on a life all its own. You'll see for yourself. In about fifteen months you'll feel loved so intensely, you'll beg God to lessen it."

Of everything said, that single statement moved me the most. I wanted to experience that kind of love. A spark of courage ignited in my soul.

We rose from our journey and stretched our legs, as if we'd been confined in a compact car. I thanked Mike more than once. We hugged and he pledged his prayers for me. Within a few days, Father Michael Dietrich would dash to Phoenix and my life would never be the same.

An hour before everybody else, I woke up the morning following Dietrich's departure. After a quick shave and injection of coffee, I slipped into a faintly lit chapel ready to undertake my first experimental meditation. I intended to merely test the waters with my big toe, but tripped and splashed into the pool.

Breaking from tradition, I sat there bookless, no prayer book, no meditation book. Silence. A pattering sanctuary flicker danced. I settled into a comfortable chair and closed my eyes. Totally unexpected, a powerful image thrust itself into my mind. Its force and graphic details startled me.

I found myself standing on an elevated hill of great height. Ankle high green grass grew thick all around. My feet were firmly set upon a cobblestone road that stretched downward and straight ahead, disappearing over a distant and vast horizon. A golden sunset lit up the whole valley before me, painting a thread of road with reflected light. A light breeze flowed over me. I stood there awestruck at the sheer beauty of the sprawling scene.

I had no idea where this image originated. I hadn't planned its creation, nor tried to construct it. It just appeared in my mind, or soul, entirely whole and intact. The more I searched its content with closed eyes, the more details I discovered.

While gazing ahead, thoroughly enjoying the panorama, I suddenly realized that Jesus stood next to me in the scene. He also adored the beauty of the moment. While we gazed into the distance, He gently took my hand in his. My heart jumped, my real heart not in the scene but in the chair. Then Jesus said something.

"Here is the best part of your life, Andy."

It felt like those words came from behind my right shoulder and from the deepest, most mysterious place within me. He was both outside and inside of me. I sat there in the chapel and cried. I believed everything. I understood that I was about to walk that road and be transformed. The experience was absolutely overwhelming.

By the time the community trickled in for formal morning prayers I was hooked. The meditation seized me. I felt instantly addicted. That first time experience filled a vacuum of beauty and meaning deep inside me. By the time Mass finished, I exited the chapel that morning with an unaccustomed feeling of hope. I bumped around that day with a vague disorientation and anticipation of good things to come.

About a week later, I was violently uprooted from Rogers Park and chaperoned back to Rome. God had accomplished his purpose. Duran had changed his mind. Mary Hudock would have to fend for herself.

An overseas phone call ordered my immediate return. I had two hours to pack before rushing to O'Hare airport. Father Duran wanted David Regan to practically hold my hand until I arrived safe and sound at Leonardo Da Vinci airport in Fiumicino, Italy.

David, the NSA cowboy from Arizona, had been temporarily residing in the Rogers Park Miles Jesu community at the time. David and I had some brief episodes of history together, Chicago in the 1980's, Ukraine in the 1990's, including intermittent happenstances in Europe and America. It was nice to spend time with him again in Rogers Park.

That autumn, David Regan trudged along in horrible physical condition. After extended years of labor in Ukraine, India, and England, he'd returned to the United States worn out and sick. He suffered flu symptoms, without the flu, and a nagging mental fatigue. Just a little exertion resulted in exhaustion. Stress accented his face. Thick, prematurely greying hair signaled the passage of time. Even so, Regan remained his jovial self.

He spent his days visiting doctors and taking medical tests, trying to get to the bottom of his health condition. The wizards and machines then discovered the congenital hole in the heart. They ordered up more tests and strongly advised David not to travel.

Not surprisingly, Father Duran downplayed the advice of the doctors. He wanted David in Rome as soon as possible. Since I couldn't be trusted to live in the Rogers Park apartment without David's oversight, and because he needed a travel companion, Duran ordered my return too. Though David had received an early heads up, I received only a two-hour notice. Perhaps Duran figured that I'd throw in the towel and head back to California if given enough time to contemplate returning back to prison in Rome.

Arriving in Rome, we each faced our destinies. I assumed house arrest again. David received the hushed assignment to help make Father Duran a bishop. Duran had convinced himself that David's persuasive personality would surely advance the push for the Institute's next level of prestige.

Following Duran's instructions, David and a sidekick went around knocking on the doors of Vatican cardinals, trying to pull the right strings to make Duran a bishop. Finding appointments hard to come by, David sat on the curbs of cardinals' residences hoping for doors to open.

David Regan eventually made his way back to Chicago. There, Doctor Kevin Dolahyde of St. Francis Hospital definitively diagnosed David Regan's life-threatening condition. A major vein from his lungs connected into the right side of David's heart instead of the left where it should have been. This birth defect resulted in a sixty or seventy percent loss of oxygenated blood circulation throughout his body. The atrial septal defect had increased the size of the heart's right side by three times. The prognosis was dismal without surgery. A baffle of some kind had to be woven into the middle wall of the heart.

To make matters worse, Miles Jesu had botched a health insurance provision for David Regan. He consequently faced a three hundred thousand dollar operation with no medical coverage whatsoever. Duran promised more than once that Miles Jesu would take care of him. "We love you David, even if we have to sell properties to care for you, we would do so," Duran said more than once. But when push came to shove, David had to beg for discounts and raise the money himself to save his own life.

# Chapter Eight

Surrounded by grunts and snores, my eyelids parted at 3:26 am. I turned to my right, reached for the cheap Casio, and clicked off the alarm before it rang. Packed like sardines, the attic dwellers would flop over and up in an hour and a half.

Five months back in Rome. With just enough light to shuffle through the darkness, I grabbed my cassock and breviary and tiptoed downstairs. I parked in the kitchen for ten minutes, swallowed a cup of strong coffee, picked like a vulture on last night's chicken carcass, and silently crept into the back of the chapel. For the next hour I'd enjoy the highpoint of my day.

I closed my eyes and imagined a vast blue stretch of Pacific horizon. An auburn sunset danced upon rhythmic waves. Shimmering clouds reflected pure beauty. Inhaling a salty breeze, warm sand ran over my feet and sifted through my toes. Sounds of distant seagulls echoed in the air. Shirtless, wearing a flowered bathing suit, reclining on a comfy bench, I lived more in my imagination than in that living room chapel.

Jesus appeared at the shore line. Seeing me, he waved and approached. He wore white tennis shorts and an unbuttoned white shirt, folded up below the elbows. Duran couldn't stand it when anyone wore a long sleeve shirt that way. With clear eyes and a big grin, Jesus looked happy to see me.

He hugged me, saying, "Andy, it's so nice to see you. How have you been, my friend?" He really meant it; I felt it. This didn't feel like prayer at all. Jesus held out his hand, "Andy, come with me. Let's take a walk today." Usually he sat next to me, sometimes silent, sometimes exchanging a few words as we basked in the peaceful sunset. I often ended up laying my head upon his left thigh, while he placed his left hand upon my heart. Today he initiated a change. Jesus held out his hand, "Come with me, Andy, I want to show you something."

We strolled along the beach for a while. Somehow, we walked up Poinciana Drive in El Cajon, California, to my childhood home. Descending the driveway, I stopped in my tracks. Was that me? A real memory. I moved closer and observed myself as a twelve-year-old boy in the deep recesses of a dark garage. The young Andy crawled upon his hands and knees and meticulously swept up the dust between storage boxes, boots, cans of oil, and all kinds of clutter. I remembered the many times I'd done that, anticipating my Dad's return from work, hoping for recognition of work well done.

Suddenly, Jesus dropped to his knees and edged next to the boy with the whisk broom. He nodded and winked, then put his hand at work with his own brush. When everything appeared tidy and clean, Jesus rose and with his hands brushed off the dirt from his clothes. He then helped the boy up, placed his hand upon him, smiled, and looked into his eyes. All the while, the adult me absorbed the amazing scene.

Growing from the deepest part of my soul I then experienced his words, "My son, you don't need to work to gain his love. I'm here. You already have my love and unconditional acceptance, Andy."

He gently pulled the adult me to himself and hugged me. I cried because I felt the warmth of his body and the beating of his heart. I understood. Already loved, there was no need to work for love, neither for my father's, nor Father Duran's, nor God's. But I experienced more than knowing this truth; I felt the awe of receiving love. I understood not by logic, but by an encounter of intimacy.

Wham! I almost jumped out of my seat. Kishore's thick meditation book, Alphonsus Rodriguez, volume II, had just belly flopped on the floor, two inches away from my left foot. "Sorry about that," he whispered, with an apology etched in his face. "Good morning, Father Sullivan," he said.

"That's okay. Good morning, Kishore."

The community meandered into the chapel for morning prayers. After the last word of Latin faded away, I immediately headed for the kitchen to hear confessions. Vested for Mass, I sat in silence, imagining Jesus hanging out on the deep freezer next to me. He seemed happy to escape the chapel, too.

I was grateful for dodging the group meditation erupting in the chapel. Father Duran ruled in there, calling people on the carpet, measuring each member's devotion by how many vocations he or she had recruited. I heard snippets of his haranguing while enjoying the protective touch of Jesus's hand.

By midmorning, the early barrage of urgencies had receded. The guys had dashed to Rome for studies. The breakfast dishes were dried and put away. Duran napped, while his bedside helper sat nearby on pins and needles. A couple other guys pounded away on fundraising letters in the basement.

The attic served as the perfect hiding place. Positioning the vacuum cleaner halfway down the stairwell, hinting at labor in progress, I retreated to the top floor and secretly devoured psychology. I read, re-read, and scratched notes from a handful of Terruwe and Baars books I'd shrewdly collected and stashed away.

After preparing and serving lunch, *al dente* carbonara with bacon chunks, garlic bread, broiled pork, mashed potatoes, salad and fresh fruit, I finished the afternoon dishes and mopped the kitchen floor. Midafternoon arrived and I panted like a restless dog, anticipating my daily walk. To my relief, Tom Walsh had received the responsibility to take me on a walk every day.

Tom Walsh exuded a grandpa aura; stability, maturity, and level-headedness shaped him. As shape goes, he struggled to keep the weight off, sometimes with success, other times stumped by defeat. Whenever a feast day arrived, he'd throw on a timeworn apron, assault the kitchen, and whip up a classic desert. Nurturing a sweet tooth, Tom could bake a tray of fudge twice as good as any found in the best bakeries. He claimed sun warmed butter as one of the secrets.

Although bushy eyebrows and a tight ear trim lent the appearance of hair, Tom's stretched forehead accentuated baldness, covered with an old golfing cap. He sported an affable mug, distinguished by a strong chin, squirrel cheek pouches, Irish green eyes, and a ready smile.

Beneath appearances, Tom packed a penetrating intellect and the gift of articulation. His synthetic mind, dry wit, and deep voice made him a genial fount of common sense, humor, and fair judgment. Walsh's great grandpa had excelled as a highly successful New York advertising executive. Tom had inherited the man's finesse at listening and solution finding.

God had provided me with the perfect walking companion. Tom was brotherly, smart, and above all else, discreet. He knew how to listen without judging, and how to keep things to himself. To my great benefit, Tom didn't follow the status quo of divulging members' confidences to Father Duran.

Sixteen years ago, Tom Walsh had joined Miles Jesu in Chicago. After passing through undergrad studies beneath the touchdown Jesus and golden dome of Notre Dame, he'd hotly pursued a Ph.D. in literature at NYU. The poetry of Edgar Allan Poe and Walt Whitman occupied his energies.

Unexpectedly, Tom experienced a life-changing conversion to God, questioned his egotistical chase of academia, and stumbled across a Miles Jesu vocation ad. I'd placed a slick "dynamic apostle" ad in New Covenant Magazine, hoping for a nibble. Seven clean cut guys on the move, coats and ties, a beautiful Chicago skyline, it was an inviting photo. A whopping fish, Tom had swallowed, hook, line, and sinker.

We broke free from the Via Tespi apartment and headed east on Via Saffo. Trying to scurry ahead of a possible recall, for the first five minutes we sped beneath shaded pine trees and through a decoratively gated and flowered neighborhood. Tom and I then hung a left and began a leisurely stroll up a slightly inclined park parallel to Via Pescatori. A five-hundred-yard passage of coddled greens and lazy pines stretched ahead. We passed some Italian yuppies playing with a Frisbee and golden retriever. A perfect seventy-degree blue sky graced the day. I paused and inhaled. It felt so good to be outside!

As usual I related my pre-dawn meditation. Tom listened to every detail. He'd joined Miles Jesu, believing that God wanted him to deny himself and embrace the ideal of sainthood. Entering Miles Jesu meant abandoning studies and simply obeying the General's directives. Fighting his personal preferences, treating himself harshly, Tom did just that. He didn't feel attracted to Father Duran; he only desired to do God's will as best he could discern.

I finished my account and we shared some ideas about my father and Duran and the way I approached work. We reached Piazza Eschilo, looped around a few storefronts on Via Menando, and made a brief stop at a supermarket to buy a few bottles of vodka for Father Duran. We then headed for Via Acilia.

As the years advanced, Tom's sharp mind and sure way with people won him the role of a Miles Jesu troubleshooter. Whenever a serious problem surfaced, anywhere in the world, Tom was sent on a mission to this or that community in crisis. Once his stabilizing influence helped to get things on track, he'd be sent somewhere else. Most recently, he'd visited Czech Republic, Ukraine, and Nigeria. At last, now stationed in Rome, he studied at the Angelicum in preparation for ordination as a priest.

We dropped down on Via Brno Molajoli, a developing street where construction debris still loitered. A newfangled sports center crowned with a glistening Olympic swimming pool strutted on our left. After a long descent, Tom and I entered a young park. Freshly planted trees, hedges, flower beds, bushes, play grounds, neatly cut lawns, and recently molded walkways filled out an enormous plot of land. Children ran about; mothers with their babies and strollers sauntered leisurely. A few older kids kicked around a soccer ball. A small crowd gathered near an ice cream stand. Life! I filled my lungs with it.

Besides affirmation meditation and daily sharing sessions with Tom, I'd adopted important therapeutic supplements. I discovered the benefit of avoiding Father Duran as much as possible. He represented a source of continuous denial of my inherent goodness. I now recognized his destructive influence, and withdrew from his presence as much as possible.

I discontinued trying to affirm myself and win love by driven work. Work shrank to a sensible proportion. I no longer allowed it to passionately seize my time and thoughts. Throughout the years, work had become an anesthetic drug and delusional promise of happiness. I put it in its place. Without apology, I took time for myself, to enjoy romantic music especially. Of course, I would have often ventured in nature if I could, but my options were limited. Such exposure to beauty was recommended by Terruwe and Baars to help open the doors to the passive reception of love.

As we looped around the park's southern end, signs of my emotional growth charged to the forefront of my mind. My fantasies of being a woman and clutching a loaded gun had been replaced with benign daydreams. The intensity of sexual urges had diminished. My ten-year thirst for alcohol and its stupor had evaporated. I could now freely bare my soul to a friend I trusted. I felt true friendship for the first time in my life. Corrections and humiliations no longer made me fall apart. The cuticles around my fingernails had healed. I no longer felt abandoned by God, but understood and loved by him. I was truly changing from the inside out, almost effortlessly.

As if from nowhere, a realization seized me. I've had an emotional disorder all my life and never knew it. Father Dietrich's therapy was really working. It was all true. The progress of the therapy proved the diagnosis correct. I could be cured! A torrent of emotion surged from my depths. I broke down. My knees hit the ground. I sobbed the hardest ever in my life. Tom Walsh placed his hand on my back to let me feel his support. I was oblivious to the stares of mothers passing by.

That moment, I couldn't express what was whirling within me. I could only cry. A violent explosion of multiple ideas and feelings ricocheted within my soul. Sheer joy rushed through me. I understood my problem and myself. Terror suffocated me. With a large part of my life over, I'd only discovered my condition now. How much of my life had I lost! Anger raged. I lived in the midst of superiors who were totally ignorant of my condition. They thought they knew everything. They understood nothing. They had attributed my sorry state to moral vices. Stupid idiots! Their treatment only served to make my condition worse and recovery less likely.

I cried so hard at that moment I felt like I was vomiting, and in a certain sense I was. I was expelling a whole life of bottled-up frustration. That day, my self-understanding took a giant leap forward. I knew what was wrong with me, and why, and how to get better. My understanding of Miles Jesu changed. I would no longer trust the guidance of my superiors. My understanding of God changed. I felt him right there beside me, rescuing me.

A few days later, a couple of new faces appeared in the chapel. Members and candidates passed through Rome all the time. One of the new faces belonged to Olha Klub, a twenty-nine-year-old woman from Ukraine.

At a naïve age of seventeen, Olha had joined Miles Jesu almost thirteen years previously. Driven by Duran's directives to comb Western Ukraine's villages for fresh vocations, she had surrendered to a Miles Jesu recruiting campaign. Father Duran had wanted the unblemished, ignorant, religious, and infinitely pliable youth sheltered in the villages.

Olha embodied everything that was good and beautiful in that delightful land. At five feet, two inches, she still possessed a shapely figure. As a priest I wasn't supposed to notice that, but I did. Her innocent face included a slender pointed nose, sharp chin, fair skin, full cheeks, and green eyes with a tinge of blue. A full body of beautiful golden hair complimented her sensual lips and inviting smile. Her small hands clutched a prayer book.

After Father Duran had ridiculed the idea of religious garb for the women of Miles Jesu, for thirty years, he extemporaneously changed his mind. He claimed an inspiration from God. Now, purely to attract vocations, they wore light blue habits. Her appearance fit neatly into a square of blue that boxed her inquisitive face. An encompassing veil covered her ears and hid every trace of hair. Nobody would openly admit the secret consensus that the habits were hated. Nobody had the guts to oppose them.

She came from a speck on a map called Dobrosyn. The scruffy village housed approximately two thousand inhabitants, mostly poor farmers clustered in the creases of gently rolling hills thirty minutes east of the Polish border.

Rolling westward on a state route to Poland, Dobrosyn bounced behind as a glimpse of life through a smudged window. A spacious cemetery and onion domed steeple leapt by on the left, followed by a government administrative building, drab and lonely. To the right, a run-down storehouse instantly gave way to a prided monument to the beloved fallen who had been snuffed out by Hitler's invading armies. Advancing towards Russia, the blood thirsty raiders had plowed through the vulnerable fields of Dobrosyn in June of 1941. With the monument and football field moving behind, a wonderful panorama of farmlands and dairy pastures crept by. The perfect photo. Two peasants watched a few dozen grazing cows on a sea of green. The villagers tag-teamed the watch of the cows.

Dobrosyn however was more than a distracted tourist's first and last impression. The village bustled with activity and breathed a challenging but satisfying lifestyle. Hard worked family plots kept kitchens loaded with cabbage, potatoes, onions, beets, and grains. The family cow provided each multi-generational household with rivers of milk, kefir, sour cream, and cheese. On Sundays and feast days especially, traditional folk dress with embroidered motifs and vibrant color patterns enlivened the village byways. Braided and flowered hair graced the happy faces of young girls. Poetry recitations and festive songs sprang from the lips of well-wishers. Tables overflowing with smoked ham and fish, fruit breads, baked duck, stewed meats, sautéed mushrooms, and plentiful bottles of vodka put smiles on every face. Olha grew up in this down to earth environment. Her father drove a tractor and her mother sweated as a construction worker. And everyone, including Olha and her younger siblings worked in the fields.

After Gorbachev's perestroika made the collective swell for liberty irreversible, Ukraine declared independence from the Soviet Union in 1991. Emerging from thirty-three years of suppression, the Catholic faith was legalized and Western Ukraine reverted to its Catholic roots.

Balancing precariously on constantly shifting grounds, the Church and society grasped at stability. The economy collapsed. It ran on barter, friendships, and bribes. The ruble crashed, replaced by a coupon which looked forebodingly like Monopoly money. The coupon had no value outside of Ukraine. Countless families lost their life savings within a year or two. Freedom proved elusive; endemic corruption filled the vacuum of law and order. A frightening mafia rose and a thriving black market permeated the culture.

The Russian Orthodox Church wrestled to keep its properties from falling into bulging Catholic congregations. Miles Jesu arrived under the cover of chaos. Free of checks and balances, the Institute wore a Byzantine face and assumed its self-appointed mission to gather vocations. Cardinal Lubachivski and the Eparchy of L'viv welcomed Miles Jesu with open arms; the resurrected Church needed all the help it could get.

Miles Jesu, David Regan and Thomas Walsh, spoke twice at the parish church in Dobrosyn before catching the serious attention of Olha Klub. At seventeen, vacillating between religious life and marriage, she wondered about her future. The comfort of a devoted spouse and children appealed to her strong maternal magnetism. A fortune teller had traced her palm and assured her of a happy future with a husband and two children. But Olha had never experienced true love with a boyfriend. Deep inside, she felt she wasn't pretty or smart enough to interest someone. Her choices of men were radically limited and nobody seemed desirable to her. Her father was a heavy drinker and so were many young men of the village.

Regan and Walsh preached a fulfilling life of meaning and love. Olha was pious and the ideal of dedicating her life to God with like-minded friends finally pulled her over the edge. So, she visited the Miles Jesu women's community in L'viv for a week. She liked the friendly atmosphere so much she joined.

The idea of a habit-free community of women appealed to Olha's innate modesty. Although drawn to community life, she didn't like habits. To her, the ostentatious garb was just another way to show off and solicit special treatment. She'd rather serve God without the pomp, and Miles Jesu appealed to her for that reason. Besides, a curiosity about traveling and seeing the world teased her to death. She wanted to unearth life beyond the village.

Like a marble in a pinball machine, after bouncing around Miles Jesu communities for a dozen years, Olha sat subdued and tired in the chapel. She suffered from indigestion of trains, trolleybuses, and planes. Drained of her natural zest, she stared vacantly at the words in the prayer book. During the past twelve months alone, Olha had changed her residence sixteen times and traveled more than thirty thousand kilometers. Passing through Rome, the idea of packing bags for a trip to Spain made her dizzy. She yearned for some solitude and stability. A college education wouldn't hurt either. Choked by the habit, Olha felt bewildered. She'd soon dash to Madrid, only to return a few weeks later.

Focused upon my therapy, I hardly noticed Olha's coming and going, and returning again. But as my emotional development advanced and my capacity for receiving and feeling and expressing love grew, Olha Klub would become a real person in my life. Heart-pounding love would soon invade me.

Throughout the latter half of 2006, my emotional and spiritual maturity moved ahead in high gear. Simultaneously, Miles Jesu in Rome descended into a confused and headless mess. My progress and the community's decline were disconnected and rapid. Paradigms raced in opposite directions. As each ran its course full circle a head-on collision became inevitable. I failed to see the clash approaching.

The twisted mind of Father Alphonsus Duran had a provocative history of abnormalities. Bishop Jerome Hastrich of Gallup, New Mexico gave his own summary calling Duran "a fugitive priest and a Jim Jones."

Jones was a cult leader who'd led nine hundred and nine followers to drink cyanide-laced Kool-Aid in Guyana, in 1978. Everybody died. It was a strong thing to say by a Catholic bishop. Duran laughed at the label and soon ordered a clandestine disappearance from the diocese. Such a magic vanishing act had its own history. Under the cover of the moon I'd helped stuff the U-Hauls a few times.

Duran's twisted mind sometimes seemed inexplicable. He liked to embrace and kiss men stripped down to their underwear. He lashed out at tearful women for yielding to natural maternal feelings. A young woman in the community had once become pregnant. Duran made her repeatedly sign a document declaring her intent of giving up the baby for adoption. His thinking: absolutely nothing should remove a woman of Miles Jesu from fulfilling her consecrated vocation. Yet, for buying an ice cream without permission in the heat of summer Duran had kicked out a community member and launched a grand investigation of pocket change.

He'd kept a group of men standing for hours in a kitchen past midnight, until someone would confess to washing a dish in the sink. At a ramshackle pig farm in Russia, Duran had commanded two members to call America all night and raise $50,000 each, within twenty-four hours as a punishment for irresponsibility. The two unfortunates sat zombie-like on a log in the snow, staring into a bonfire, frantically searching for phone numbers. Duran practically drained the $700,000 seminary fund to buy luxury apartments in Saint Petersburg. The list of the bizarre was endless.

Throughout the years of Duran's governance members endured the craziness of community life mostly due to a rock bottom acceptance of Miles Jesu's approval by the Church. Confident of the tough love, orthodoxy, and evangelical goals that impregnated the scrappy but elite members, everyone believed in a personal divine calling to the group. Everybody found security in the inspiring quips of bishops, cardinals, even the Pope, about the excellence of membership. Miles Jesu believed its own propaganda; none of these prelates had actually lived in community.

The community's strange customs blurred with the highest ideals of consecrated life. Good and bad, truth and lie, carrot and stick blended indiscernibly together. Duran's crazed obsessions were tolerated as the eccentricities of a holy founder. His inner circle of co-dependents shielded his drinking, drug abuse and sexual indiscretions.

But ideals alone lacked the adhesive power to bind members together. Fear was the glue that cemented unity. Fear of God's punishment for unfaithfulness, fear of the outside world, fear of Father Duran permeated and fused the followers into a group-think family.

Toward the end of 2006, the apartment environment in Rome tumbled into an Alice in Wonderland version of consecrated life. Raisa was the first victim. Named after Gorbachev's wife, she was the house dog, a yellow-gold Great Dane with shadows of black around the nose and ears.

Convinced that the thing was a nuisance requiring a severe blow, Duran had locked onto the poor dog.

"This dog is a serious problem. We have to get rid of it," he'd repeat.

The demise of Raisa was sometimes lumped together with mentions about poisoning the fluffy Pomeranian across the street. That white rat dog was the terror of the neighborhood, according to Duran.

Raisa was a gentle giant, playful and good natured. She'd nudge you when she wanted to be petted and sometimes knock down a flower vase with her tail. She was stuck in the wrong house at the wrong time.

I'd befriended Raisa as a part of my therapy. It was the first time in my life I'd treated a defenseless creature with respect and tenderness and let an animal's goodness penetrate me. Raisa could neither judge nor reproach me; I allowed her friendliness and beauty to be enjoyed. Hidden from the community, Raisa and I had developed a healing relationship. I'd learned that a man's love could be measured by how he relates to the most vulnerable of creatures. A radical shift from Duran's way of thinking, I'd developed a friendship with the dog.

Duran's fixation about Raisa came to a head. Riding shotgun, he instructed his entourage to throw the dog into the back of the Ford Transit. Duran and his insiders ripped down the highway and arrived at the woods of Sabaudia, an hour and a half south of Rome. Tricked by a round of play, Raisa darted into a forested area while Sean Brennan ran the opposite direction.

Tangled in thistles, the pitiful dog yelped. Duran banged on the car door.

"Get in! Get in! Hurry! Let's go!"

Speeding homebound, they recalled the shock in Raisa's eyes and laughed. Duran's humor often erupted at the misfortune of others. In the face of Italian laws, thoroughly protective of animals, everyone was sworn to secrecy. The lie was articulated and agreed upon that poor old Raisa had run away. I felt Raisa's absence the next morning and somehow knew the truth.

An obsession about the devil settled like a blanket of fog over the apartment. Duran felt demonic evils lurked everywhere. Enslaved by his uncontrolled imagination, the priest saw the devil out to destroy him, Gelson, and Miles Jesu.

Father Duran's whole being seemed to gravitate in this direction, as Father Gelson's health declined. Marcus Gelson's body and soul had progressively manifested the signs of a nervous breakdown. The yoke of service to Duran had finally cracked him. Gelson could hardly function.

Insomnia, irritability, anger, depression, guilt, exhaustion, and the inability to focus upon any task at hand converged and choked his capacity to shoulder responsibilities. The guy couldn't even read for five minutes. Drowning, Gelson fled the apartment whenever possible. A shell of his former Southern Louisiana sunshine, the victim hoarded morning walks, days off, and trips. Vodka and Xanax became his coping friends.

The man had reached his limit; years of impossible expectations had conquered. Shouldering relentless health emergencies, he'd persevered as Father Duran's caregiver. Frequently covering for Duran's bed bound condition, Gelson had presumed the daily operations of the global Institute. Additional wear and tear resulted from Duran's insensitive treatment. Gelson was abused as a scapegoat and manipulated as Duran's right hand of injustice. Suffering in silence, Marc had pushed himself to his limit.

Strangely enough, Father Duran was unable to comprehend the cause of Marc Gelson's decline. Duran demanded Marc's continuous presence day and night and worked him almost to death. The needy and picky Spaniard had no idea the he was the primary cause of Gelson's breakdown. At last, getting to the bottom of things, Father Duran concluded that the devil was loose, targeting Father Gelson.

Father Duran spared no expense to connect Gelson with the best exorcist. He rushed the broken priest to a noted exorcist sheltered within the oldest Cistercian monastery in the world.

Holy Cross Abby nestled in a lush valley at the western tip of the Vienna Woods, a veritable enchanted forest. Deep within the nexus of Gothic halls and Romanesque buildings, Duran and Gelson tried to feel comfortable as they sat before a black and white robed monk reciting exorcist prayers. A whorl of frigid air petrified them. A prayer book leapt from Marc's hands and flew across the room. The monk confirmed that the devil indeed was attacking Miles Jesu and its Vicar Director, Father Marcus Gelson.

After the two had returned to Rome, the harrowing account was impressed upon the community. But was the story true or exaggerated? It was often difficult to tell with Duran. Apparently, everybody believed. Any doubt would have provoked the wrath of God to come crashing down.

Gelson next began visits with a respected Vatican exorcist. Duran then pulled everyone into the waxing fray. The community started a daily recitation of a lengthy exorcism formula. Before long, the dreaded thing had to be recited twice a day. The mantra kept repeating, ending with a line of creeping penitents kneeling before Duran. Each member kissed the relic of the holy cross, received a blessing, made a sign of the cross, and absorbed a splash of holy water in the face. The atmosphere couldn't be escaped, Duran's demonic fixation spread to every room of the apartment.

Duran manifested other signs of slipping into fantasy. Stuffed boxes of all sizes littered the rooms. Convinced that the community would almost immediately move, Duran had ordered everyone to pack up books, clothes, pots, pans, office supplies, chapel supplies, sheets, and pillows, practically everything. Everyone knew it was ridiculous. Nobody resisted. Obedience. As if this didn't make life difficult enough; the phones had to be unplugged and locked away, along with the computers and TV. The unbridled use of the phones required a drastic move. Every sign of functional life lay sealed and buried beneath a mountain of cardboard boxes reaching the ceiling. The apartment morphed into a shell waiting for moving trucks. But there were no trucks and no plan to move.

Up in Father Duran's bedroom another obsession developed. Between enemas, Father Duran frequently shuffled around on his balcony, smoking cigarettes and sucking Hall's cough drops. Now, a monster rat with beady eyes lurked behind a nearby tree. It possessed a large slender body, a long tail, reddish-brown fur, and enormous claws. The thing slithered around at night and scared the dickens out of the decrepit priest. Duran became convinced the elusive creature represented the devil. It had to be hunted down and shot.

Reluctantly, sacrificing his valet's help, Duran assigned Sean Brennan to kill the haunting creature. Sean knew the thing was nothing more than a tree shrew. He'd dealt with the varmints on his dad's golf course. But an acting role had to be maintained and proven with an outward face of concern. For months, equipped with a flashlight, air rifle and scope, Sean watched on the balcony, biting at the bit to pull the trigger. Except for the loss of sleep, he didn't mind; it was actually liberating outside of the apartment.

He'd occasionally step back into Duran's bedroom to report on the kill mission. Although a flood of global matters waned, Duran actively monitored Sean's progress.

"Sean, did you get him?"

"No, not yet."

"Do you think he's still out there?" Duran knew he was.

"Sure he is." Sean had no idea and really didn't care. It was nice to be outside in the fresh air.

Duran shook his head, rubbed his face, and tightened his lips, conveying a momentary look of determination. He instructed Sean to fetch some cough drops, discussed the probable hiding place of the critter, and adjusted hunting strategy ideas. Sean skated back outside and resumed his monotonous post. Everyone grew weary of the devil rat saga. The tree shrew survived.

As 2006 ran down, Duran exhibited increased signs of deterioration. The poo march marked a low point.

Father Duran and Petro strolled on the balcony. The unshaven priest puffed away and scooted along with baby steps. Supporting the man, Petro inched on the left. Petro Shevchuk was a no nonsense Ukrainian farmer with a broken nose from a bar fight years ago. The blond haired and passionate young man now lived in the Tespi apartment as a Miles Jesu seminarian. I'd helped recruit him into the Ukrainian community when the kid was eighteen. This dark morning, he assisted Father Duran. Gelson and Brennan couldn't take it anymore; they'd escaped for a break and begged Petro to take over for a few hours.

"Petro stop. Stop! What are you doing?"

Duran had been picking on Petro for months now. The Ukrainian could do nothing right.

"I'm stopping."

"No you're not. You're stubborn and proud."

The priest then began to pull down his pants and underwear. He wanted to urinate.

"What are you doing Father?"

"What do you mean? Do I need to tell you what I'm doing? Who are you Petro? Who do you think you are?" Duran was extra feisty this morning.

"If you need to go to the bathroom we can go inside."

"Are you telling me what to do?"

"No, I am trying to help you. We can go inside to use the bathroom."

"Okay, let's go." Something momentarily clicked.

They entered the blue tiled bathroom; Duran sat on the toilet. Petro parked himself on the edge of the bathtub. This was a normal situation. Father Duran often sat on the pot for lengthy stretches of time, conducting meetings with members perched on the bathtub. Often, a small group of people crowded into the bathroom, some sitting, some standing, as business jarred forward, backward, and forward again in a different direction.

After twenty minutes, Duran had an idea.

"Petro, go down to the chapel and bring back a couple of candles. We must confront the devil."

Petro returned with the candles, without the faintest idea of Duran's plan. He walked into the bathroom and contempt rushed into the eyes of the General. Duran exploded.

"Petro, what is this?"

"Here are the candles, Father."

"Did I ask for candles? You never listen, do you? I asked for two candles and two candlesticks. And two candlesticks! Where are the candlesticks? Go get the candlesticks." Duran grabbed the candles. He'd only asked for candles.

Petro returned and the tragic comedy resumed. It wasn't funny to Petro. The tall white candles were inserted into the brass candlestick holders and Father Duran revealed his strategy to thwart the devil.

"Petro, we are going to make a procession with the candles and the relic of the true cross. Go get the relic on the tabernacle and call Father Kroll and Vasyl. I have to take a crap and the devil is blocking me up."

"Okay, Father."

Turning around, heading for the door, Petro rolled his eyes and slightly shook his head. Good thing Duran didn't see it.

The pious crowd assembled in the bathroom. Kroll had been busy tallying income slips from the Vatican Bank. Vasyl, a cheerful Ukrainian recruit, had been cramming for an exam. Everyone came together; Duran organized things.

"Petro, go ahead and light the candles."

A match was struck and Father Duran lost it.

"Petro," he yelled, "What are you doing? What are you doing? Don't light the candle that way!"

"I'm lighting the candles."

"You're doing it all wrong. Use the toilet paper."

"Use the toilet paper?"

Duran looked to Father Kroll and insulted Petro.

"What do you think Father Kroll? Petro has no idea of what to do, a farm boy with nothing in his head."

Kroll took the toilet paper and discreetly agreed.

"Yes, I can help." He pulled a long line of paper and twisted it into a straight candle lighter, lit the end, and then lit the candles.

Duran's frustrated face broke with a smile.

"See, Petro, that's how to do it. Do you understand now? No. You'll never understand."

Petro stood there and swallowed. His only consolation was that his shift would soon end.

Father Jerry Kroll now threw on a stole and vestment; they lined up, and began the procession. Burning candles floated around the room with the relic held up high. The faithful marched around, with Duran in a bath robe swaggering from the rear.

After a few circles, the prayers fell silent and the procession halted. Everybody disbanded except for Vasyl and Duran. Vasyl winked and nodded at Petro. Relief had arrived. Petro felt a wave of thankfulness for his friend and silently slipped into the hallway. Vasyl lead Duran back into the bedroom.

# CHAPTER NINE

B eneath a crescent moon, nine taxed apostles snoozed in the attic at Via Tespi. Army bunk beds with plywood and three-inch-thick mattresses held up the drained bodies. I turned and woke sufficiently for consciousness to spark. Suddenly, the powerful presence of Jesus seized me. Not again! I swear I could feel the impression of his weight upon my mattress and the heat of his body next to me.

Happiness shot through me. Closing my eyes, I could feel his head resting on my breast and his hand upon my heart. "Good morning Andy. I love you. Just let me be here," he whispered. Hearing him, I filled with a love so piercing I couldn't hold back the tears, and immediately pushed the pillow into my face so nobody would hear my sobs of pure joy.

Miles Jesu kept tumbling down the rabbit hole, but prayer therapy detached me from the chaos. By the end of 2006, after fifteen months and almost six hundred hours of affirmation meditations, I not only survived but flourished in a wonderfully disassociated world. Still imprisoned physically, in the midst of craziness I enjoyed heaven.

It seemed like ages ago, five thousand miles away, Father Dietrich had said that within fifteen months the power of love would come crashing into my life. It had, exactly as he'd estimated. For two weeks now, love had shaken me awake in the dark and left me crying for hours. Love had gushed into me so forcefully that it felt my heart would burst open. It actually hurt. My chest and ribs ached. I begged Jesus to tone it down.

"Jesus, please. It's too much! I can't take it. Please! I beg you."

My eyes were soaked and my breathing erratic. The almost nightly experience would continue for months. I lost a lot of sleep.

This intense reception of love rooted in my soul. It flowed from count-less hours of affirmation meditations, each organically linked in a chain of love episodes, together making a mysterious whole that had taken on a life all its own. I hadn't charted a systematic course to follow. Love had its way with me. Day by day, I merely saw and felt myself being loved, usually on a beach with a sparkling sunset. I hadn't planned to go anywhere, but Jesus whisked me everywhere in the world, regardless of borders and time itself. Each morning, I'd hide in the chapel, close my eyes, enjoy the beach with my friend, and off we'd go.

We fished in Minnesota, conversed over a morning coffee in a Tennessee café, strolled the shores of Southern Italy, and perched on a castle wall overlooking a lush valley in Northern Spain. We hiked, swam, traveled, relaxed on the decks of cruise ships, and developed a real friendship. Sharing stories and feelings, we bonded intimately together. As Miles Jesu went wild I lost myself in a honeymoon life.

I suffered bouts of anger with Jesus too, lashing out at his indifference throughout the years. He absorbed my accusations with a smile, sometimes with tears, sorry that I'd suffered so much. He'd look me in the eyes, place his hand upon mine, sympathize and apologize. Though he didn't need to say it, I needed to hear it. Then he'd promise, "I'll make everything up to you, Andy."

Like the ghost of Christmas past, Jesus took me to my childhood, not to mourn, but to see his loving presence revealed. As I smashed the ball at soccer matches, I discovered his face in the crowd. He cheered for me from the sideline. My father never attended a single game; Jesus never missed one.

He shepherded me to the most distressing moment of my childhood. Floating overhead, we observed a teenage Andy devastated at the loss of Linda Hughes. Mom had forbidden me from seeing her, and I lay in bed crying. Jesus came and sat next to me on the bed. He placed his hand upon me and spoke.

"My poor Andy, let me console you. I hear you my friend. I will answer your prayers, in time. I promise you'll know love."

The teenage Andy perceived nothing, but now I witnessed everything from above. I witnessed the entire picture of reality. He was really there listening! He always had been. The wound healed and the memory became a source of comfort whenever recalled.

Visiting the abuses and traumas of my life, a wave of profound healing washed over me. For the most part, each therapeutic encounter followed a similar pattern. I'd initially experience a memory which would evoke a few days of emotional upheaval. Once this internal retching ran its course, I'd somehow discover Jesus embedded in the memory. His presence always surprised me. I'd never seen him there before. I'd then witness his unveiled solicitude, his understanding, his compassionate response. After sharing our feelings about the wound, and there's nothing like sharing intimate feelings to seal a relationship, the memory would transform into a wellspring of gratitude. I'd receive a gift, unwrap it, and find meaning and enrichment flowing from the suffering. The wound would close up and the memory would lodge itself in my heart as another sign of God's love. Hundreds upon hundreds of these love-proofs overwhelmed me.

Jesus was there in my family's home when Fred and Paul had come to recruit me; he tried to slow them down. He was there at the picnic table in Virginia when my innocence had been manipulated; he promised my rescue.

He was there in the chapel when I'd despaired at facing ordination the next day; he took me by the hand and simply walked me through an insurmountable wall into a breathtaking garden. We enjoyed three days on the other side of the wall, sitting near a babbling brook, beneath a sun radiating dancing beams through swaying greenery. We entertained conversations about marriage. The rapid succession of healing experiences and the intensity of scenes broke me down and simultaneously reconstructed me.

He was there revealing my soul to me and protecting me from harm at each instance of healing. He was there in Ukraine where despair climaxed in sexual intercourse; there next to me wherever Duran shamed me publicly; there at a dock on Catalina Island at three in the morning. I had sat there grieving, hungry for the smallest morsel of intimacy in my life. Jesus appeared, sat next to me, put his arms around me, and soothed me with consolations.

"My dear friend, I've been looking for you. I'm here. You don't need to wander about looking for love. I love you. You'll soon receive an outpouring of love. Hold on a little more." I fell asleep in his arms.

By December 2006, receiving love precipitated my psychic birth, terribly late in life, but finally coming. I wiggled forward past the midpoint of a birth canal.

Dr. Anna Terruwe and Dr. Conrad Baars defined psychic birth as a second birth, not physical but psychological. As human development naturally unfolds, a psychological birth results gradually from an interplay of love between mother and infant. With her caresses, kisses, gazes of adoration, the mother lavishes pure love and acceptance. The baby absorbs this loving presence through the senses and responds with enjoyment, satisfaction, and overtures for more. This intimate love-exchange leads to an affirming communion of persons and a child's internal sense of being loved and wanted, lovable and worthwhile. From these deeply planted core feelings, further nurtured during the growth period of childhood, sprout homogeneous beliefs and thoughts. A psychologically stable person is born, gifted with genuine self-confidence and a worthy self-image.

From a clinical perspective, when an emotionally affirming relationship is lacking, psychic birth is abnormally and indefinitely delayed. This frustrated condition may last a lifetime, condemning the adult to an emotionally crippled existence. But given the proper conditions, it's never too late to grow. Once the passive reception of affirming love invades the heart, emotional development resumes, reaching its maturity with a whole new way of feeling and thinking and self-perceiving.

The crowning glory of emotional growth, psychic birth opens the beloved's eyes to an astounding personal awareness. The old-newborn at last feels he is loved not for what he does but for who he is. He no longer tries to convince himself that he is loved; he feels it, knows it. A new frontier of understanding comes into view and the neophyte receives the gift of himself from the unconditional lover.

For the first time, I experienced the awesome truth of my own inherent goodness. Flooded with this inner light, the world felt different.

The morning of December 21, 2006 I felt compelled to flee the chapel. Father Duran had established the custom of indulging the exorcism formula immediately after everyone received Holy Communion. The most precious moments of the day created for sublime sharing with God, were now routinely squandered on rebuking the Prince of Darkness. After months of frustration I couldn't take this lunacy. I rose, mumbled a lame excuse, and discreetly exited the chapel. A few turned heads wondered what the hell had gotten into me. Good thing Duran wasn't there.

I descended into the basement and locked myself in the bathroom. Practically tearing off my vestments and bundling them into a clump, I hurled them at the washing machine. Emotions and images took over. At the base of the toilet, inches away from a dead cockroach sprawled upon its back, I buried my face in a towel on the floor, and cried.

Then I felt his presence, his hand upon my back. Always a surprise, he appeared anywhere and everywhere now. Jesus knelt next to me, bent low, and whispered into my ear.

"It is time my son. Go. Go to the Vatican and I will lead you to my friends."

It wasn't the first time I'd heard this, but it was the first time the words penetrated with irresistible force.

The thought of going to the Vatican alarmed me. Curled up on the floor, I grappled with the risk of defying Father Duran. Admittedly, it helped that the man didn't function with a full deck.

Even so, it was the scariest moment of my life. I feared Father Duran and the consequences of getting caught. Dread crept from the pit of my stomach. I didn't want the inspiration. My breathing constricted.

I sat up, rested my right arm on the toilet seat and stared inward. Ruminating over Miles Jesu's ineptitude to help me, a rush of determination shot through me. No matter the cost, I'd pursue my complete emotional healing to the end. Nothing would stop me. At that moment, fear lost its domination over me. I would break through the forbidden barrier. I shut my eyes.

"Okay, Jesus, I'll go. Today."

A couple hours later, after the students had left for the day, and Duran had fallen into his usual drug induced slumber, I grabbed the keys to the white Fiat Tipo and slipped out the front door. A few minutes later, I flew northeast along Via del Mare toward the Vatican. Speed. I'd allotted an hour for driving there and back and an hour for a meeting with someone, anyone. Jesus would have to keep his word because I had no idea who to see.

Just beyond the reach of the twisting Tiber, the Vatican sat west of central Rome. In ancient times, toga clad mourners had gathered there to weep at a pagan cemetery on a hillside. As Roman law had prohibited the burial of the deceased in the city, Vatican hill functioned as a necropolis outside urban boundaries. Marking the turnaround spot with a majestic rosy obelisk from Egypt, Nero's Circus lounged at the foot of the slope. Saint Peter had been martyred there, his body carried up the hill and buried.

Two thousand years later, the Vatican had resurrected. Rome bulged with six million inhabitants and Vatican City teamed with living people. Sheltering briefcases stuffed with important documents, Brazilians, Indians, and Ethiopians, people from all corners of the planet bumped about, checking their watches to keep appointments with princes of the Church.

Checking my watch and scanning for police, I ripped up the right-hand side of the Tiber. By 1929, Pope Pius XI and Mussolini had agreed upon the boundaries and character of the smallest city-country in the world: Vatican State. Behind Renaissance walls, the cobblestoned wonderland would operate as a Catholic theocracy, as its own country within a host country.

Apart from ample supplemental properties scattered throughout the city of Rome, Vatican State claimed a mere one hundred and ten acres of land. Arrayed with fountains and sculptures, manicured trees and exotic plants from a multitude of countries, the Vatican gardens appropriated fifty-seven acres. This left fifty-three acres for the rest of the country.

Near Ponte Mazzini I slowed, held up by backed up traffic. An opening emerged; I hit the clutch, pushed the stick into third, curved to the right and whipped pass a few parked cars in the left lane. Broken glass sparkled beneath their bumpers, doors hung open, drivers stood their ground, arguing with dramatic hand gestures. I hit a green light and accelerated.

Monolithic structures, Saint Peter's Square and Basilica, the Vatican library, museum, archives, bank, the papal residence, all vied for a sliver of the precious remaining acreage. Swimming in the wake of such indispensable institutions a thousand dwellers, including a hundred Swiss Guard, occupied the nooks and crannies. Most of the population consisted of clergy with prestigious Vatican jobs, and their envied families. The grocery store, pharmacy, parish church, and post office devoured the last scraps of space. With no room for foreign embassies, the world's ambassadors to the Holy See had to scrounge for prestige elsewhere.

Decked with legislative, executive, and judicial powers, the Pope reigned over Vatican State. Delegating the bulk of national affairs to a Secretary of State, the Pope somehow found the time to govern a billion strong Roman Catholic Church, diffused world-wide. Over millennia this vast task grew more and more dependent upon a central governing apparatus. The administrative structure now consisted of a bureaucratic web of congregations, tribunals, Pontifical councils, commissions, and a curia. A nexus of delegated power concentrated in thousands of offices scattered within Vatican City and throughout the city of Rome.

I hung a left at Vittorio Emanuele II and clipped over a bridge lined with stubby obelisks and naked statues. Bumping down a decline, turning left again, the stunning facade of Saint Peter's Basilica came into view. Blurring past quaint outside cafés and waves of tourists, I sprinted toward the end of Via Conciliazione and hit the brakes in the piazza.

The Piazza of Pius XII enjoyed a prime plot of land adjacent to the entrance of Saint Peter's Square. Talk about location! The street piazza functioned as a virtual diving board into an expansive tourist fairyland, distinguished by Bernini's colonnade, mushroomed fountains, a cool obelisk, and the famed basilica. Symmetrical five-story office buildings flanked each side of Pius XII square, representing Vatican overflow spilling into Rome.

I jammed the Tipo into a tight fitting parking space on the right side of the piazza, near the Holy See Press Office. Slamming the door shut, stepping up the curb, I walked to the towering twenty-foot-high double doors of the Vatican monster. Pausing, looking around, time momentarily froze. Everything seemed familiar, the hot dog stand and religious article store to my left, the convoluted phone booth, the tourist buses, the Vatican's pilgrimage business to the right.

The papal tiara and crisscrossed keys over the lentil forced a moment of reflection. *What am I getting myself into? Why did I come here?* Suddenly, nothing felt familiar at all. But the clock kept ticking, and I sensed Jesus urging me forward.

Through the doors, up the flight of stairs on the left, I cracked open a stately portal and passed under a granite chiseled plaque: *Congregatio pro Institutis Consecratae et Societatibus Vitae Apostolicae.* I'd been here many times in the shadow of Father Duran, most often to confer with his old friend from seminary days. Typically, I sat nearby while they jabbered in Spanish.

The primary door opened into a spacious entrance hall with a tiny desk. Sixty feet of polished marble reflected the sun illuminating a high ceiling. At each end of the hall additional double doors led to labyrinths of private offices. Each office represented an assigned worker bee with a Roman collar, some sort of specialty of drudgery, and an eternal allotment of deadlines.

I knew the receptionist at the desk, at least by sight. He had a giraffe neck, beak nose, tight haircut, and welcoming smile. Luigi turned his head, offered a sincere *"buon giorno,"* and waited. We recognized each other. Did he wonder why I was alone? Would he tell on me? Ignoring my paranoia, I shot from the hip and improvised.

"Good Morning," I returned. "I'd like to see the priest from America. I'm sorry, I can't remember his name."

Many Vatican beehives employed an American priest or two. My chances were good of getting a sympathetic priest capable of conversing in English.

"Maybe it was Monsignor Murphy?" asked Luigi.

"Yes, that's it."

Luigi continued, "Do you have an appointment?"

"No, but I'm sure he'd see me."

I hoped he would see me. Throughout the years I'd learned that many less noticeable Vatican officials welcomed visitors without appointments. Duran had known this and pushed the possibilities to the limit. He'd show up with a group of members to see a bishop, purposefully making it difficult for a secretary to send everyone away.

I divulged my name and waited. After indicating where I should stand, Luigi picked up the phone, punched a memorized extension, and exchanged a few laughs with the monsignor.

Hanging up, the receptionist assured me that the monsignor would see me. Luigi pointed to a door and instructed me to take an immediate left and walk to the end of the hallway.

"Before another corridor opens left, the monsignor's office is the last door on the right." It must have been a fifty-yard walk.

Monsignor Bret Murphy wore an unblemished white shirt, trimmed with elegant gold cufflinks. Snapped behind his waist and neck, a formal clerical bib hung neatly over his chest and stomach. A Midwestern prairie boy from the cascades of the Big Sioux River, the priest radiated innocence, good manners, and neighborliness. He had light-brown hair, full cheeks, squinty eyes, a soft voice, and a genuine smile. Nearing the end of an eight-year stint, Murphy was on loan to the Vatican from the Diocese of Sioux Falls, South Dakota.

We met just outside his office door. The Monsignor gave me a firm handshake and warm greeting.

"Hello, I'm Monsignor Murphy. Come this way."

He insisted I enter first. I introduced myself and walked through the doorway into a small but tasteful office. No clutter, comfortable chairs, the faint smell of wood polish hung in the air. A perfectly ordered desk sat near a marble edged window; a beautiful painting of the Blessed Virgin Mary hung on the wall. We each grabbed a chair. Facing each other, the priest lent the impression that I was the center of attention and he had all the time in the world. A real gentleman.

Not realizing it yet, God had guided me to a man eminently capable of understanding and advising me. As Miles Jesu prohibited spiritual direction with outsiders, this was a first for me. Monsignor Murphy shined as a prolific theologian, a star canon lawyer, and a shrewd Vatican counselor. His expertise fixated on the consecrated vocation and exclaustrations. Somehow, exactly the man I needed.

After some small talk about our families and how we each had ended up in Rome, the Monsignor got down to business.

"So, Father Sullivan, what brings you here today? What can I do for you?"

"I need some advice. I'm a member of a new group called Miles Jesu. It's headquartered in Axa, a suburb of Rome."

His lawyer mind sought a simple clarification. "What's the canonical status of Miles Jesu?"

"In 2002 it was approved as an Ecclesial Family of Consecrated Life."

The Monsignor instantly perceived the generic characteristics of the group's newly carved category. It was a group then, mixed with men and women, consecrated and non-consecrated lay members, priests and lay followers, community members and those detached from community life. The Ecclesial Family was a medley of everyone who wanted to love God. Under canon 605, it was designated as an experimental form of consecrated life. Only a handful existed.

"I see, so the Congregation established Miles Jesu as an Ecclesial Family?"

"No, the Vicariate did, after working out the details with the Congregation."

The Monsignor thought that unusual. Thus far, it had been the Congregation that erected Ecclesial Families of Consecrated Life.

"That would make Miles Jesu not a pontifical, but a diocesan institute," he said.

"Yes."

"Then, Cardinal Ruini is the external superior of Miles Jesu."

"Yes."

It felt weird to say. It was seldom acknowledged in community. The emphasis always pointed to the Holy Father as the ultimate superior of Miles Jesu, as if a chain of command hardly mattered.

The monsignor pressed further, politely inquiring about my incardination. According to canon law, incardination ties the priest to a particular ecclesial superior. No priest can move around and operate in a free-lance kind of way. Without assuming, Murphy wanted to understand which bishop held jurisdiction over the priests of Miles Jesu.

"Father Sullivan, may I ask where you are incardinated?"

"I'm incardinated in Miles Jesu."

"What was that? Really? In diocesan institutes the priests are incardinated in the diocese itself, under the local bishop." He shook his head and licked his lips. "That's unusual."

At the risk of making things muddier, I tried to explain further.

"I was originally incardinated in the Diocese of Ponce, Puerto Rico, when the Institute had been erected there, and then released to Miles Jesu. Within six months after my ordination, Miles Jesu had been re-established here in the Diocese of Rome. In January 2002, Cardinal Ruini erected Miles Jesu in Rome, with a five-year approval of an experimental set of constitutions. In his decree the clerics of Miles Jesu shifted to incardination in Miles Jesu."

Monsignor Murphy wiggled in his chair. Scratching his head, he tried to grasp something normally simple and straight forward.

"So, the clerics are incardinated in the diocesan institute itself? Okay."

He turned his head slightly and lifted his eyebrows.

"Again, this is not normal. But the General Director? What is his name?"

"Father Alphonsus Duran."

"In Cardinal Ruini's decree was anything stipulated about the incardination of Father Duran?"

"No, I don't think so."

"It seems Father Duran's incardination would fall under the jurisdiction of Cardinal Ruini," said Murphy.

"I don't know. I suppose it would. It's not the kind of thing ever brought up or specified in Miles Jesu." It struck me that instant; I'd been in Miles Jesu twenty-eight years and didn't have a precise idea about who functioned as Father Duran's ecclesial superior.

Monsignor Murphy momentarily stared at me, now unsure of pursuing his own clarifications. He had brushed against the tip of an iceberg and sensed a mountain of irregularities lurking beneath. His curiosity peaked and he adjusted his approach. Encouraging me to express my needs, the neighbor from Sioux Falls held his horses and decided to tilt back and listen.

"Tell me Father Sullivan; what can I do for you? What brings you here this morning?"

I exhaled, slipped deeper into the chair, and proceeded to relate the story of my life. The monsignor's alarm escalated as I uncovered the rogue way Duran flew under the radar, mis-governed Miles Jesu, and traumatized me. I tried to focus on my own emotional immaturity, its discovery, and the amazing healing I'd experienced. Monsignor Murphy slumped, dumbfounded at the results of my therapeutic prayer. He stroked his chin, impressed at the power of the passive reception of love. It had overwhelmed me, empowered emotional development, and thrust me into his office.

It took almost an hour to sketch a provisional profile of my life. I looked at my watch and imagined hell breaking loose upon my return to the Miles Jesu apartment.

The monsignor perceived my anxiety. "Father Sullivan, are you okay with the time?" He couldn't have been more polite.

"I'm okay, but don't have much time left."

"Do you have another appointment somewhere else?"

"No, I don't." I paused. *What the hell.* "I'm here this morning because I secretly escaped from the community house. Nobody in Miles Jesu knows I'm here and I have to return soon if I'm not to be caught."

Murphy's eyes opened. He scooted to the edge of his chair and placed his hands on his knees.

"I don't understand. What do you mean, you escaped?"

"I've been under house arrest for over three years now. I'm not allowed to leave the Miles Jesu apartment in Axa." Disbelief washed over the monsignor's face.

"What do you mean?"

"By obedience, I absolutely can't leave the apartment, unless I have the express permission of Father Duran, who assigns someone to practically hold my hand."

Monsignor Bret Murphy stared at me. Anger began to bubble.

"This is absurd. We don't live in the middle ages. This is not how people are treated in consecrated life."

"Yes, I know." But did I really know? I scrunched my shoulders, lifted up my hands, and waggled my head in agreement. "I know the theory of consecrated life. But Miles Jesu is the only way of consecrated life I've ever experienced. Almost thirty years of it. Miles Jesu has always operated outside of the norms."

"Father Sullivan, are authorities aware of Father Duran's manner of governing?"

"Are you kidding? Of course not."

Silence descended. Mental activity ricocheted in Murphy's skull. I fixated on my watch, calculating a dash for Via Tespi. Where did all the time go? Restlessness gripped me. I had to leave, but couldn't. Touching upon the essence of my visit, a few nagging questions persisted.

"Monsignor, I hadn't planned to use so much time talking about Miles Jesu. I actually came here for personal advice. My therapeutic prayer and emotional growth have resulted in a strong desire for objectivity. Although I know how to initiate emotional growth, I don't know how things end. My meditations are so powerful my imagined world often seems more real than reality itself. I feel a need for feedback from a competent psychotherapist."

"Well, given your unique situation, that's probably a good idea. Your desire for outside objectivity is a good sign in itself, in my opinion."

"I want to find a psychotherapist and start psychotherapy, but don't see how this is possible. Father Duran doesn't believe in psychotherapy. He laughs at the idea of paying for it. Does a religious order have an obligation to care for the psychological needs of its professed members?"

"Yes, any institute of consecrated life has an obligation to care for its own. This is a general principle that applies to psychological help. If a member has a legitimate need for psychological counseling the institute must allow for this kind of care and pay for it too. Even more, an order can neither impose psychological counseling, nor require a revelation of conscience to the superior. Whatever is discussed between a psychotherapist and a member of an order is personal and not subject to intrusion by superiors."

I chewed on the monsignor's words and let out a laugh.

"When Father Duran might send a hopeless member to a shrink he'd tell that person what to say and then demand an account of what was discussed. The whole purpose would be to gather information and twist it in favor of whatever he believed to be true." The monsignor shook his head.

"That's hideous. It helps nobody."

I didn't have much time and changed the subject.

"My other question concerns morals. Given my circumstances, I'm not sure what to do. I believe I need psychotherapy, but Miles Jesu stands in the way. What would you recommend?"

"You should try to find a competent psychotherapist and get permission from a superior. You'll need permission if Miles Jesu is going to pay for therapy. Try to follow the standard way of proceeding. If that doesn't work, then you could consider other options. Besides Father Duran, is there another superior you could approach for help?"

"Yes, maybe Father Gelson."

"Who is he?"

"He's the Vicar Director of Miles Jesu. He'd most likely lend more help than Father Duran. Still, it would take a miracle to pin down Father Gelson, express my need, and lobby permission. I'll see what's possible. But if things don't work out, I'd like to consult a good moral theologian. I want to know my grounds if I must do things without permission."

"I'd recommend Monsignor Harrison across the street in the Congregation for Bishops. He'd give excellent advice. He's a good friend of mine and will treat whatever you tell him in the strictest of confidence."

The Pope had recently designated Father John Harrison a monsignor. An American priest from the diocese of Allentown, Pennsylvania, a five year Vatican appointee as a proficient moral theologian, Harrison advised a multitude of bishops. I'd seen him a few times at the Angelicum, where he lectured occasionally as a guest professor.

"Okay, great. May I use your name if I see Monsignor Harrison?"

"Yes, of course. Just say that I recommended you see him."

"Good. I guess that about does it. I really have to go."

Handing me his business card, Murphy made a gesture of kindness.

"Father Sullivan, my door is always open if you should have more needs."

I held up the card in gratitude. "I appreciate it Monsignor."

I uncrossed my legs and started to get up. At that instant, the monsignor threw an unexpected curve ball.

"Father Sullivan, given your circumstances, you might want to consider an exclaustration."

"An exclaustration?"

Holding back my gut reaction, I knew this implied a war with Miles Jesu.

"I'll research it and give it some thought. I really have to go." "I understand," he said.

We rose and shook hands. I stepped out the door, said a quick farewell, and hurried down the corridor.

The delightful Italian countryside blurred by; fear pressed my foot heavy upon the accelerator. Flying down Via del Mare, my mind exploded in countless directions. I planned the lie I might use if caught. Then wonder dominated. Amazement swelled within me, drowning every worry. I could hardly believe what I just did, what God did. Imagining the possibilities of healing, a feeling of hope comforted me.

Then reality struck me. How on earth is this going to work? Shaking my head, I had no idea. Psychotherapy seemed impossible. His presence suddenly riding shotgun promised a good destiny. Jesus looked ahead and encouraged me, "Do not be afraid, Andy. I will heal you."

Twirling into the back lot, I skidded to a stop. I slammed the car door shut and dashed for the men's apartment. The idea of wiping my fingerprints from the steering wheel put a grin on my face and made me laugh. *What the hell? I didn't do anything illegal. Don't I have a right to real advice?*

Carefully, silently, I turned the knob, cracked open the front door, and slipped into the apartment. Nobody. I skipped into the kitchen, threw on an apron, and started to peel a batch of potatoes. Had anyone noticed my disappearance?

Within minutes, Tomas Jedlicka appeared in the kitchen. I almost had a heart attack. He was a member of Miles Jesu and a medical doctor from Czech Republic. Tomas had the munchies and like a rabbit pawed a nearby carrot and nibbled away.

"Good morning Father Sullivan. How are you today?"

"I'm fine, thanks."

He made some small talk about Duran's night and looked at his watch.

"I have to go back up to Father's room and sit there. He better not wake up without me next to him."

I offered Tomas another carrot; he happily grabbed it, thanked me, and headed for the stairs. I stopped peeling and stared out the kitchen window. A tremendous wave of relief washed over me. Nobody had noticed anything. Opening the window, I let out a deep sigh and inhaled the fresh air. My defiance that morning emboldened me to seek healing outside of Miles Jesu.

A Spanish galleon sailed over the crest of a massive wave, fell and smashed into a watery grave. The dreadful impact shook the proud vessel. While the perishing crew hung on for life, a submerged bow momentarily fought for air.

About a football field away, Jesus and I stood shoulder deep in calm water, close to a lazy shore. A soft golden glow surrounded us, protected us. The storm rose about fifty yards out. We watched the tragedy unfold before us, as if from the comfort of front row seats. The horrendous scene riveted our attention.

Darkness descended upon the warship, tossed about, drenched, struggling to escape sinking. Torrential rain, lightning strikes, high-pitched winds unleashed their fury. Loose rigging sloshed about wherever the sea invaded bow or stern. The cracking and splintering of the masts, rendering crushing thuds upon the deck sent terrified men scrambling for cover. I could hear faint wails for help. I recognized the voices.

Hit by a breaker from hell, popping the ship's seams, the sea washed into a gaping fracture. Knowing all was lost, men panicked and leapt overboard. Some perished; others barely survived, grasping onto floating pieces of wreckage. The ship floundered; the stern sank into raging waters. Towering high in the sky, the bow hopelessly surrendered. Hidden in wet blackness and buffeted by gale-force winds, lightning photographed and illuminated in stark and terrifying beauty, the ship's terminal plunge.

Our feet bounced weightlessly upon the sand. Speechless, Jesus and I stared. We knew the meaning of the drama. Familiar with the faces and voices of the survivors we witnessed the approaching fate of Miles Jesu. I cared little, felt little for the ship. Yet my heart grieved for the souls who'd lost all they knew.

Clack, clack, clack, thud! The kneeler wobbled. Someone began to say something, rudely demanding my attention. The meditation was so graphic, so captivating, it was difficult to grasp the reality of the moment. From the other side of the confessional screen, Olha Klub exposed her sins.

Toward the end of January, 2007, I sat in the kitchen at Via Tespi, enjoying a scrap of solitude in a makeshift confessional. Olha appeared from nowhere. Her softly spoken words mingled with the residual image of a sinking ship that still begged for my attention.

Olha wanted a moment of solace from an erratic life. She almost rested her head against the metal confessional grate, but held back. A light blue veil flowed from a precarious white strip of plastic covering her forehead. The slightest pressure in the wrong place might pop the head piece open. The plastic was a jimmy-rigged flap cut from an ice cream container. Father Duran thought it looked elegant, unaware of its origin. The women kept buying ice cream for the perfectly shaped white plastic curve.

Her words penetrated my vulnerable heart. I could now receive and feel the tears of another person. For decades, my heart had sealed shut like an impenetrable rock, now it enjoyed countless opened passageways like a sponge. It had grown accustomed to absorbing beauty and goodness and love, feeling compassion, and empathizing. I felt like a real human being.

The habit of receiving love had radically changed my feelings and beliefs about love. Love was no longer Duran's twisted idea. It was not a presumed and platonic good violently forced upon a person, regardless of its welcome or not. No. Love breathed. It inhaled and exhaled. It journeyed into an open heart, expanded the heart, warmed and relished the inner world. Then, once love filled that heart to the brim it effortlessly overflowed back into the world. I experienced this and let it have its way with me. Receiving love taught me how to give love. Presumption and force had no place in loving. Love respected the sentiments, desires, and limits of the receiver. It took its time and didn't care if it took a while.

Olha's words sank into my soul. On my side of the confessional screen tears trickled down my face. She soon finished her list of iniquities and fell silent. I briefly encouraged her, traced the sign of the cross in the air, and imparted the formula of absolution.

"I absolve you from your sins in the name of the Father, and of the Son, and of the Holy Spirit."

Ignoring canon law, Father Duran had forbidden Miles Jesu confessors from advising internal community members. Not a word of spiritual direction could pass through the priest's lips. Apparently, Duran didn't want his priests to compete with his undisputed control of ideas and principles. At the same time, if the penitent was a potential vocation or benefactor the priest could lavish guidance and swim in the art of persuasion.

Olha thanked me, stood up, and turned away. I listened to her heels clack upon the floor and fade away as she returned to the chapel. I let her go, but my heart rebelled. I promised myself that no matter the cost, I'd find a way to help this woman. My determination to reach out to her had nothing to do with the specific confession she had made, but everything to do with her innocence and the damaging treatment Olha had endured from Miles Jesu.

I remembered the first time I'd encountered her. Thirteen years ago, she'd appeared in the bedroom of a humble home in an isolated Ukrainian village. Shivering, despairing, hiding in a bed, I was sick as a dog and on the verge of leaving Miles Jesu. Olha was the newest member of the women's community. She was a happy and enthusiastic young recruit. Thoroughly broken by Miles Jesu, I looked at Olha and felt sorry for her, knowing she'd be destroyed.

After her confession, Olha sat in the back of the men's chapel at Via Tespi and waited for Mass to begin. Feeling sorry for herself, she distractedly fixated on her superior.

She remembered her superior pressuring her to profess perpetual vows. Olha resented the coercion and manipulation to do what she didn't want to do.

The chapel door swung open. Everyone popped up as Father Duran and his priests and altar servers progressed into the chapel. I was one of those priests. The opening hymn burst forth. Trying to shake the memory from her head, Olha opened her eyes, found a songbook next to her, and rose at a snail's pace.

The Mass sped along without fuss, until the sermon. Oblivious to the real entrapment Olha experienced within her, Duran harangued about his latest crusade. Nothing energized him more than a good fight.

The *L'osservatore Romano*, the Vatican's illustrious newspaper had published an article referring to the Epiphany Feast as a 'little Christmas.' This had enraged Duran and set in motion a newly formed Miles Jesu committee to draft a detailed response to the editor. Although Jesus had spared me a place among the weary researchers and writers, it was impossible not to be a spectator of the fiasco. Duran spearheaded a veritable war to topple the 'thoughtless and ignorant journalist' from his throne.

Like a captain at the helm of an advancing warship, Duran stood defiantly at the chapel podium, demanding to know the status of the ever expanding letter. A lone sailor read the damn thing. Public corrections and additions followed. Everyone sat there in silence nodding in agreement, guarding their true feelings. The entire affair felt exaggerated and tiresome.

The ostentatious spread of Christmas decorations, broad brush strokes of red and gold tinsel flowing everywhere, the baby Jesus on angel hair in the middle of the room on the last day of January suggested an out of touch backdrop. Outside, Christmas had come and gone more than a month ago. Despising cultural expediencies, numb to the inner world of distraught members, Duran thrived in his own universe.

A spirited defense of the Epiphany marched unchecked like a thousand troops heading into battle. Citing festive traditions and quoting ancient big shots, elegant words of defiance hung in the air. Duran's face glowed with approval. If Duran had his way, the journalist would have been fired.

I raised my head and looked past the altar to the other side of the chapel, twenty-five feet away. My wondering eyes discovered Olha looking back at me. We caught each other looking. When a vital conclusion echoed in the room, I tilted my head and raised my eyebrows in phony surprise. Duran didn't notice. Olha welcomed my playfulness and giggled.

For an instant, our souls communicated. We experienced a passing solidarity of some sort. We recognized our survival together in the same plummeting boat. A spark of mutual attraction ignited.

As the rickety cage-elevator crept upward, I caught sight of my face on a polished bronze plate of buttons. Two months of cloak and dagger visits to Vatican offices had a backbone firming effect. Floating above the black and white Roman collar, my face reflected courage and deliberate intent. More grey hair, too. I'd grown accustomed to skirting around house arrest at Via Tespi.

Now, on an overcast Friday morning, escaping from the Miles Jesu apartment, February 9, 2007 marked my first visit with a psychotherapist.

The elevator rattled to an abrupt halt. I pulled open the narrow double doors, pushed through a second set of outwardly swinging doors and stepped forward onto the fourth floor. Immediately to my left I spotted the correct suite. Here was a new threshold in life and I was more than ready. I rang the bell beneath the number forty-two and waited on an exquisite marble landing.

I'd finished my homework and felt confident. During the past few weeks I'd made fifty-three covert phone calls from the men's basement at Via Tespi to psychiatrists and psychotherapists located in the city of Rome. Knowing the kind of therapy and therapist I required to complete my growth into emotional adulthood, I had searched for the right person.

I didn't want cognitive or behavioral therapies, but an approach that stressed affective presence, as close to affirmation therapy as possible. I hoped to find a loving heart capable of understanding and accepting everything about me, and favorable to the prayer method that had already generated astounding emotional growth.

Each doctor had expressed his or her opinion. Some made sense, some oozed stuffy prejudices, some were nuts. Scrawling notes, I discerned the dispositions and attitudes of the unaware contenders. After studying pages of replies and reactions, Ambra Treichler had topped the list.

She had suffered and grown past her own emotional immaturity. She'd conveyed an affirming bearing and humble confidence.

"I've personally experienced what you are going through," she'd said. "I know how to help you." I'd felt the embrace of her maternal care over the phone.

The door swung open to reveal an elderly woman with an amiable face. Clothed in a white dress with thin green and blue bubbles, Grandma bowed her head, offered a hand, and spoke softly.

"Good Morning. How may I help you? My name is Maria."

She juggled her duties as a receptionist, cook, and secretary. Actually, she was another psychotherapist. I shook her hand.

"Yes. My name is Father Andrew Sullivan. I have an appointment with Ambra Treichler at ten."

Ambra had indicated on the phone that the initial visit was free and that she'd make room for me between two other clients.

Maria looked me over.

"Good. She's with someone at the moment. Mrs. Teichler is looking forward to meeting you, Father Sullivan. Please come in." We spoke in Italian. Her words flowed like butter; mine jumped about, loaded down by everything American.

"*Grazie,*" I replied. Maria then motioned where I should walk. She tucked me into a nearby waiting room.

"It won't be long. Please make yourself at home." Maria smiled and gently shut the door, but not entirely. She turned away and made haste down the hallway. A tea kettle whistled in the distance.

The sun filtered through light brown sugar curtains, dispersing a golden glow everywhere. To my left, two grand impressionist paintings hogged the wall space. A Paris sidewalk café. The Eiffel Tower with strolling lovers in a foggy foreground. The right hand wall swelled with neatly organized books from floor to ceiling.

Turning my back on the black leather chairs, paintings and vases with flowers, I felt the magnetism of the books. Scanning a row at shoulder height, I discovered a collection of classics, mostly in Italian, some in German, a few in English: *War and Peace, A Christmas Carol, The Travels of Marco Polo, The Origin of Species, Huckleberry Finn, The Prince.* Everything you'd ever want to read neatly displayed on a handful of room-length shelves. This prohibited wall of humanities represented a void in my education. For decades, Miles Jesu indoctrination had limited my time and oriented my interests to whatever pertained to obedience and getting things done. For countless years, day to day, I barely had time to crap, let alone indulge in a classic.

The door swung open and Ambra Treichler entered. She took a few steps forward, offered her hand, shimmering bracelets and all, and welcomed me. A subtle disturbance of air blanketed me with the scent of perfume.

Ambra was a real knock out, auburn hair down to her shoulders, a perfectly proportioned face, beautiful tanned skin, big blue eyes. "Welcome Father Sullivan. I hope you didn't wait long." Her English vibrated with a slight German accent.

"No, I've only been here a few minutes."

"Good."

With plump lips, she flashed a natural smile. Dolce & Gabbana glasses hung on a delicate chain draping her neck. A floral designed dress exploded with colors, toned down with a white silk scarf flowing over her shoulders. The fifty-year-old widow appeared classy, suggestive, but conservative. The dress manifested a moderate neck line with unadventurous boundaries at the elbows and just below the knees. Her watch and ring smacked of good taste.

Ambra Treichler was born in Zermatt, Switzerland, in a predominately German speaking municipality, ten kilometers north of the Italian border and a stone's throw from the famed Matterhorn. Her passion for lush green valleys, snowcapped peaks, hiking and skiing had persisted into adulthood. She took advantage of every opportunity to explore the beauty of Italy, the peaceful countryside, art, music, and delectable cuisine. She preferred the mountains more than the sea.

Besides her lifelong passion for outdoor adventure, Ambra's childhood faith endured too. Despite her baptism into Jungian analytical psychology, she retained her Swiss reformed faith. She treasured occasional retreats into the quite wonderlands of the grand Catholic churches of Rome, where she'd occasionally wind down and reflect on the meaning of things, and pray a little.

We exited the waiting room, turned right, and entered her small office. Showing me the way, she insisted I go first. No degrees hung on the walls. Ambra never felt the urge to aggrandize her capacities. A few simple paintings of seashores and mountain peaks softened the atmosphere.

"Right here Father Sullivan. Please take this chair." I sat down in a padded black leather chair; she circled around and positioned herself on the other side of an almost bare mahogany desk, strategically arranged to prevent physical proximity.

We agreed to call each other by first names and made introductory chatter. Ambra then invited me to express my needs.

"Andy, tell me why you've come to visit me this morning."

She rested her hands upon the desk, smiled, playfully wiggled her nose, and with a slight nod communicated for me to start. We instantly liked each other. She already felt like a friend. Chemistry sparked between us and I suddenly felt like I could say anything. A seasoned psychotherapist, Ambra was ready for anything I could possible divulge.

Overlapping circumstances converged to peak my trust in Ambra: I trusted my own research; Miles Jesu lacked the competence to help me; daily meditations had refined my receptive disposition; confiding in Tom Walsh had gradually loosened my tongue and taught me how to reveal myself; Jesus had pushed me to discover Ambra.

It took thirty-five minutes to rip through the essentials. I explained my abusive treatment by Miles Jesu, my discovery of emotional deprivation disorder, and the radically transforming practice of affirmation meditation. I then crowned the summary with my need.

"I feel that I need the objectivity of a proficient psychotherapist." Warmed by the sun through the window she soaked up the abbreviation of my life. Ambra had studied at the University of Vienna, an illustrious institution with a long list of legendary scholars and Nobel Prize Laureates.

She had the brains to walk the same halls where visionaries had pioneered, where Carnap, Freud, Frankl, Husserl, Mendal, and Popper had nourished their unique contributions to the world.

Within this broad-minded milieu, Ambra had specialized in Jungian symbols and dream interpretation, and in the therapeutic approach of Donald Winnicott, an English pediatrician and psychoanalyst. This made her adept at discerning the images of the soul and skilled at recognizing and encouraging the emotional and psychological stages of development. Providentially, her personal experience and professional education coincided perfectly with my need.

"Andy, it sounds like you've been systematically traumatized."

"Well said. I'd agree to that."

"Tell me, what finally moved you to come to me today?"

"A few days ago, I started to experience some startling revelations about my mother and my relationship with her."

"And how did this happen?"

"It was through the meditations I've described to you."

"Tell me what you experienced."

"The meditations took a few days to play out. They each began around three in the morning. Each morning, I woke and realized Jesus was at my bedside. He bent over and whispered in my ear how much he loved me. The feeling of receiving love immediately overwhelmed me. I felt so loved I cried. I couldn't take the intensity.

"Each morning this happened, I dressed and went to the chapel as soon as I could. I sat and imagined my bare feet warmed in the sand, playing with the grains as they filtered through my toes. I heard the waves breaking upon the shore and the seagulls screeching overhead. I breathed the salty air, scanned the sea line, and saw the reflection of the glistening sun on the water. Jesus then appeared."

Ambra smiled. She absorbed every image and description and noted the movement of my feelings. She shook her head in amazement. Was this really prayer or some kind of psychological escape from trauma?

Sunlight cracked through the window behind Ambra and lit up her ring and bracelet. I continued with my narrative.

"The first morning I learned about my mother I laid there on my side with my head nestled in Jesus's lap. His left hand hung casually over my side; his right caressed my ear and fingered my hair. I slowly opened my eyes and saw the living room of my childhood. Jesus and I were on the couch. We saw my brothers and sisters crawling about and my mother sitting in a chair holding a baby.

"Suddenly, I was a naked infant; the Mother of Jesus knelt before me. She gazed at me with adoration in her eyes, kissed me on the cheek and caressed my face. Jesus observed and grinned, enjoying the interaction between his Mother and me.

"At that instant, it felt like a dam broke inside of me and a torrent of emotions gushed everywhere. I curled up like an infant. 'My mommy, mommy, my mommy,' I cried out. My body shook. I felt weak. Imagination and reality blurred together. I fell on my knees, placed my head on the rug in the chapel, and wailed with the full force of my lungs. 'Mommy, mommy,' I kept crying. I felt naked. Jesus and Mary knelt there on each side, caressing and consoling me.

"A raw barrage of ideas exploded in my head. I didn't receive enough tenderness, sensual affection, affirming presence from my own mother as a child. Physical and emotional contact between us had lacked depth and time. Preoccupation and business had colored everything. Twelve children had needed attention. I barely remembered caresses, hugs, and kisses. I had almost died at birth, strangled by my own umbilical cord. I realized that the relationship with my mother was not affective, but effective.

"Emptiness eviscerated my soul. I felt like I'd just lost the deepest part of me, somebody precious to me, my own mother. Yet, in the midst of this loss, clarity appeared in my mind. Long separated puzzle pieces of life fluently joined together. I understood. My adult life was marked not only with a deprivation of paternal affirmation, but a void of maternal intimacy. Dumbfounded, I collapsed on the rug and blubbered. Jesus consoled me.

"My meditations had already taught me that I used work and achievements to win the love of an emotionally distanced father; now I realized a lifelong grasping for the tender embrace of my mother. Everything made sense, the addictions to pornography and masturbation, the attractions to women's clothing, the propensities to confide in older women. I wasn't looking for sex, but a mother. I dried my tears, lifted myself from the floor, plopped in a chair, and stared into the darkness. Shocked, I'd hardly sleep for the next two nights."

Silence seized the room. As my words echoed, I looked up at the Black Forest cuckoo clock on the wall. Ambra sat pensive and motionless, sidetracked with Jungian concepts flashing in her brain. Active imagination, individualization, self-realization. She scrutinized the broken priest sitting before her, a priest who'd tapped into an inner world that was radically transforming him. Was the finger of the supernatural really at work here? Ambra perceived the power of my prayer, even if she couldn't yet unravel its mystery.

Time had dead ended for both of us. Her next client waited in the adjacent room. I hoped that Father Duran still lay incapacitated in a drugged stupor. Ambra returned to reality with a sparkle in her eye. She had to wrap things up, pleasantly and proficiently.

"Andy, it seems that you're drawn to a woman psychotherapist?"

"I didn't think so until I'd experienced these recent meditations about my mother. They pushed me to see you."

"I think it's fair to encourage you to meet a few other psychotherapists before making a decision about us. You see, the success of psychotherapy depends very much on a natural rapport between the psychotherapist and the client. You may want to test the waters first with a few other therapists."

"That won't be necessary Ambra. Our rapport is fine. But there's a problem about me starting psychotherapy."

"Oh, and what would that be?"

"I have no money and I need permission from my superior, who's prejudiced against psychotherapy."

"I don't understand. Then how were you able to come this morning?"

"It's a long story, but since I'm not allowed outside of the community house, I secretly escaped to come here. My plan was to first meet you, as a step toward asking for permission."

Her eyes focused tightly. My situation was worse than she'd imagined, and she had no time left. Ambra took a deep breath. She felt sorry for me, but held firm.

"Andy, I'm sorry to hear of your predicament, but we couldn't possibly proceed with psychotherapy in secret. You must get permission; everything must be properly done. Once you get permission, only then can you come back for ongoing psychotherapy. We could make a half price arrangement, for twice a week visits. Maybe this might influence your superior to agree." Ambra normally charged one hundred euros an hour.

"Okay then, I'll work on getting permission. I don't know when, but I'll be back."

Each feeling the pressure of the moment, we politely hurried to the studio entrance and bid quick farewells. When the door shut, Ambra rushed to the kitchen for a five-minute tea. I flew down the stairs, ran to the car, and bounded into chaotic Roman traffic.

# CHAPTER TEN

Spring marked the resurrection of life, beauty, and tourism in Rome. The glow of a waking sun illuminated the majestic facade of Saint Peter's Basilica. Contrasted with a crisp blue sky and an imposing obelisk rising from the cobblestone, a stunning panorama begged for adoration.

After a few pastries and cappuccinos, early-bird tourists bogged down with backpacks and cameras waddled into Saint Peter's Square, where gurgling fountains and Swiss Guards displayed sparkle and color. Showing off their blue and yellow pajama-uniforms, the guards clicked their heels whenever a priest passed by. Bunches of hungry pigeons scratched for breakfast. Seagulls floated far above. European Robins darted about on the statues. Not a cloud in the sky. Another gorgeous day.

Twenty-five kilometers southwest of the Vatican, a few days past the ides of March, Father Duran shuffled around on his balcony at Via Tespi. His dying world seemed a thousand miles away from the invigorating life of Rome. Sean Brennan propped him up from behind. Duran twisted the wrong way and a stab of pain shot through his body. Beneath his abdominal muscles, a small pump released a dose of morphine through a catheter and needle inserted into the priest's spinal fluid space. Surrounded by pink orchids, violet lilies, and a surge of oleanders, Duran narrowed his eyes and puffed a Pall Mall Red to the end. The scent of nearby chrysanthemums, the Italian's flower of death, mixed with a bouquet of smoke snaking upward.

It was spring in the Catholic Church too, a symbolic catch phrase articulated by Pope John Paul II. It referred to the proliferation of divinely inspired new groups that promised a renewal of holiness and evangelization for an increasingly godless planet. Within this broad context, Miles Jesu sprouted amidst thousands of charismatic upstarts popping up everywhere during the latter half of the twentieth century.

Sean yanked the sliding glass door and Father Duran baby stepped inside. Drained of energy, Duran sat on a bed. Absent-minded, he stared, and breathed. Whipping out a finely ironed hanky, the soldier wiped sweat from the General's neck and forehead. After years of corrections, Sean had been conditioned to anticipate every desire of Father Duran. The ailing priest stretched his neck; he liked that he didn't have to ask. It was time for the first enema of the day.

The General and his subordinate slid like two snails toward the bathroom. Rogue aberrations represented the downside of the new groups. Their proper development required vigilant supervision by diocesan authorities. Having flown beneath the scan of ecclesial radar for forty-three years, Father Duran and Miles Jesu typified the rogue weed growing wild beside otherwise somewhat healthy Church institutions.

Canon law spells out the bishop's supervisory role over emerging new groups within his jurisdiction. The exercise of this oversight assumes a traditional process of continual tweaking of the founders and neophytes. Of course, such ecclesial solicitude entails the rooting of an institute in a diocese.

Charismatic founders feel the inspiration of God to launch innovative ways of life. Their attempts to address the needs of the times are met with legal resistance by ecclesial lawyers safeguarding polished categories. A tug of war ensues until mutual terms of peace eventually settle. The lawyers rewrite a few things and the founders get a few things, accepting some boundaries. Father Duran used to joke about this inconvenience.

"The Holy Spirit inspires something new, and the Church disapproves it."

Actually, both sides laid claim to a double-sided truth. The founders envision the removal of obstacles to more effectively Christianize ever-changing cultures and societies. The legal apparatus of the Church reacts to this and delineates fresh canonical parameters to limit overreach and protect the rights and goods of everyone involved. Wild inspiration is somewhat domesticated.

Father Duran had dodged the appropriate investigations of regulatory bishops for untold years. He'd evaded psychological and moral scrutiny and shielded the real inner workings of his Institute from outside intrusions. He walked back from the bathroom, parked on the bed, and asked for his shoe box of drugs. For decades he had danced through the raindrops of checks and balances; now he sat a shattered and bewildered soul.

Sean gave him the box and Duran abruptly objected.

"What do I need the box for?"

Sean was a pro. Taking the box, he immediately agreed, and proceeded to cluster a handful of pills for the morning routine: diazepam, valium, Xanax, Lorazepam, a diuretic, an extra morphine pill, and a few other assorted M&Ms. Duran wanted some vodka too. Accustomed to the fine art of managing Duran, Brennan put aside the liquor, convincing Duran that he wanted it later, after a morning nap. Duran swallowed the pills and Sean meticulously recorded the time, drugs, and dosages in a small black notebook.

The nurturing process of a consecrated institute implies years of fertilizing and pruning by a bishop, who has the right and duty to scrutinize, discern, adjust, and articulate the unique gift of a sprouting group, and draw boundaries too. He exercises the role of monitoring the step by step progression of the group, seeking to preserve the good of the members and secure the harmonious functioning of the upstart in relation to his own diocese.

Duran wanted a shower. Sean picked up the phone, punched the intercom, and voiced the usual announcement.

"Father General will now take a shower. Do not use the hot water. I repeat. Do not use the hot water!"

Every phone speaker had its volume cranked to high; nobody wanted to miss any word booming from the office of Father General. The words echoed from the basement to the third floor loft. The warning gave just enough time for grown men to scramble for cover.

As Sean and Father General emerged from the staircase and walked past packed boxes, community members on the top floor discreetly moved from the priest's sight of vision in fear of the unknown. Depending on his erratic mood, there was no telling what the General might do. His sight of a recently targeted person or focus upon an incongruous object might ignite a tirade of criticism that would last for days. Or it might provoke a time-consuming organizing and cleaning blitz, or occasion a two-hour meeting to humiliate someone or get to the bottom of something. It was best to hide away and prevent a ridiculous scene of some kind. Sean understood. He knew the art of pointing Duran here or there, or distracting him as needed to prevent an upheaval.

Worn down and drugged, Father Duran slept a lot. His existence was a blur of smokes, craps, long naps, balcony shuffles, and symbolic meetings where he thought he governed. Actually, Brennan and Gelson managed him, letting him feel the illusion of decision making. Most of the major needs of Miles Jesu circled in a holding pattern. The experimental status of the constitutions expired months ago; nobody bothered. Duran received lip service and heard selected news from his handlers. Good news only.

Absolutely vital decisions were manipulated out of him under whatever pretext. He got a taste of his own style of manipulation of people. The man often forgot or confused whatever decision he'd made anyway. Miles Jesu flopped headless.

The handlers' philosophy was straightforward. Keep Duran pacified. Minimize his involvement. Contain the damage of an erratic and obsessive temper by steering clear from explosive topics. Keep him drugged. Let him enjoy his vodka.

Duran's driven personality still lingered. The General, who once coveted the adrenaline of driving and feared the vulnerability of flying, still had to feel the levers of control. Otherwise paranoia would kick in and the priest would demand the exercise of power, even if purely symbolic.

Meanwhile, hope, the belief in change, kept the caregivers persevering. At some point in the future when Duran would be out of the equation, the puzzle pieces of Miles Jesu could be gathered and reconstructed, many thought. Pontifical approval could be acquired, the constitutions definitively set, a formation program finally put in place. Members could be educated; graduates could enjoy employment in the world as real secular apostles. At present, only a few members held secular jobs as a punishment, an embarrassing perversion of the Miles Jesu ideal. Scott Fremont, a balding airline pilot was the exception. He worked outside of community as a cash cow and poster boy for recruiting. Nonetheless, the elusive dream of a better Miles Jesu kept everyone hanging.

Brennan and Duran returned from the upstairs shower and entered the bedroom. Vasyl Mikula waited. The shift change. After exchanging a few wet kisses on cheeks, Sean left and Duran turned to Vasyl.

"Good morning, Father." Vasyl's youthful demeanor and cheery face offered a warm greeting.

Somehow, this rubbed Duran the wrong way. "You are always smiling Vasyl. Life is not a joke. Vasyl, I'm in pain."

"Where, Father?"

"Everywhere."

"How can I help?"

"How can you help?" The priest sneered, skeptical of the young man's capacity to understand suffering. "Vasyl, open your eyes. Can't you see how much pain I'm in? And you're smiling? I'm dumbfounded. I'm in pain everywhere. Can't you see it?"

A minute of silence passed. Duran pointed to the bottle he had started last night.

"Pour me a glass of wine."

Mikula corked open the half empty bottle of Merlot and started to pour it. Duran urged him to fill up the glass.

"That's enough" Duran said. "Put the glass on the dresser and cover it with a handkerchief, so the alcohol doesn't evaporate."

Without a personal opinion, the Ukrainian go-lucky simply obeyed.

Duran now wanted to scoot around on the balcony and take a smoke. Afterwards, maybe he'd do another enema. They stepped onto the balcony and paced its length a few times. The priest stopped and stared at the tree where the devil rat had once resided.

"The devil is after us Vasyl. He is striking at the head. Now, go get the glass of wine."

Only a minute later, by the time Mikula returned with the glass, Father Duran had forgotten everything about the wine. Somehow, his brain had short circuited. Seeing Vasyl approaching, offering the glass, Duran flicked away his smoke and erupted with rage.

"What are you doing? You son of a bitch! Get that away from me!"

"I thought you wanted the wine."

"What wine? You want to know everything. You want to see me drink it. I should never have brought you from Ukraine. You're a KGB. You're KGB aren't you? Why are you giving me a glass of wine? Why? Answer me! Why do you need to know what I'm drinking? Who are you reporting to?"

As his silk red robe waved in a soft breeze, the whiskered General mopped the floor with Vasyl Mikula. His shouts of anger caught the ears of the lady next door. A down to earth Texan widow, Terri passionately hated Duran because he'd written a nasty letter to her. The letter had warned her not to contact Miles Jesu for help when her dog died. Duran's temper filled the air. The rounded blond smiled and shut the door behind her. Vasyl stood flabbergasted, knowing that any explanation would just make things worse.

The volcano would blow for the next three days. Cinders and ashes would fall everywhere. With the priest propped up in his bed, witnesses would be escorted before him. Trusted stooges would be called upon to drill Vasyl and falsely accuse him. Lies and exaggerated stories would be told of him, and then he'd be banished from the General's presence for a three-day punishment. Hiding his relief, Vasyl welcomed the exile.

Before sending Vasyl away, Duran ordered him to fetch Petro Shevchuk, the next guy on shift. Mikula was not to return. Petro dropped everything, rushed to Duran's side, and helped the upset priest to his bed. The spat about the wine had drained away Father Duran's energies. He collapsed on his bed and stewed. Nothing but complaints against Vasyl passed through his lips. Petro sat nearby and tried to look concerned, walking the high wire between siding and not siding with the General. Vasyl and Petro were best friends.

A forty-three-year crusade left Father Duran defeated, squirming in bed, outside the ancient walls of Rome. The erratic General had uprooted and replanted the headquarters of Miles Jesu no less than six times: Arizona, Kentucky, Virginia, New Mexico, Illinois, Puerto Rico, and Italy. Claiming escapes from liberals, Miles Jesu had repeatedly dodged ecclesial oversight.

I'd been personally involved in such covert operations from the beginning of my membership. Not long after joining I had helped Miles Jesu escape from Front Royal, Virginia. Duran had been prohibited from governing the Institute by Bishop Welsh of the Arlington Diocese. The Bishop had ordered Duran to a treatment center that specialized in treating sexually addicted priests in Albuquerque, New Mexico.

Stretching the length of his central nervous system, the effect of the morphine finally won. Relaxation, drowsiness, and a warm euphoria conquered. Father Duran closed his eyes and rested his head upon two stacked pillows. Sitting at the General's bedside, Petro breathed a sigh of relief.

The Very Reverend Father Alphonsus Duran lacked the competency to govern Miles Jesu, yet his grasp of power endured without question. His rule by fear and his tenacious character had much to do with this. But absolute rule went deeper.

Miles Jesu instilled a culture of blind obedience and internal problem solving. Anything wrong with Miles Jesu had to be hidden from the outside world and resolved inside the community, without external feedback or influence. It was God's will, backed by the constitutions. Miles Jesu guarded an enclosed system of group think, supported with a self-serving theological justification. Nobody in the world could possibly understand the unique Miles Jesu vocation.

While Father Duran slept, I shouldered the responsibility of answering the phone. My instructions were explicit. If anyone inquired about Father Duran, I should confirm his excellent health. I did as I was told, and it had become repugnant.

Excommunication is the most serious punishment Catholic authority may inflict on a delinquent Church member. This penalty is so severe it exiles the offender to the realm of the spiritually dead, barring participation in the sacraments. It supposes a grave offense with terrible consequences. The idea of excommunication is to shake the reprobate to his or her senses and motivate a repentant return to communion with the Church. Granted, it may or may not achieve its end.

Historically, the application or threat of excommunication enjoyed great extension. Many years ago, bishops overused this amputation-like penalty to exact fasts, coerce tithes, and extract revelations of matrimonial impediments from frightful villagers. Eventually, such abusive patterns of governing were brought under the sway of sobriety and moderation. Today, the dreaded penalty is customarily reserved only for the gravest offenses.

The 1983 Code of Canon Law distinguishes between two fundamental types of excommunication. Basically, someone may be excommunicated by a bishop's juridical act, or an unfortunate soul may incur the curse automatically, simply for doing something really bad.

In the latter case, excommunication happens as an automatic effect of transgressing certain laws. Accordingly, canon law attaches the penalty to a predetermined list of evil deeds. Simply do one of these deeds, and poof, you're excommunicated. No juridical judgment and public pronouncement is necessary. This list includes such wickedness as physically attacking the Pope, impersonating a priest hearing confessions, handing over the Eucharist for sacrilegious purposes, preforming an abortion, or apostatizing. The list goes on.

Generally speaking, when automatic excommunication occurs the offender must approach the local bishop and humbly ask for the penalty to be lifted. The sinner may do this personally or anonymously through a priest confessor. Directly or indirectly, the bishop then hands down a penance to remit the excommunication. The penance is done and the excommunication is taken away. Once the penalty is lifted, the offender may then receive sacramental absolution and participate in the spiritual life of the Church again. Some automatic excommunications are so bad they must be referred to the Pope for mending.

March 17, 2007. It was a lazy Saturday, by immovable custom a cleaning day. Duran slept. Community members ran errands, dusted, scrubbed, swept, mopped, each soldier his assigned area. In the adjacent Tespi apartment, Olha Klub vacuumed the women's chapel on the second floor.

I decided to rescue her that day. Who cared about the risks? I no longer did. I met Olha in the chapel and inadvertently stepped upon a path that would lead to my automatic excommunication. It would take about six weeks to fall head over heels in love with her and get kicked out of the Catholic Church.

The women's chapel felt like a dainty closet with incense hanging nimbly in the air. Actually a bedroom, the space had been modified into a tight sanctuary with an altar surrounded by cushioned chairs. A Persian rug cuddled the floor. Fine religious art with delicate gold leafed frames hung on the walls. A small service table in the back left corner occupied needed space. A Spanish Lladro, crystal cruets from Bohemia, and an alabaster key-box sat on the table.

It was two in the afternoon and the sun had just passed overhead, withdrawing its rays of light piercing through the sliding glass door. Without a choice in the matter, Olha wore her light blue habit, overlaid with a wax-splattered cleaning apron. Vibrating with a hint of defiance, she had left the constraining head piece on her bed. She wound up the vacuum cleaner cord; golden hair danced on her shoulders.

Two days past, I'd experienced a bewildering meditation about Olha Klub, shortly after three in the morning. I'd woken to darkness and instantly felt Jesus kneeling at my side. He placed his hand upon my face and I received an electrifying bolt of love. I wouldn't be able to sleep any longer. Then he spoke.

"Andy, you have a purpose for being in this world. I will give my love to others through you."

"Jesus, it's so late in my life," I whispered back. He ignored my words.

"Your suffering was not only to let me in, but to open the doors for others to enter into me. I will give you a special gift today."

I imagined Jesus turning around, descending the stairs, and walking into the chapel. I got up, dressed, flew down stairs, and slipped into the chapel. As soon as I closed my eyes the scene of the family room back home flooded into my mind.

Every detail stood out, the trophies on the shelves, the yellow and green spray painted piano, the bust of John F. Kennedy, the reddish shag carpet, the bed where I'd cried like a baby, begging Jesus to let me marry Linda Hughes. It was the same room where I'd bid farewell to my father, who had turned away with a tear in his eye. It was the same room where Fred Bach and Paul Vota had escorted me away to join Miles Jesu. In recent meditations, it was the same room flooded with colored lights and healing waters.

Burning logs crackled in the fireplace. In a comfortable high back chair, the Blessed Mother held me, a newborn infant feeding at her breast. Then I noticed the others, Jesus, Thomas Walsh, Father Dietrich, and Ambra Treichler. Immersed in an atmosphere of love and security, among a family of friends who really loved me, I felt flooded with gratefulness. There in the chapel, tears rolled down my face. I felt loved by a family. The doorbell rang. Jesus rose, walked to the door, and opened it.

Dressed in her blue habit, Olha Klub stood there soaked to the bone. A downpour ravished the street behind her. Dad's drenched Toyota sat in the driveway. Jesus took Olha by the hand and welcomed her into the warmth of the family room. He shut the door and she turned to him and said, "I want to be a part of this family. I feel love here."

Jesus gazed at her with love and put his hand on her face; she felt his affection warm her. He then removed the soggy headpiece, laid it to the side, and led her to an adjacent room. Knowing she was coming, he had earlier draped a snug cotton nightgown in there, white with a yellow flowered pattern.

With his help she undressed and slipped on the gown. Upon returning to the family room, Jesus sat on the far left side of a couch facing the fire. Olha stretched out with no reservation and rested her head in his lap. He placed his left hand on her forehead and caressed her. She shut her eyes; Jesus stared into the fire and curled her hair around his finger. He then laid his right hand softly upon her heart.

My attention refocused on the Blessed Virgin Mary. I saw myself as an infant wrapped in her arms. Absorbed, I drew milk from her breast. Suddenly, Jesus's face was right there. He kissed me on the forehead.

"My dear Andy, wait a little longer."

I wasn't sure if he referred to my growth or Olha's welcome into the family.

That meditation provoked two days of reflection. It was Saturday, the third day now. What the hell? It was time to reach out to Olha. She and I agreed to meet in the woman's chapel at two in the afternoon.

She placed the vacuum cleaner near the door, blew out the sanctuary flame, and carefully lifted the glass-cased candle out of the red sheath near the tabernacle. After replacing and relighting a new candle, Olha sat in a chair between the balcony's sliding door and the altar. Hoping I'd arrive soon, she checked her watch.

Mikhail Gorbachev's perestroika had opened the doors for Miles Jesu to pluck Olha Klub from a humble village in Western Ukraine. After thirteen years of life as a pawn in the grand Miles Jesu chess game, Olha now studied canon law in Rome.

Duran had wanted a couple of canon lawyers to advance the prerogatives of the Institute worldwide. His idea was to push the rights of the Institute to the limits, not so much to defend the personal rights of the members. Olha had been one of the two women picked for the mission. Her mind raced ahead toward the challenge; her heart lagged behind.

Olha sat there with anxiety in her eyes. Miles Jesu did not permit unchaperoned encounters between the sexes. A male and female member meeting alone was anathema. I didn't care. Olha knew she was breaking the rule too, but her instinct to survive Miles Jesu prevailed.

Over the past few months, she'd noticed a profound change in me. I'd grown more compassionate and caring. I'd gone out of my way to answer the phones when it was her shift. I'd spent extra time helping her fundraise, to protect her from the shame of unproductivity. She had a reason to believe that my overture to her was sincere and that I was capable of offering genuine help. She knew that I exposed myself to harsh discipline if caught alone with her. But she had come to believe in me and was willing to take a risk.

Olha's trust ran deeper than a growing appreciation and attraction toward me. At the end of her rope, she was desperate. Though she knew community life was finished for her, she couldn't find the courage to pack her bags and leave. Miles Jesu had a track record of fraught members escaping in the middle of the night and hiding from bounty hunters sent after them. Olha hadn't the guts to suffer that nightmare.

The Miles Jesu environment had pushed Olha Klub to the brink of suicide. Restrictive, ultra-authoritarian, fear-imbued, mindless living conditions had ensnared her spirit in an envelope of despair. Discarded and disgraced, she felt trapped, with no hope of change. As the sacristan, Olha had access to the altar wine. Backstairs drinking helped calm her nerves, so she told herself. But dulling the mind seemed to compound the futility of the situation.

At her worst moments, Olha's imagination wandered into ways of ending it all. She imagined a plan of slitting her wrists and bleeding to death, when, where, how. Silence forced violence into her fantasies. Sometimes, she'd visualize opening the door of a speeding car and throwing herself onto a racing highway. Only the moral presence of her grandmother restrained Olha from catastrophe. Judgment and the eternal fires of hell sobered her each time she felt the lure of temptation, yet offered no escape from the agonies of daily life.

I pushed open the chapel door and saw Olha sitting behind the altar. My cleaning assignment allowed me to wear Levis, sneakers, and an old grey pullover. What a refreshing feeling! I hated wearing that tight fitting black cassock. Covering my bases, I'd deliberately left the men's second story bathroom in a mess, suggesting that I'd stepped out of a hairy job for a breather. I'd removed a floor plate and snaked a plumber's auger deep into the guts of a disgusting pipe. After throwing some dirty rags, wrenches, and screwdrivers on the floor, I had simply disappeared. A splash of bleach in the bathtub hinted at work in progress. Olha greeted me with an eager smile. I sat next to her and started.

I remembered that I'd once walked Olha's same path of darkness. But life was now entirely different for me. Love roared ahead, unrestrained, at a wild pace. The intense reception of love had engendered emotional backbone and removed the blinders from my eyes to see the truth of the Miles Jesu environment.

I shared my journey with Olha, the drinking, the despair, the discovery of receiving love, the explosion of love within me, the profound interior changes. With wide eyes, she listened intently. Nobody had ever revealed himself to her like this.

Sometimes, the relentless drive of the meditations was unbearable. A powerful meditative life had hijacked me. It was often difficult to know which life was more real. Was it the prison life surrounding me or the inner paradise in my heart? Submitting to the direction of the meditations, I felt like a swaying ribbon hanging for dear life from the rear end of an unstoppable freight train. I had no idea of my destiny. I only knew that God was leading me. My sincerity and complete trust surprised and soothed Olha.

We confided in each other. To prove the transforming power of my prayer, I exposed some personal details of my life. She spoke of her deplorable treatment and how death seemed desirable. I'd seen it all. We instantly bonded. Love ignited. I felt drawn to rescue and care for her; she experienced the magnetism of my tenderness. I knew how to save her from her despairs and gratitude surged within her.

Then, reservedly, timidly, she asked for my blessing. Deep inside, she screamed for it. Olha wanted my touch. She hungered for it. We rose and stood before the altar. Facing one another, we each felt an irresistible attraction to hug. But we held back at this first encounter.

I placed my hand on her cheek, looked into her eyes, and blessed her. At that instant she felt a current of love rush through her body; warmth invaded her heart. I felt given over to her and it demanded every ounce of discipline not to lose myself. I didn't realize it at that moment, but I blessed her exactly as Jesus so many times had blessed me in my meditations.

That instant, an intimate relationship was born. It would grow at a ferocious pace. Her parched heart throbbed to life and tears trickled down her face. Olha had not felt sincere love for very many years. I'd been permeated with love and ached to lavish it upon a trusting soul disposed to welcome it. It was a perfect match. She wanted to receive love; I wanted to give it. And it was no longer a puzzle or chore to give love; it simply overflowed from an unmanageable fullness within me.

It would take six weeks for our secret relationship to sink roots. During that time, we'd meet often, wherever and whenever we could slip away unnoticed. The chaotic condition of the communities facilitated our disappearances. We'd confide in one another and share every thought and feeling. Eventually, intimate conversations would lead to touches, and then caresses and hugs. We'd even dare to go to the beach and once to the cinema. At forty-six, it would be the first time I'd take a girlfriend to the movies.

About six weeks past our Saturday morning talk in the women's chapel, we lay hidden in uncut grass. An umbrella pine towered over us. It was two in the morning, pitch black except for the half-moon and stars twinkling at us through swaying branches. A gentle Mediterranean breeze passed over us.

Our heads touched. Lost in a paradise of good feelings, we joked about life and death in Miles Jesu. We giggled about Duran's obsessions and then sparked anger at how he damaged lives. Holding hands and gazing up to the heavens we wondered aloud about our futures.

"Olha, what's going to happen to us?"

"I don't know. I just know that I want to be with you," she said.

"I love being with you too." I squeezed her hand. "But our situation can't last. I'm going to ask for an exclaustration soon."

"An exclaustration? What's that?"

There were complicated canonical ways to explain an exclaustration. I decided to side step the details.

"It's basically a permitted long break from Miles Jesu. For the sake of my emotional health, I have to get away from community life."

"What do you mean?" Anxiety colored her face. "How long?"

"Maybe two or three years."

I'd figured that after three years of healing I could possibly resume life in Miles Jesu. But I wasn't really sure.

Olha, skeptical, couldn't hold back a burst of laughter.

"You? Father Duran would never allow that."

"Well, I'm going to give it my best shot. Come push or shove, I think Miles Jesu will grant me the exclaustration if I appeal to higher Church authorities. The friend I made in the Vatican thinks so too."

"Right. You guys are crazy. No way! Remember? We live in Miles Jesu. We're not normal, Andy. Miles Jesu is not normal."

I neither appreciated nor accepted her words at that moment, but Olha's uneducated opinion would end up more accurate than the professional consultant in the Vatican.

It was time to go. I turned to Olha with a request.

"My love, let me rest my head on your breast."

Without any hesitation, she lay upon her back and invited me.

"Just for a few minutes," she said.

Resting there, listening to her heart, I wondered aloud.

"It must be deeply satisfying to be married. It must be wonderful to belong to each other, to sleep together, to caress each other without guilt, to enjoy God's blessing on it all. I wish we could marry Olha, but it's impossible. When I joined Miles Jesu I'd wanted to get married."

I paused and thought about what I'd just said. My words penetrated our hearts. Then I felt sorry for us.

"I've finally discovered human love, and it's too late."

I didn't think of it at that moment, but the idea of marriage had permeated my meditations for more than a year. Hundreds of scenes had presumed a marital relationship between Jesus and me. Long ago, we'd placed rings on each other's fingers and promised ourselves to one another. Countless encounters had subtly flashed fleeting images of our hands with the rings glistening here or there. Working its own purpose within my soul, a mysterious power had reconnected me with my childhood craving to be married, a never discussed longing that had been swept under the rug when I joined Miles Jesu. Was that mysterious, inner power persuading me? Was it God? Was it me? Was it both of us?

"I'd wanted to get married too, Andy. Don't you think there's any chance at all for us to get married?"

"I don't see how, Olha. I'm a Catholic priest and you're a consecrated virgin."

We clung to each other and yielded to the pleasure. After a stretch of silence, a bittersweet fog crept into our souls. Accepting the impossibility of marriage, tears trickled from our eyes. She rested her left hand upon the side of my face and we each felt the deep frustration of Miles Jesu entrapment. Trauma and chaos had flung us into each other's arms. It was hard to swallow that our deepening friendship had no future.

Then it happened. Swimming in swaying grass, enjoying the soft brush of a peaceful breeze, we embraced like there'd never be another moment together. Lying upon our sides, we gazed into each other's wet eyes. I wiped away her tears; Olha did the same to mine. We spontaneously allowed ourselves a tender kiss, an intimate embrace. Olha and I should have known better. We did know better. Passion ignited and rushed through our bodies. Temperatures climbed, caresses, kisses, heavy breathing. Breaking loose from years of self-control, raw desire emerged. An eternal moment of lust consumed us.

Before that irrevocable moment spun entirely out of control, we consciously made the effort to slow down and hold ourselves back.

Though we'd stopped short of sexual intercourse, we'd certainly leapt over forbidden moral boundaries.

Her hair a mess, she found her bra and blouse. Grabbing hold of my wrist, Olha checked the time.

"Andy, it's late. We have to get back right away, before everyone wakes up."

"Yeah, I know."

I rolled up the beach towel and then paused and gave her a glance. "Olha, I'm sorry for that."

"That's okay. You don't have to apologize. I'm sorry too. I guess we've been tied to the doghouse for too many years."

We couldn't help but laugh. Mixed feelings swirled within us: the exhilaration of bodily love, the remorse of sin. Emotions liberated our spirits; tender consciences accused us.

Just before setting out for Via Tespi I got a crazy, absolutely insane idea. Perhaps it was the dumbest thing I'd ever do. Time will tell. It hardly mattered that it sprang from a good intention.

"Hey Olha, what if I hear your confession and give you absolution? I could do it if you want."

"Are you sure?"

"Yes, canon law says that a priest cannot absolve his partner in sexual intercourse. Since we didn't do that, I can give you absolution."

"Really?"

Of course, I was dead wrong and didn't know it. The law actually states that, "the absolution of an accomplice in a sin against the sixth commandment of the Decalogue is invalid."

That covered a lot more ground than sexual intercourse. I'd somehow lost sight of that crucial distinction. Though Olha was a student of canon law she didn't have a handle on the details either.

She rubbed her chin with her fingers and gave my proposal some thought, just for a minute. The reflection didn't last long. The clock was ticking. Olha then readily agreed, knelt down, bowed her head, and confessed the sin we both knew. When she finished, I voiced the official formula, traced the sign of the cross in the air, and absolved her. I thought I was so smart dancing around a legal, sacramental technicality.

Now in a rush, we started out for the Miles Jesu apartments. Olha felt relieved that she wouldn't have to confess to any other priest; I felt content that I'd made things easy for her. A five-minute walk left us on the street adjacent to the apartments. Shielded by an oleander bush, we swapped a well-behaved good night kiss. Our hands separated and we each made an independent tiptoe back into our respective apartments.

Expanding upon my abuse of sacramental power, the law wasn't finished with me. Under the section on penalties, canon law spells out that whoever absolves his accomplice incurs an automatic excommunication, reserved to the Apostolic See. This meant that the Pope had to rectify my mess. I had no idea.

Lying in bed, I stared at the bottom of the upper bunk and reflected. Somebody sawed logs on the other side of the loft. I felt the excitement of human love. I repented of my sin, thanked Jesus for the feeling of love, both divine and human, begged for forgiveness, and humbly asked for an exclaustration. When the excitement finally subsided, my weary eyelids closed. The community would be up within the hour.

A priest is bound by the seal of confession. He therefore cannot reveal sins confessed to him. The penitent however is not bound by this seal and enjoys the freedom to disclose whatever sins confessed. The penitent may exercise this liberty personally or through somebody else. By documented consent, Olha declared her intention to make public her confessed sin and its aftermath.

On a cloudless Roman morning, Monsignor Luigi Moretti labored at his overloaded desk. The fifty-eight-year-old cleric crouched like a bulldog, pawing his papers. He looked the dog too: big nose, bushy eyebrows, pudgy mouth, sagging cheeks, roundish chin and balding head, only lacking the flappy ears and stubby tail. Thick rimmed glasses teetered on the tip of his nose, blurring the bags under his eyes and mirroring rapidly flipping pages of sensitive material. Licking his thumb, a breakfast belch slunk out.

The monsignor knew how to scan mountainous documents and abstract the essence of things. He'd mastered the art of gleaning the facts for his superior, Cardinal Ruini. After four years of troubleshooting and crisis management, the prematurely aging monsignor wore the thick skin of the office.

From a bird's eye view, two streams of delegated authority gurgled from the Pope. His person was the starting and linking point of two grand power structures. The Vatican represented the Pope's instrument for global governing, both at secular and religious levels. The Vicariate functioned as an apparatus for administering the Pope's own diocese of Rome. Delegated authority gushed from the Pope's right and left hands into the robed princes of these two kingdoms.

Cardinal Camillo Ruini, an acclaimed conservative with a long face and teeth-filled smile, sat at the head of the Vicariate. Appointed by the Pope, Ruini served as the Vicar General of the Diocese of Rome. Monsignor Luigi Moretti was the next guy down on the totem pole: the Vice-Gerent for the Vicariate of Rome.

Even if called a monsignor, Moretti was really a bishop. His position demanded it. While the Pope dealt with the world and the Cardinal with the Italian press, Moretti pounded away as the plumber who rolled up his sleeves and wrestled with the complexities of administering the most distinguished archdiocese on the planet. Others got the credit; Moretti did the work. He certainly had his hands full. The Vicariate covered 880 square kilometers of territory and included 340 parishes, 8,500 priests from throughout the world, and two and a half million faithful.

The jurisdiction of Moretti's stewardship pulsated from an ancient Papal residence, still conspicuous for its enduring magnificence. It didn't matter. The monsignor's intense duties overshadowed the beauty and glory that hedged him in. He sat at his desk and worked like a dog, oblivious to Saint John Lateran's splendor, the old Papal throne, priceless frescos, Papal tombs, irreplaceable statues, fountains, and a monster four-hundred and fifty-five ton red-granite Egyptian obelisk soaring outside his office window.

While Monsignor Moretti scribbled a reminder note and slipped a paper clip on a wad of documents, I sat in a waiting room on the other side of his office wall. It was April 27, 2007, a few days past my midnight encounter with Olha Klub.

During the past few months, I'd assimilated a handful of eye-opening meetings with Murphy and Harrison in their Vatican offices. These snail paced consultations eventually lead me to the conclusion that an exclaustration from Miles Jesu would be best. Monsignor Murphy had advised me to present my unique situation to Monsignor Moretti.

A young Italian cleric with a military cut approached and escorted me into the monsignor's office. I noted a fat desk weighed down with piles of documents. A tastefully framed photo of Moretti and the Pope hung on the wall. It looked like they were buddies. But many Church officials dangled the same photo-honors on their own walls. Following a quick and firm handshake, I sat in one of the two plush chairs directly opposite Moretti's desk. The crew cut left and shut the door behind him.

Thankfully, politely, Moretti launched the conversation in English. Skipping pleasantries, he telegraphed his wish to speed through this meeting.

"What can I do for you Father Sullivan?"

"Both Monsignor Harrison at the Congregation for Bishops and Monsignor Murphy at the Congregation for Consecrated Life advised me to see you. I'm interested in an exclaustration from my community, but my superiors cannot possibly process my request in the appropriate way regulated by canon law."

Murphy had coached me how to present my case. Name drop and then cut to the chase. Moretti would be time conscious.

"Father Sullivan, tell me about your Institute and your status."

"I'm incardinated in an Institute of Consecrated Life that is erected here in the Diocese of Rome."

"What's the name of the Institute?"

"Miles Jesu."

"Miles what?"

"Miles Jesu."

"I've never heard of it."

"It was approved here in 2002 as an Ecclesial Family of Consecrated Life."

"I've never heard of this group. We've had a moratorium on the recognition of new diocesan groups."

The diocese had been burned in the past by well-intentioned but windswept new groups. He rubbed his chin and shook his head. An old headache returned. *How the hell did a new group get approved by Cardinal Ruini?*

I leaned forward in my chair and added some details.

"In January of 2002, Miles Jesu was recognized by Cardinal Ruini with a five-year experimental set of constitutions, now expired."

Moretti inhaled slowly, blinked his eyes, and deliberately blew air through his lips. Maybe changing the subject would help.

"Normally, a request of exclaustration is a simple matter. I don't understand why you're here to resolve this need. This is a matter for your general superior."

"That's why I'm here. I urgently need an exclaustration because community life in Miles Jesu is emotionally damaging me. I can't request an exclaustration from my superior because he's incapable of processing my request."

"What do you mean by that?"

"For the most part, he lives in a drugged state of mind and can barely function and make sound decisions. Besides, I want my reasons for requesting an exclaustration to remain confidential. Father Duran is not capable of respecting this right. He customarily makes members' confidentialities publicly known, often as a way to humiliate. I have a right to request an exclaustration without such treatment and to have my need respectfully and canonically handled."

I remembered the appeal I'd written requesting not to be ordained a priest, but bit my tongue.

"Who is Father Duran?"

Trying to calm his annoyance, Moretti's voice grew louder.

"He's the General Superior of Miles Jesu," I said.

Moretti looked for the easiest way to help me.

"Can you approach the vicar of your Institute to handle your need?"

"He's not approachable either. He's living in an apartment outside of the community because he can't function around Father Duran. Besides, the community would be prejudiced to an exclaustration for me."

"Why's that?"

"I've been living under house arrest now for over three years. I'm able to see you this morning because I escaped from the house. Monsignor, Miles Jesu is crazy. An exclaustration would be categorically denied. They don't believe in exclaustrations."

"What! Exclaustrations are not a matter of belief. They're a matter of canon law!"

Moretti had enough. His antennae had gathered sufficient information. Everything smelled fishy: a covertly approved group, a drugged superior, an emotionally damaging environment, a disregard for confidentiality and human decency, an incarcerated priest.

"*Basta!*" (Enough!)

Experience ran through his veins and he knew exactly what he needed to do. To his credit, Moretti refused to shrug his sense of responsibility. In his shrewd way, the bulldog wanted to dig to the bottom of things.

"Father Sullivan, does anybody know that you've come to see me?"

"Nobody in Miles Jesu."

"Good. Let's keep in that way. This is what I'd like you to do. I want you to write a request for exclaustration. Address it to Cardinal Ruini. Mention our meeting today as a point of reference. Include the instructions I'm now giving you. I want you to detail the reasons for your extraordinary request and hand deliver it to me. I want all the pertinent background why you can't ask for an exclaustration from your general superior."

Bishop Moretti stared at me with determination.

"Do you understand all these points?"

"Yes."

"Do not let your superiors know what you are doing. Bypass them and do not let them see the document you prepare. Do not give this document to anyone in my office. I emphasize this. Personally place it in my hand."

"I understand."

He looked at his watch.

"Good. I'm sorry for your situation, Father Sullivan. The sooner you can make your request, the sooner we can try to resolve your need."

I thanked him and he encouraged me. Moving toward the door, Moretti apologized for his time constraint. I followed his lead. We shook hands and agreed to meet sometime in the future. I stepped into the corridor; Moretti pulled the door shut and immediately returned to other high priority disasters.

I now focused on my watch. Really? The meeting took only twelve minutes. Great! I calculated the times and distances for the mad dash back home and headed for the car.

# CHAPTER ELEVEN

Father Marcus Gelson was supposed to govern the Institute whenever Father Duran couldn't. For months now Gelson had removed himself from community life because he could no longer stomach Duran's presence. Gelson was Duran's chief confidant and preeminent casualty.

Marcus, once a jovial young man who oozed the best of Southern hospitality, now struggled to make it through each day. Years of psychological abuse and dysfunctional modes of operating had left him traumatized. A psychologist suggested a treatment center for post-traumatic patients and warned him to stay away from Father Duran.

Tucked away in a secret apartment not far from Via Tespi, under Tom Walsh's care, Gelson struggled to recover. He only visited the Miles Jesu apartment when it was absolutely required. Otherwise all kinds of stories and lies were fed to Duran to justify Marc's absence. Escaping the Institute's ground zero, Marc attempted to live a normal life, resting, recreating, cooking, taking walks. He found therapeutic relief reconnecting with his alienated habit of cooking meals on a Mississippi dredge boat. He could barely read, but he could chop onions and garnish a plate with parsley. Brandy and Xanax kept him relatively calm, until the dreads of night.

Because he bloodied his knuckles, Gelson slumbered with protective gloves. Whenever he'd slip into a half-conscious state, darkness would explode with screams and curses against the devil and Duran. Despairing cries would fill the bedroom where he'd kick and punch the walls. The dreadful scene erupted each night.

One evening, Gelson stood on the three-story balcony and stared down at the ground. Trembling with despair, he wrestled with the devil and the temptation to cast himself into the tranquil embrace of death.

Ironically, believing himself an expert in discerning psychological dispositions, Duran had no idea that he was the cause of Marc's breakdown.

The General blamed the devil. Despising psychotherapy, he pushed the exorcism prayers to throw out the demonic from Father Gelson's soul. Nobody had the education or guts to oppose Duran's cock-eyed treatment. He approached Marc's ordeal with a mindset firmly rooted in the Middle Ages.

At last, kept secret from Duran, Father Gelson's rage could only be alleviated by the feminine touch of the Vicar Directress, Jeni Staus. Day and night, she showed up to help with her embraces and caresses.

Jeni was forty-five and respected by the women's branch of Miles Jesu. The daughter of a doctor in Madison, Wisconsin, and smart as a whip, she'd been denied an education by Father Duran. Of course, nothing personal; a discontinuation of education was the norm for practically anyone who joined. Thoroughly indoctrinated, her thinking mirrored that of Duran. But in this messy and no-win situation, Jeni broke the rules to reach out to Father Gelson. If it called for her maternal tenderness, so be it. Duran would never know.

Commanding an envied location, the Casa del Clero sat between Piazza San Pietro and Castel San't Angelo. To its immediate left, the six-flat red-brick building hugged an antiquated Papal escape route that connected the Vatican with the Castel. The towering, thirty meter arched walkway gave the Pope a path to save his neck in a worst case scenario. In ages past, if the Vatican suffered an attack the Pope could sprint in the sky to the safety of a military stronghold.

At cobblestone level, the Casa looked like any other modest building in the area. Sliced granite encapsulated the ground floor. With graffiti splotched here and there, pollution accented the natural pit lines of the grainy slabs. Students frequented a similar looking building across the street. Italian babes in tank tops and curly haired students with goatees and motor scooters lounged about. Burdened with obligations, visiting clergy entered and exited the hotel all hours of the day. Housing international visitors, the Casa operated as a strategic hub for getting things done in the Vatican.

Setting down my luggage, I watched Father Kroll speed away in the distance. A couple of bishops passed behind me heading toward Michelangelo's dome. Kroll hung a right, clipped past *Radio Vaticana*, bounced onto the Trastevere, and headed back home. I stood there dumbfounded. A small miracle had just taken place. I'd received permission to relax, all by myself at the Casa for two weeks.

A few days earlier, I'd asked Sean Brennan for permission to take a break from community life. With Duran and Gelson out of the picture, there was nobody else to ask. The last standing man of the general government in Rome, a fatigued Brennan tried to orchestrate Duran's caregivers and hold Miles Jesu together. Spinning plates on sticks, Sean jumped from one crisis to another.

I'd explained my inability to stomach the house atmosphere any longer: the governance by fear, the obsession with the demonic, the reckless decisions from a demented mind. Sean immediately understood, agreed, and instructed me to make arrangements to stay at the Casa del Clero on Traspontina near the Vatican. He promised to cover for me with Duran. Any lie would do. It had seemed all too easy; I'd learn why later.

Friday, May 4, 2007, ten days after my sexual encounter with Olha Klub, seven days after my meeting with Monsignor Moretti in the Vicariate, I picked up my bags, entered the building, and checked in at the front desk. My pre-arrangement included a two week stay in a second floor room with three squares a day in the basement dining room. The hotel management had no problems with billing Miles Jesu at a later date. Religious orders typically had fat Vatican bank accounts and honored their pledges. Before leaving the Miles Jesu apartment, Brennan had slipped me sixty euros for pocket change, promising that he'd scrounge something more in a few days.

Finding my room, I unlocked the door and pushed it open. Giddy with disbelief, I beheld a spacious room with a big window overlooking the front street of the Casa. After twenty-eight years of shared second-hand arrangements, including more than three years of punitive confinement, the simple room felt like a palace.

Everything smelled fresh and felt squeaky clean. Marble floors, a real bed, a chair and desk, a private bath. Sunshine poured through the window. I back floated upon the bed, cradled the back of my head in my hands, and stared up at the light. A feeling of release, freedom rushed through me and a sigh of relief whooshed from my lungs. Solitude tasted wonderful. Closing my eyes, tears trickled toward my ears. I imagined Jesus kneeling at my bedside.

Suddenly, a barrage of random photographs of my life flew through my mind: shaking John Paul II's hand; getting thrown off a train by the KGB in Russia; hitchhiking through an ocean of Iowa cornfields.

My spirit thumbed through almost three decades of memories.

Snapshots shuffled in rapid succession: delivering grappa to Vatican cardinals; standing next to Father Duran bribing a Vatican official; surrendering to deportation from India; begging for a side of beef in a sea of suspended carcasses; singing before thousands in Ukraine; talking in a teenage-packed gymnasium in Michigan; ladling soup for Navajo Indians in New Mexico; watching Duran wake a young man with wet kisses on the lips in Texas; giggling with Cardinal Ratzinger in his office not far from the Vatican. The flood of memories then settled on the smiling face of Olha Klub. I felt liberated in that room and my spirit ran wild.

Seeing the swaying grass, her smiling face illuminated by the moon, I stared at the motion picture of our passionate kisses. I remembered her bowed head and the sacramental absolution traced in the air. That instant, stretched out on the bed, it hit me. Not born of the tedious logic of reason, a flash of intuition popped my eyes wide open.

"Oh my God," I whispered. "I'm excommunicated!"

Without conscious participation, my subconscious had dug up the truth. It had only required my unfettered spirit to roam freely. Momentarily stunned, shaking my head in amazement, a hint of laughter broke the silence. "Shit!" I already had more than enough to do.

Sean Brennan had inadvertently placed me at the throbbing heart of the Catholic Church where I could finish my exclaustration request with hustle. It seemed that God had cleared a path for me to dash for the end zone. I'd seize every spare minute to write, consult, and rewrite. But the excommunication would now complicate things. I'd have to juggle two sticks of dynamite.

Wide awake, I bounced off the bed and walked into the bathroom to splash water in my face. Distractedly, I glanced at my watch. Damn! Lunch time and I was late. I dried my face, threw the towel, grabbed my keys, locked the door behind me, and took off for the basement. The elevator sank and banged to a halt; I jumped out and followed my nose.

Pushing open the dining room door, I momentarily froze: a thriving restaurant, served by women religious in bleached white habits. The lip smacking aroma hit me in the face. But I couldn't move forward. Hundreds of priest-collared spaghetti-eaters. My heart sank. No thanks. I didn't feel like finding a vacant chair. That instant, churning inside of me, I felt an indigestion of clergy and a repulsion of Church superiors.

Turning around, I found my way out of the building and into the street. Peering through the arch on my right, I saw a tourist-swamped hot dog cart. Reaching down into my pocket, I grabbed the euros from Brennan.

"Thank you, Jesus."

Like chess pieces locking into place, the days and episodes at the Casa marked both the end of an old life and beginning of a new. Almost daily, consecutive events unfolded that progressively weaned me from Miles Jesu, sealed the fate of the rogue cult, and thrust me into unbelievable new possibilities.

That first weekend, free of a schedule, wonderfully alone, I spent many hours sitting at the base of a pillar in Saint Peter's Square. I loved to sit there and inhale the beautiful landscape: the cobblestone stretching everywhere, the mushroomed fountains, two hundred eighty-four pillars, one hundred forty statues, an Egyptian obelisk, and enthusiastic tourists. Perched on a cold stone, I slogged there with a clipboard and pen in hand, feverishly scribbling my exclaustration request. Between blasts of ideas I'd break and scatter crumbs to the pigeons.

Each day ended at a nearby internet café where the day's work found its way to a cheap memory stick. Day after day, darkness fell outside the window of a thriving family business where a crowd of computer addicts gathered, young and old, foreign and domestic. It was a clean and bright place with a couple dozen terminals pampered by an amiable Indian staff. A few euros got me an hour of frantic typing. I'd save money and print my swelling document someday in Murphy's Vatican office.

With the exclaustration request advancing, I focused next on getting back into the Catholic Church. Ironically, my feverish writing aimed at securing a break from it.

Early Monday morning, May 7, 2007, I located Father Lorenzo Angioli at a popular student bookstore near the Vatican. Apparently, he owned the place. Ambra Treichler had told me about the man and where to find him. I wanted to consult him about resolving my excommunication. While I waited outside a locked door, the cleric arrived on a Vespa.

The clean shaven priest with welcoming eyes doubled as a psychoanalyst. With a paternal demeanor about him, Father Angioli radiated a gentleman in every sense of the word: cultured, smart, pleasant, polite, and funny too. A man of principle. Long ago, he turned down a Papal invitation to wear the cardinal's hat. Nope. Lorenzo cherished his liberty and solidarity with the simple people, and his mountain of books. He knew the Catholic Church and its ways, inside and out. Knowledgeable and outside the circle of ecclesial authority, Father Lorenzo seemed the perfect consultant for my sensitive matter.

We introduced ourselves to each other, scampered up a staircase, and found some chairs in his dinky office. He didn't seem to mind his donation of time. After a handful of probing questions that confirmed my excommunication, Father Lorenzo advised a simple course of action. "Father Sullivan, go to the Apostolic Penitentiary, explain the case and follow their instructions. But do it anonymously. Find a lower positioned cleric and say that you're unofficially inquiring about the procedure for a priest who lives in Rome."

The Apostolic Penitentiary is one of the three tribunals of the Roman Curia. Together, these tribunals operate as an administrative branch for the Pope. The Apostolic Signatura functions as the highest judicial apparatus; the Roman Rota as the highest appellate body, the Penitentiary as the Pope's mechanism to grant the absolution of censures reserved to the Holy See. In my case, burdened with an automatic excommunication reserved to the Pope, the Apostolic Penitentiary offered the established avenue for forgiveness and reunion with the Church.

The next day, I arrived at the arched entrance of the Penitentiary. A congestion of tightly parked cars, mopeds, and hungry tourists at sidewalk tables filled the scene. The three story building overflowed with layers of arched windows. High above the entrance, the chiseled words *Corte Imperiali*" flaunted an elegant tradition. Winged lions and eight-tipped stars ushered me into an enclosed cobblestoned courtyard encircled with majestic pillars. During my school years, I'd passed this place almost daily, clueless to its function.

I climbed the stairs, stepped through the main door, and turned to the receptionist.

"Good morning, Father," I said. "I'd like to consult with any English speaking cleric about a confidential matter. It shouldn't take much time."

I wore my Roman collar. Priests received preferential treatment at such offices.

The receptionist looked like the model German soldier, only dressed as a priest. Tightly cut, blond hair, a perfectly proportioned face, baby blue eyes. No questions asked, the priest immediately obliged and instructed me to follow him to a waiting room.

"Make yourself comfortable, it will take a minute."

Responding to me in English, he couldn't hide his German accent. As soon as the door closed, it reopened. An American priest practically rushed to me. It felt like the black-suited guys had been playing tag team in the hallway. The untypical efficiency of a Vatican office caught me off guard. Father Smith stuck out his hand, smiled and greeted me.

"Good morning Father. How may I help you?"

Superbly dressed in shiny clerics, with wire framed glasses suspended on a stubby nose, the Vatican employee exuded a brainy first impression. We sat in comfortable chairs and after a nameless introduction I spoke directly.

"Father, I came to inquire for a third party. A priest has incurred an automatic excommunication by absolving his partner of a sin against the sixth commandment. This priest lives in Rome and wants to know the easiest way to lift the excommunication."

Did Smith see right through me? It was a first grade theology question and I didn't realize it until I'd actually asked it. The cleric wore a poker face, just as he was trained to do.

He crossed his legs and scratched his ear. Baby stuff. A gold cuff link twinkled as the priest folded his hands in his lap.

"Well, since the penitent does live in Rome, he could bypass this office and go directly to Saint Peter's Basilica." A get out of jail free card. "There's a specially trained confessor there who could handle everything."

"Really? And how does the priest find this confessor?"

"There's a confessional box across from the cupola entrance, near the altar of Saint Josephat. This confessor sits in that box every morning. Obviously, there's no need for an appointment."

Bull's-eye! I knew the exact confessional box Father Smith described. Now I knew what to do. It had only taken a minute with the right man. Smith then threw in something extra.

"You can reassure the priest that the process is simple. Although the Apostolic Penitentiary is sometimes perceived as a chiding institution, it's really a tribunal of mercy. The essential purpose of this office is to offer forgiveness."

Did he say this for my sake? Maybe. Following a minute of small talk, I thanked Smith and exited the building. The whole thing had taken only five minutes. I pocketed the information and planned to visit the priest in the box another day. Walking back to the Casa, passing the display windows of papa and mama shops, my thoughts shifted to the remaining sections of my exclaustration request to Cardinal Ruini.

Three days later, Friday evening, May 11, 2007, I left the internet café with the definitive version of the exclaustration request on my memory stick. Dodging captivated tourists and lovers strolling hand in hand, I walked into a bar for a symbolic celebration: a slice of pizza and a gin and tonic. I asked for a single piece of something genuinely Italian: a concoction of mozzarella, green olives, fresh cherry tomatoes, rugetta and sweet basil.

Wedged in a crowd of guys and beers, I found a niche at a table near a big screen television blasting a raging soccer match. Not accustomed to the rowdy atmosphere, my mind refused to relax. Chewing away, watching the game, I kept planning the tasks at hand. Tomorrow, I'd go to the confessor in Saint Peter's Basilica, stop by Murphy's office to print a hard copy of the exclaustration request, and try to make an appointment to see Bishop Moretti in the Vicariate. I'd then find a way to arrange for a meeting with Olha. It didn't really feel like a celebration. The Romans seized their first goal and the bar erupted with cheers. Twenty minutes later I exited and headed for the Casa.

Meanwhile, that same eve marked the tragic end of a whirlwind week back at Via Tespi. While Duran slept, the general government of Miles Jesu lost its chief functioning member: Sean Brennan, the swashbuckling, ex-rock star.

During the past week, Brennan had sided with Tom Walsh in an attempt to solicit the full support of the general government for a Vatican intervention. Brennan and Walsh knew that the chaos of Miles Jesu had to be subjected to high superiors. By Friday however, the majority of general government members dug in their heels and resisted. Predictably, they clung to the Institute's praxis of evading the scrutiny of external observers. Brennan and Walsh lost the fight. After they failed to win general government support they withdrew and explored the idea of making an independent appeal for an intervention.

The idea of seeking a Vatican intervention actually grew out of a series of discreet consultations primarily between Tom Walsh, Sean Brennan and Professor Patrick Molony. These meetings had launched about a month ago at the University of Saint Thomas Aquinas. After a class on the spirituality of Saint Teresa of Avila, Brennan, Walsh, and Molony had met in a private room, where two desperate souls revealed the bizarre world of Miles Jesu to a veteran listener.

Professor Molony, fifty-four years old, wore an ankle-length white tunic with a tapered and pointed hood that trailed down the crease of his back. A thick black belt and drooping rosary distinguished his habit as a sign of commitment to God. Round glasses, full beard, Irish-green eyes, and a touch of balding on the top and greying on the sides, Molony discharged a countenance full of laughs.

After fifteen years of probing the depths of spirituality, the eloquent professor had mastered everything pertaining to community life. He knew the theory and practice, the canon law, the psychology and theology permeating it. Throughout the years, the professor's approachable nature and horse sense had won the trust of many students seeking advice. Molony had the hush-hushed reputation of knowing how to help religious students hurting in irregular communities. By experience, the professor knew how to navigate the Vatican offices and persuade authorities to effect relief for the victims of bad superiors. Brennan and Walsh had found their man.

As shocking disclosures mounted and consultations advanced, an intervention plan gradually took shape. Breaking through years of conditioned fears, Brennan and Walsh smashed the ironclad law of Miles Jesu prohibiting the revelation of family problems to outsiders. But they felt they had no other options to manage their crumbling world. They knew that the governing body of Miles Jesu couldn't fix itself; it couldn't even understand the dangers of its own self-serving principles.

Molony had engendered the trust of Brennan and Walsh, and everything spewed forth: sexual abuse; tyrannical power; financial misappropriations; sickening humiliations; paralyzing fear. More than once, the professor had stressed the need to disclose the whole truth.

"We must shine the light of Christ upon this human tragedy to bring genuine healing to everyone." He also had warned of terrible things to come. "Brace yourselves brothers, things will get worse before they get better."

The strategy had developed to win the cooperation of the Miles Jesu general government, except for Father Duran, of course. Brennan and Walsh had gradually introduced the government members to Molony, who tried to persuade each person to yield to a reasonable course of action. Some members had started to come around until Gelson showed up at the critical moment.

That Friday evening the plan collapsed. Gelson was the pivotal man to win over; he wouldn't budge. Once the meeting concluded the band regrouped and Gelson strengthened his wobbly-kneed companions.

"Molony can't be trusted. There's no way on earth we'll expose things to the Vatican. We'll go to Cardinal Castrillon Hoyos and Father Torres." Father Duran's friends. "We'll solve things on our own."

Gelson's course of action would follow the long established defective pattern of problem resolution. A sanitized version of the problem would be shared and any response would be filtered and manipulated to represent whatever Miles Jesu wanted. The tragedy would end with a band-aid on a heart attack.

After the government receded, Brennan vented his frustration.

"Hell! They're not going to do anything. It's the same old shit again. Tom, we can't deal with these people!"

Tom Walsh bit his upper lip, not allowing his emotions to spin out of control. He was the logical thinker of the duo, and wanted to keep his brain free from emotional influence. After Sean's knee jerk reaction, Tom summarized things.

"Yep, I know what you mean, Sean. Looks like we're on our own.

If anything's going to happen, the ball's in our court now."

They both knew what had to be done: an independent and simultaneous appeal to the Vatican and the Vicariate to intervene and stop the absurdity of Miles Jesu. But even at this moment Walsh hesitated. Circumspection and a meticulous disposition made up the deepest part of his nature. Tom never acted rashly. He thought. Never play Axis and Allies with him! Although Sean revved his engine to push forward, Tom Walsh tapped the brakes. He insisted they sleep on it for a few more days.

Early Saturday morning, May 12, 2007, another perfect day in Rome. I passed through the portal of Saint Peter's Basilica and headed toward the confessional near the altar of Saint Josephat. The glory and splendor of this renaissance church never ceased to amaze me. From the front door to the back wall, the interior stretched two football fields in length. The interior space shot upward a hundred thirty meters high. Imposing mosaics and herculean statues floated by. My black shoes skipped over flawless interlocking patterns of colored marble. Where three massive rays of light pierced the air and hit the floor, polished stone reflected an explosion of light. Pausing, I inhaled the beauty surrounding me and whispered to my friend.

"Jesus, I'm here. What do you have for me today?"

His response immediately resounded. Not hearing words with my ears, I felt them move inside of me.

"Andy, tell this confessor everything. I will speak to you through him."

The prayer soon passed. I turned to my right and saw the confessional where Father Smith was indicated. The fifteen-foot-high structure sat on a wooden platform. Although the thing looked like a finely carved single unit, it actually divided into three sections. Behind swinging doors, the middle section enclosed the confessor. To his right and left, entrance niches with kneelers butted up against the confessor's capsule. A sign hung above the central doors: "English, Italiano." I stepped into the niche on the right and knelt down. A creak echoed throughout the Basilica.

The panel slid open. Through a perforated confessional screen, the faint silhouette of a hunched priest appeared. I'd been to confession somewhere around two-thousand times in my life. This confession would soar above the ordinary. Within thirty minutes, I'd receive the hope of a new kind of life.

"Father, I'm a priest living here in Rome and I believe that I'm excommunicated. After consulting at the Apostolic Penitentiary, they instructed me to come to you."

"Can you tell me why you think you're excommunicated?"

"I absolved my partner of a sin against the sixth commandment. But I did it, mistakenly thinking that the penalty applied only if there was sexual intercourse."

"There was no sexual intercourse?"

"No, Father."

He coughed and cleared his throat.

"Well, you're right. You are excommunicated, regardless of your ignorance. But because you were ignorant the offense is not as serious as it could have been. We can handle everything between us, without the need to refer back to the Apostolic Penitentiary. If you are willing to accept a penance to lift the excommunication, we can move on to confession. Is this okay with you?"

Feeling good about the simplicity of it all, I spoke into the screen. "Yes, that's fine. I'll accept whatever penance you give."

"Good. For your penance you can say a rosary every day for a week."

"That's my penance?" It seemed too easy.

"Yes, that's all. We can now proceed with the sacrament of confession. How long has it been since you last confessed?"

"Hum, it's been about a couple weeks since my last confession."

Straight away, I confessed my open criticisms of church superiors, sins of the flesh with Olha, my presumptions of God's favors. The priest asked a few questions here and there; I responded with bare bones answers.

Although that morning encounter could have ended abruptly with an additional penance and quick absolution, God Himself seemed to intervene for his own purpose. I suddenly felt the urge to open my heart completely and share the burdens and the freedoms and the craziness of my life. As if from nowhere, a spontaneous and intense need for real spiritual direction surfaced in my soul. Did Jesus want me to receive impartial counsel from a master of the spiritual life, from a man who knew how to sew a torn life back together? I surrendered to the unexpected opportunity of the moment.

Perhaps my sudden desire for genuine counsel was little more than a rebellious kick against twenty-eight years of Miles Jesu spiritual direction. Its practice had strangled any impulse to speak freely and colored every conversation with caution.

By its principles and regulations, Miles Jesu spiritual direction was designed to keep you in the community and make you unconditionally loyal to Father Alphonsus Duran. You couldn't seek guidance outside of the group. The counsel given had to conform to the paradigm of Father Duran and be guided by his specific instructions. He chose your director for you. Nothing was confidential. Through the demand of obedience, Duran could access anything shared between two members and use the information to publicly humiliate or coerce conformity. For the most part, spiritual directors were uneducated laymen. Priests were forbidden to impart counsel. The overriding custom had nothing to do with competence and everything to do with parroting Duran's viewpoint and instilling loyalty. Of course, the practice was buttressed with biblical principles and Church approvals promulgated by Duran. Beneath the pretense of exceptional spirituality, Duran's internal system was a manipulation to entrap souls.

I swallowed. Here it goes.

"Father, there's something else I'd like to talk about."

"Yes, please. Go ahead. We're not in a rush. We have all the time in the world."

I appreciated his attitude. There were now a few penitents in line.

"I'm having a real crisis in life. I've just removed myself from community life because I can't take it any longer. During the past seventeen months I've been going through drastic changes in my ways of thinking and feeling. It's like I'm growing up overnight and discovering how damaging my community environment really is. My community is a new form of consecrated life here in Rome.

"How long have you lived in this community?"

"Twenty-eight years."

That sank in. After the silence settled, the surgeon of the soul re-gripped his scalpel and executed another scrutinized incision.

"Tell me why you decided to leave."

His invitation reached deep into me and unlocked a long history of abuses that had climaxed with three years of apartment imprisonment and a suicidal death wish. A torrent of explanations burst forth from my soul.

"I joined the group when I was eighteen years old. At that time, I thought of being a priest and was told that I would study. This was the carrot that had persuaded me to join. But I didn't start college until sixteen years later. When I joined I had mixed feelings about marriage, but lacking any kind of unbiased and competent discernment process, my consecrated vocation was simply presumed. I then made what I understood to be a morally irreversible commitment to the community.

"There was no formation program; no novitiate to prepare me for consecrated life, even if documents said such things existed. Sixteen years later, after I'd decided to leave the community, my studies were the result of the General Director's manipulation to keep me in the Institute.

"I'd requested in writing not to be ordained a priest and my appeal was publically ridiculed and then categorically ignored. I subsequently went through ordination without the courage to oppose it. Now, I'm a discarded priest, without pastoral experience. I've spent the past six years as a priest either fundraising or doing menial jobs. For the last three years I'm living under house arrest, locked up in an apartment."

"And why did you leave the community?"

"After living in despair for years, a priest revealed to me that I had emotional deprivation disorder, and showed me a therapeutic kind of prayer to help me grow out of it. I've spent seventeen months practicing this prayer and I'm a different person now."

We talked about emotional deprivation disorder and Doctor Baars. The confessor was familiar with the psychotherapist's summation and corresponding therapy. He agreed with the Papal theologian's favorable stance regarding the doctor's therapeutic approach. I continued to explain the result of my therapeutic meditations.

"I'm experiencing an overwhelming intensity of receiving God's love. It's like an explosion of love inside of me. I'd always believed that God loved me, but hardly felt it. Now, my emotions correspond better with my intellect. I actually feel God's love. This experience has made my emotional life grow and given me a new outlook on life. It has opened my eyes to the damaging nature of the environment where I live. These changes finally brought me to the conclusion that I must remove myself from my community if I want to complete my emotional growth and healing. A monsignor in the Vatican has told me the same thing.

"So far, I have a temporary permission to live outside of community, but this arrangement will soon run out and I can't bear going back into that environment. In this regard, I really don't know what to do."

"It sounds to me like you ought to ask for an exclaustration from your community at this point. This would give you the independence and the time you need to finish growing up and to reassess your calling in life. Then you could freely choose your vocation, free from any kind of coercion. You might want to consider some psychotherapy to help in this process."

With Tom Walsh's help, I'd recently received Gelson's permission to start psychotherapy.

"Father, I'll be submitting my request for exclaustration this coming week, and I've just started psychotherapy."

"These are good signs." He launched in another direction. "Your community is a sinking ship. Either jump the ship or go down with it. God could not possibly want you in that place."

"And why's that?"

I felt God speaking to me. The many meditations depicting Miles Jesu as a sinking ship flashed in my mind.

"See what that community has done to you. God does not will the systematic destruction of a person. Continue to get your exclaustration and finish your first analysis and then you'll be free to discern your vocation and follow it."

"What do you mean?"

"You lacked the maturity to freely choose your vocation. You joined your community by deception and remained in it by coercion. You lacked the opportunity to discern your vocation objectively. You had no formation program and no novitiate; you lacked a thorough understanding of the way of life you chose. Once you finish your emotional development, your healing of emotional trauma, you're free to choose whatever vocation you might discern, including the priesthood or marriage."

"Marriage?"

"If you finish your therapy and discern it as your calling, then yes, even marriage."

My outlook on life changed that instant. Up until that moment, I'd been obsessed about getting out of a harmful environment. Suddenly, a wider picture came into view: the possibility of a brand new kind of life after Miles Jesu. Marriage. The impossible had just become possible and I felt stunned.

The confessor added a few blurry remarks, tacked on an additional penance, and gave sacramental absolution. I was now back in the life of the Catholic Church and it felt good. And the hope of marrying Olha felt wonderful. In a daze, I made the sign of the cross, stepped out of the confessional, and drifted into the breeze and sun of Saint Peter's Square. I found my familiar pillar, sat down, looked around, and saw nothing. My exclaustration request had just taken on a new meaning and my whole life too.

"Oh my God! I can't believe it! Thank you Jesus." I grasped my memory stick and cried.

The next day, Sunday, May 13, 2007, proved a pivotal day for Tom Walsh. He felt the divine push to launch an independent appeal to the Vatican and Vicariate for the intervention. Standing near the southern edge of the Castel San Angelo, not far from the bridge of the angels stretching over the Tiber, Tom looked up and saw a chopper overhead. Inspiration sparked inside of him and compelled him to follow the bird.

A snow white Agusta Westland 139, the Pope's helicopter swept westward over Piazza Navona and the Lungotevere. A blue double streak slashed across the body of the slick twin engine executive transport. The copter headed toward the fortress-like pad tucked high on the western tip of Vatican City.

Flying in from Da Vinci airport in Fiumicino, the fifteen passenger helicopter carried the pilgrim virgin statue of Our Lady of Fatima for a special celebration at Saint Peter's Square. Hearing the thunder of the blades, Tom felt an inner prompting to follow the sign into the piazza. He'd been wandering around, uncertain of the solution to his moral quagmire.

Arriving in the square, Tom discovered the famed statue and attended a special Mass in honor of the Blessed Virgin. Over and over, he kept experiencing a refrain from the Song of Songs: "Who is she that comes forth as the morning rising, fair as the moon, bright as the sun, terrible as an army set in battle array?"

Miles Jesu prayed this phrase every day, but at this instance the words assumed an entirely new meaning for Tom. They resounded in his soul, cleared his mind, and fortified him. He felt the confidence to go to the Church authorities without delay. The Mother of God was going to lead the way and rescue her suffering children.

There was another phrase that pounded in his head and reverberated throughout his big body. At the moment, he forgot its origin. A friend would later identify the quip as the final line of the film *Jesus of Nazareth* uttered by a Roman at the empty tomb: "now it begins."

# CHAPTER TWELVE

O ur brisk steps tramped upon the marble corridors and echoed off the frescos above our heads. D-day. Tuesday morning, May 15, 2007. It felt like hitting the beach running. We headed toward the Vicariate office of Monsignor Luigi Moretti. Rick charged ahead with a dispensation appeal in hand. I held my exclaustration request.

Rick Wolowicz was a fit, handsome, soft-spoken guy. Thirty-one years old, deep green eyes, a ready smile. Leaving behind his hard earned profession as a pharmacist, the New Jersey gentleman had joined Miles Jesu eight years ago. Rick had wanted to offer his life to God. Duran had taken it, wanting the innocent man available for a myriad of odds and ends assignments.

Wolowicz and I met at the Vicariate that morning. Throughout the past month we'd been talking on the sly. I'd shared candid advice and introduced him to a batch of Church documents and canon law so he could measure the aberrations of Miles Jesu. His eyes had been opened to participating in a rogue cult gone wild, and now he wanted out. After eight years of deceit, fear, and coercion, he wanted his freedom.

We entered the receptionist's office and greeted a beautiful, brunette secretary. She stood, bent forward, and held out her hand. Behind her, the official portrait of Pope Benedict XVI seemed to crack a Mona Lisa grin.

"Good morning. How may I help you?" she asked.

I offered my hand. "My name is Father Andrew Sullivan. This is Rick Wolowicz. I have an appointment with Monsignor Moretti at ten."

She bent her head a little and shrugged her shoulders.

"Oh, the monsignor just left. But he did ask if you could come to his residence. Do you know how to get there?"

"No, I've never been there." Rick just shook his head.

A five-minute walk. Shooting through the Vicariate archway, noting the obelisk on our right, we passed an old red church and found the fifteen-foot high iron barricade topped with ornate spear tips. This marked the gateway of Lateran University, where two hundred professors cranked out perpetual ranks of canon lawyers destined for hot spots far and wide. We skirted the boundaries of a vibrant campus, crowded with students loaded down with backpacks and books. A few more twists and turns between buildings, and we stood before the monsignor's front door.

We rang the bell and waited.

The monsignor himself opened the door and stepped forward onto the welcome mat. His frame seemed a bit pudgier than I remembered. Everything else appeared the same: double chin, wire-rimmed glasses, balding, greying on the sides, a black jacket and grey clerical shirt, and a stubby bishop's ring.

"Good morning Father Sullivan," he greeted me. "Thank you for coming over. I have a busy morning and had to come back here to get started. Please come inside."

I could barely squeeze in the obligatory introduction of Rick.

Unfortunately, Moretti was in a rush. I'd anticipated a meeting of some kind, but that wasn't going to happen. He just wanted to snatch my document and disappear.

I held out my exclaustration request. He grabbed it, offered a distracted "thank you," shook our hands, and ushered us back outside. But before he could close the door, I let the monsignor know that Rick's dispensation request was included.

Moretti acknowledged the information and gave a reassurance.

"Father Sullivan, and Rick, please excuse the rush, but I'll read your documents and be in touch. It won't take long." The door shut. After a long day, the monsignor read my exclaustration request beneath the light of his kitchen table. Under normal conditions, an exclaustration request is a simple matter. A brief explanation of a need for temporary independence is submitted to a major superior. He then hashes over terms with his counsel, tweaks a circumscribed response, and issues a one-pager granting permission. Within a week, the routine blink of administration is resolved and tucked away in a file, and the needy soul unpacks his belongings in a new environment.

But I was not dealing with a normal institute, not even a functional or sane institute. And the circumstances were anything but ordinary. My need was urgent, superiors incompetent, and a big shot bishop in Rome wanted to leverage my request to hunt down a clandestine new group hidden in the peripheral fold of a jam-packed diocese.

Addressed to Cardinal Ruini, I slapped on an over-sized title in bold at the top of page one. It unambiguously identified the document: "REQUEST: FOR AN INDULT OF EXCLAUSTRATION FOR A RESIDENT PRIEST OF ROME UNDER EXTRAORDINARY CIRCUMSTANCES." A three-page letter and thirty-one pages of single-spaced appendix material followed.

The outrageous length of the appeal reflected my desperation. There was no way on earth I wouldn't get that exclaustration! So, I crammed the document with every possible argument to secure the new environment needed to thrive. The bottom line was that I needed a place to emotionally mature and heal from trauma. I had to stay in Rome for therapy, and this demanded financial support. Of course, I could have simply abandoned the whole effort and took off, and I thought about this more than once, but inspiration led me in another direction, in agreement with my conscience. I wanted to follow the established canonical procedure for exclaustration, even though Miles Jesu had no such provision in its own constitutions.

Regardless of the Miles Jesu implosion back at Via Tespi, I focused upon my health. I couldn't help it if the breakdown of Duran and Gelson and the blossoming of my own healthy self-love coincided.

In a nutshell, the request and appendixes amounted to a naked revelation of my soul, born of immaturity, methodically wounded by an inhumane environment.

The first appendix described the broken and incompetent state of my superiors. The second was a letter to Cardinal Ruini written by my psychotherapist to verify my psychological diagnosis and validate a therapeutic need.

The third appendix told the story of my disorder, its discovery, its provisional self-treatment by affirmation meditation, and how I came to the decision to seek an exclaustration.

This appendix included a description of the manipulative recruitment and indoctrination techniques of the group and a summary of the emotional environment. It indicated that regardless of the endorsements of bishops and cardinals, even the Pope, the testimonies of prelates served as window dressing. Quips and quotes of prestigious Church officials unwittingly sheltered a damaging way of life behind closed doors.

I described an environment that used false promises and fear to recruit, coercion to advance premature commitments, and the virtue of blind obedience to discontinue education. Two pages sketched an ambiance saturated with fear, humiliation, and senselessness. Miles Jesu community life nurtured thoughts and feelings that attacked the foundations of human interaction. Subjected to Duran's scrutiny and criticism, true friendships broke under the weight of unconditional loyalty to Father General.

Privacy and solitude couldn't possibly survive. Solitude was selfish. Letters, phone calls, walks, slumber, encounters with family members, travels, practically every human activity required another person's presence to safeguard the vocation. Human feelings were viewed as enemies, except those orientated toward the realization of Duran's interests. Education was viewed with great suspicion. Women and marriage were ridiculed and held in contempt.

The later part of the third appendix dropped the bombshell. Six pages identified Miles Jesu as a cult. I presented two respected sources to evaluate the cult-like thinking and behavior of the group. The first was Father Francis Morrisey, OMI, a known professor of canon law and former Vatican consultant. He'd established fifteen warning signs generally acknowledged as a guide when assessing new associations within the Catholic Church. The second source was Doctor Michael Langone, a thirty-year cult researcher and the Executive Director of the International Cultic Studies Association. He'd assembled the criteria by which experts judge a group to be a cult. An adapted version of Langone's criteria applied to Catholic associations.

Morrisey's list consisted of fifteen points. Miles Jesu exhibited eleven of them. Langone's adapted list for Catholic associations consisted of five points. Miles Jesu exhibited all five. That's sixteen of twenty indicators of cult manifestation. In hindsight, after learning of Duran's sexual abuse of members, Miles Jesu possessed seventeen of the twenty warning signs.

I indicated and described each cult-like attribute embedded in Miles Jesu culture. This list included: preoccupation with recruiting new members; obsession with fundraising; elitism; induction of guilt and fear as a way to control members; severance of links with the family and outside world; special secretive vows to preserve the interests of the authority structure; secrecy imposed on members to restrict communication with authorities outside of Miles Jesu; control over the choice of confessors and spiritual directors, including the content of private discussions that result from such relationships; weird and severe penances; special treatment of the founder, who lives above the confines of the law; making use of falsehoods to obtain approvals and advance agendas; no sense of connectedness with the local church; too soon an insistence on placing all goods in common; absolute obedience to the Pope and General Director of Miles Jesu, seen as two sides of the same coin.

The fourth appendix underlined specific Miles Jesu policies that fostered injustice and impeded human development. I listed twenty practices that opposed emotional and intellectual development.

This list exposed an environment that withheld the basic goods needed for human growth. Customarily, the Miles Jesu drive to recruit members and get them involved in Duran's latest apostolate overwhelmed formation and education considerations. Miles Jesu provided no formation program, no properly trained formation directors, no location dedicated to formation, no psychological evaluation of candidates, no vocation discernment by competent and impartial directors, no novitiate, no priestly formation program headed by a competent director. Of course, Miles Jesu had plenty of written documentation that such things existed.

The fifth and final appendix was a supportive letter from my brother, Jim. He'd spent four years in Miles Jesu and escaped in the middle of the night, in the summer of 2003. I included his testimony to provide an outsider's perspective, but from someone who'd experienced the internal dynamics of the community:

"Those in a position of trust, priests and the General Director personally, abused trust in different ways that were psychologically harmful. I was humiliated repeatedly in public and private. I was told to accomplish certain tasks without any means of accomplishing those tasks, then ridiculed and humiliated severely in front of others for not being successful. I was told that I just needed more grace and that pride was preventing me from doing anything.

"I witnessed members, including priests of Miles Jesu, tell young men and women that their chances of going to hell were very great if they did not join the organization. That thought brought me into Miles Jesu. I had made a retreat with the community many years before, but the threat of hell had remained in my mind. In my experience, discernment retreats or discernment time spent at a Miles Jesu community amounted to nothing less than, 'Join Miles Jesu or go to hell.'"

I sealed the letter of request with my signature, adding a few details to persuade serious consideration. I'd been a member of Miles Jesu since 1979 and an advisor within the general government for nine years. Besides, I'd served as the General Secretary and Provincial of Eastern Europe.

Two days later, Thursday, May 17, 2007, Olha Klub tiptoed out of the woman's apartment. She silently sealed the front door, skipped down the stairs, and cut to the right. Heading up the driveway, she ducked beneath the eyes of the apartment windows. Overgrown oleanders shielded her passage.

Weaving through the cars in the back parking lot, the woman slipped through a hole in a chain-link fence and stepped upon the beaten path that encircled a beautiful park. A sweet sensation of liberation relaxed her tense body and put a smile on her face. The date and time of our secret rendezvous arrived at last. Clothed in an out of style green dress, without lipstick, earrings, or makeup of any kind, she kept the date. With an eager heart, Olha got to the oak tree first.

She kicked off her sandals and sat in the shade. Searching for me, she scanned the horizon. Alone, waiting, Olha's mind wandered to the day she had left home. At a pivotal moment in life, her mother's words had impressed a lasting memory. Mom's wisdom never seemed to go away.

Seventeen years ago, when Olha was seventeen, she had stood beneath the porch extension of the family home. A light rain dampened the ground, rousing the chickens to scratch for fresh grub. Olha and her mom lingered, looking at the ducks waddle along the base of the barn, followed by a line of ducklings trying to keep pace. They observed grandma's stroll back into the house. The aged woman carried a fresh pale of milk and wore a wide smile as she passed by her daughter, and her daughter's daughter.

Wrapping up their conversation, Mom turned to Olha and repeated herself.

"Olha, in the end, it's your choice. It's your life." Although Miles Jesu had been pressing Olha to join, her mother had given the girl a feeling of genuine freedom to make her own decision. Olha had appreciated her mother's attitude.

"Don't worry about the crops. If you decide to go, we'll find a way to get things done."

Olha's thoughts jumped to the present. Mom's words still echoed. "It's your choice." Olha sensed that her days were now numbered. Miles Jesu was falling apart and she wouldn't last much longer. "It's your life."

Seeing me in the distance, Olha jumped to her feet and practically ran to me. I wore sneakers, Levis, and a blue pullover. We met with an embrace and a kiss. The hug energized us and brightened our faces. It felt wonderful to be together again, to squeeze and smell each other, to feel the warm softness of our bodies pressed together.

Although I'd all the time in the world, Olha was constrained by the clock. I understood. Been there, done that. She had about an hour and a half before the two distracted community members in the apartment might start looking for her.

I brushed aside some hair hanging over her face.

"Hi Olha. It's so good to see you! How are you?"

"I'm fine, now that you're here. How are you, Andy?"

"I feel good today. I'm nervous about the Casa bill, but feel great living on my own."

We made some small talk about her escape from the apartment, who was home, how she got out. I asked about Duran and Gelson. They were just as dysfunctional as ever. We sat on thick grass and nudged close to one another.

"So how about your exclaustration request? Did you turn it in?"

"Yea, I gave it to Monsignor Moretti two days ago."

"That's great. What did he say?"

"Nothing really. He was in a rush. He said he'd read it and have an answer soon."

"That's good."

"I can hardly wait. It can't be fast enough. I hate living in limbo."

"But what's your impression? Do you think you'll get it?"

"I think I'll get it in a few days. I don't see how the Vicariate can read my request and refuse to grant it."

A breeze allowed flickering sun streams to dance upon our bodies. Olha wondered where this would leave her. She was happy for me, but worried for herself. If I was free from community life and Miles Jesu continued to crumble away, where would that leave her? What would she do? How would she survive?

I reached out and gently took her hand. Leaving aside the prefaces, I started with the bottom line. She hated dramatic teasing.

"Olha, there's bigger news. There's a possibility that we could get married."

"What? Really?" Absolute shock.

"Yes, really."

"I don't understand. We said it was impossible."

"It's a long story."

"Andy!" Her big green eyes scrutinized my face. Impatience grabbed hold of her. "Tell me everything! Don't leave out the details."

From beginning to end, I told the whole story: how I discovered my excommunication and confirmed it with Father Angioli; how I consulted with Father Smith at the Apostolic Penitentiary, how I confessed to the priest in Saint Peter's Basilica. I shared the conversation between the confessor and me.

As I neared the end of the story Olha exploded with interior joy. She could hardly contain herself. Her heart pounded. Tears trickled down her face. Silence settled upon us and we embraced. Her time had run out.

Playfully, she blurted out her raw feelings.

"See, I told you not to give me absolution."

"No, you didn't."

"Yes, I did."

"No, you didn't, Honey. You agreed."

"Maybe, but I didn't feel it was right."

I laughed, and she cracked a big grin and hugged me again.

"But I'm glad it happened."

"So am I."

Then, I remembered a passing word of advice imparted by the confessor somewhere toward the end of the confession.

"Olha, the priest at Saint Peter's also said that we really shouldn't meet again."

"Oh, what does he know?" We laughed again.

I agreed, and tightened my embrace.

Mindful of the time, I concluded with a few sobering thoughts.

"Olha, of course, marriage could only be in the distant future. I first have to finish my psychotherapy. After that, the confessor said I'm free to choose my vocation."

"I understand. It's a long process."

Everything's a long process. Olha was not an overly optimistic person. She was a realist. She felt sad about a long waiting period, but hopeful of a new life with me. Still, the details of the future remained just as blurry as ever: how, when, where.

Time had run out. She had to return to the apartment. It was hard to say our good-byes. It seemed we had met for only five minutes, but it was an hour and a half. We kissed and promised to meet again in a week, near the Piazza del Quirinale in Rome.

I watched her walk away and slip through the hole in the fence. I had no idea that I wouldn't see her again for a full two months, a thousand miles away.

A canonical visitation is an extraordinary intervention by the Holy See to evaluate and fix a broken Church institution. Welcoming criticisms, investigating crimes, and checking on the proper execution of duties, it aims at a thorough examination of the conduct of individual members and the operation of an institute as a whole. The probe concludes with a summary of discoveries and recommendations.

Under regular circumstances, a bishop or major superior requests a canonical visitation of whatever church entity. Even when the Pope initiates it, he proceeds through a delegate authority connected by jurisdiction to the mess at hand. Things were different with Miles Jesu. Lacking an authoritative voice, the visitation request sprouted at the grass roots level of an imploding Church institution. It had a good chance of working because of its shocking content and because it threatened a fresh scandal in the Pope's back yard. Church hierarchs scramble when public image weighs in the balance.

Tom Walsh's five-page letter started with the names and addresses of the two recipients: Camillo Cardinal Ruini, the Vicar General of His Holiness; and Cardinal Rode, the Prefect for the Congregation for Institutes of Consecrated Life and Societies of Apostolic Life. Two birds with one stone.

Page five concluded with ten signatures from veteran members of Miles Jesu. A note indicated two anonymous members willing to cooperate to resolve the Miles Jesu crisis. I was one of them. Tom didn't want my signature because of a prejudicial perception by the internal superiors of Miles Jesu that I was not emotionally sound.

The day after my rendezvous with Olha, Friday, May 18, 2007, Tom Walsh handed the canonical visitation appeal to Monsignor Moretti. The reluctant bishop half-heartedly grabbed the thing out of Walsh's hands. The monsignor had to take seriously anything addressed to his boss, Cardinal Ruini. Earlier that same morning, Walsh had left a copy for Cardinal Rode at the Vatican.

Brennan, Walsh, and Molony had hatched the idea of a canonical visitation a month ago. Gelson almost killed the thing, until Walsh found the courage to plow ahead regardless of Miles Jesu leadership. It took a four-day barrage of labor. Murphy provided the good counsel and cheer leading; Walsh birthed the document; Brennan recruited the signers.

Following an introductory plea for help, the letter divided into three sections of disclosure. The first addressed the sexual seduction and attempted sexual seduction of younger male members and candidates by the Founder and General Director, and attempted cover-up by the Vicar Director and other members. The second exposed the physical and psychological state of the highest superiors of Miles Jesu. The third section abbreviated five kinds of abuse of power and psychological abuse inflicted by the Founder and General Director. Overall, the letter uncovered a freshly approved institute with systemic dysfunctional dynamics.

A quick read included references to a dozen alarming cases. The first section told the stories of a sexual seduction and an attempted sexual seduction. In Ukraine, Duran had been caught with his hands on the hips of a Miles Jesu candidate stripped to his underwear. Two senior members of Miles Jesu were then sent to Church authorities to protect Duran by discrediting the young man. The candidate was so traumatized he left the Catholic Church.

Another case in Rome alleged that Duran had seduced a member of the community with French-kissing, oral sex and masturbation. The victim was subsequently sent to the Miles Jesu community in Spain. Tom Walsh and the victim received gag orders never to tell anyone, under obedience.

The second section offered a succinct appraisal of Duran's physical and mental incapacities, Gelson's trauma, and Jeni Staus's psychological impairment. After illustrating Duran's disconnect with reality and Gelson's need for psychotherapy, the remaining six members of the general government were categorized as deformed superiors. They were profoundly affected by decades of suffering which flowed from the dysfunctional issues of the Founder, and by a fear-based, secretive, and Machiavellian mode of operating.

The third section portrayed Father Alphonsus Maria Duran as an independent trailblazer. His charm, sway, manipulation, and domination over his followers seemed like a second nature woven into his psyche. Placing himself above the constitutions and customs, he governed in a bubble of pervasive lack of accountability and transparency.

This section listed habits of the Founder that scarred souls for life. He forced matters of confidentiality into the open and laughed at the most sensitive and precious thoughts guarded in a person's soul. He compelled members to rebuke and humiliate each other. He purged positions of authority to keep the inner core of Miles Jesu unconditionally loyal to himself. He criticized black people as smelly, sneaky, and lazy. He entirely neglected the formational and educational needs of members. He convinced everyone that Miles Jesu was an instrument par excellence in the hands of Holy Mother Church, that every hardship and discipline was really the love of God purifying imperfections, that no other congregation or seminary could possibly compare, and that hell awaited anyone who left. This section concluded with the idea that bonding to the group might be likened to a syndrome noted in cult-like groups.

The document ended with a request for anonymity by the signers, if at all possible. A note added that three of the signers were scheduled for priestly ordination within the month, and that if an intervention would necessitate a cancelation of the ceremony, the turn of events would be accepted. In advance, Cardinal Ruini was thanked for his consideration of the crisis at hand.

After helping Tom deliver his intervention request to Moretti, that same Friday afternoon I returned to my safe haven at the Casa del Clero. Exhausted, I locked the door, stripped naked, and poured a gin and tonic in the bathroom. I'd just participated in the second bombing raid of Miles Jesu and felt frazzled. Soothed by the cool marble beneath my feet, I twisted the knob and let the water gush. A good soak in a hot tub. Nothing else mattered at the moment.

Parked on the toilet lid, staring into the swirling waters, I nursed my drink and imagined how soon I might be exclaustrated. Just the thought of freedom calmed me. Then the phone rang. As if from nowhere visceral terror pulsated throughout my body. Adrenaline squirted into my heart and I began to sweat. I still needed healing from countless traumatic phone calls with Father Duran barking insults and commands. I turned off the water, scurried into the bedroom, and grabbed the outdated handset.

"Hi, Father Sullivan." It was Father Kroll, former school buddy and now community bean counter.

"Hi, Jerry. What's up?" I tried to sound calm, but my heart raced. "Hope you're having a good day."

He turned his back to a snooping concierge and spoke softly into the mouthpiece.

"We've taken a look at your email requests for money and everything seems fine. I came to help with the Casa del Clero bill."

Since arriving at the Casa, I'd been sending emails asking for financial assistance. As requested by Father Kroll, this morning's email provided a budget and an explanation of my need to live outside of community. It also suggested an escalating desperation. Following instructions from Father Gelson, Kroll had consulted with a lawyer about my predicament.

"Could we get together and talk? I'm in the lobby. I could come up or wait for you down here."

In the lobby! "You want to talk right now?"

"Yes. I have two documents for you."

"Documents?"

"Yea. When we meet I can explain everything," he said.

Bullshit! There were always strings attached. I stood there in the raw, vulnerable and defiant, starting to get mad.

"No. Tell me what you have. What are the documents? I can't meet with you. Tell me what kind of documents you have."

Father Kroll frowned and tried to remain focused. His mission wobbled on the brink of failure.

"Since your time outside of community is over, one document orders you back home. The other requires your signature. It's a statement that you are responsible for your own actions. I'm supposed to leave with your signature."

"I can't give a signature right now. I'll need some time to think about it. Just leave the documents at the front desk and I'll consult with a canon lawyer in the morning."

That was enough for Kroll. "Okay, have a nice day." He slammed down the phone.

I hung up and studied the hands of my watch. Fueled by anger, the wheels in my brain did the math. Kroll had miscalculated his time. He'd planned on a meeting that didn't take place. Twenty minutes to dash to the Vatican for advice. I grabbed my underwear and dressed as fast as I could.

Stopping at the hotel desk, I asked the concierge if a priest had left any documents for me. Glancing over his bifocals, he looked confused. The pudgy man shrugged, tilted his head, and raised his eyebrows.

"Father Sullivan, I saw an American priest, a short guy, who wanted to see you. We let him borrow the phone and then he vanished. I assume he spoke with you."

"Yes, but did he leave anything for me."

"I don't think so. He had papers in his hands, but he took them with him."

"Okay. Thank you."

Once Kroll heard that I'd see a lawyer, he changed his plan. He didn't want a paper trail and a Vatican lawyer scrutinizing his documents. At this point, I didn't care if he left them or not. I exited the hotel, determined to fight. I was not going to be intimidated any more.

Beneath the shadow of the Papal escape route, I ran over the cobble-stones to the Square of Pius XII. Tourists turned their heads, surprised to see a priest sprinting toward Saint Peter's Basilica. At the end of Via dei

Corridori I cut into a high class tourist trap and popped out the other side into a busy piazza. Hanging left, I passed through the doors of the Vatican refuge and flew up stairs.

The light-haired prairie boy with a Midwestern work ethic, Monsignor Murphy sat at his desk drafting an important document. Every day he clocked his service with precision. I walked into his office; he stood up with a smile and handshake. During the past months, we'd become friends.

"Hi, Monsignor Murphy. How are you today?"

"I'm fine Andy, and you?"

"Well enough I suppose. Monsignor, I'm in a rush to ask for advice and then run across the piazza to see Monsignor Harrison before his office closes. I've got about five minutes."

"My time is yours. What's on your mind?"

"My superiors want me to sign a statement saying that I'm responsible for my actions."

He shook his head and let out a laugh.

"That sounds strange. This is true for anyone, and it doesn't need a signature to confirm it. There's no doubt that you're responsible for your actions. I'm responsible for mine, too."

"I don't want to sign it."

"That's your choice. It's just not necessary. Maybe they want some kind of legal leverage in case you become a liability. Seems they don't trust you."

"That's no surprise. Or maybe they're planning to pin the Casa del Clero bill on me."

"That's a possibility."

"It's a probability."

"I wouldn't recommend signing it Andy. It's neither necessary, nor does it benefit you. Your best course of action is to do nothing. And they can't use obedience to make you sign it either."

"That's enough for me. I'm sorry, I have to go. Thanks again for your advice, Monsignor."

"Anytime. You have about eight minutes before they close the Bishop's Congregation."

I said goodbye, shook his hand, fled down the hall, dropped down the stairs, and burst into a congested piazza. After weaving through hardly moving traffic, I entered the twin Vatican office building on the other side of the square. During the past months, I'd seen Monsignor Harrison a few times.

One of twelve children, John Harrison had a slender face, pointed chin, and high forehead stuffed with a big brain. Green eyes hid behind black wire-framed glasses and a warm grin revealed a few out of place teeth. He buzzed with the energy of an athletic forty-one-year-old and emanated the down to earth sense of an inhabitant of rural Pennsylvania.

I liked this priest professor. Loaded with conviction, he was the first Vatican official who stressed my moral duty to expose Miles Jesu to Church authorities. He'd served in the Vatican for six years, with two more to go.

The desk clerk stuck me in a waiting room adorned with exquisite religious art. Almost immediately Monsignor Harrison entered through the open door.

"Hello Father Sullivan. You caught me just in time. I was just packing my briefcase for the day."

"Good timing then. Hope you had a nice day?" "Thank God it's Friday! What can I do for you?" "I only need five minutes.

"Let's sit down." He waved his hand and indicated where.

We slid into a couple of posh chairs. An elegant chandelier dangled over the Sylvia marble floor. My body refused to relax. I leaned forward and launched the conversation.

"Cutting to the chase, my superior is ordering me back to the community. But I'm not capable of living in that environment. It's damaging to me, emotionally and psychologically. Am I obliged to obey, or not? Am I morally justified to refuse to return?"

"You're absolutely justified. You don't have to obey that command."

"And why? What's the rationale?"

"You see, a superior can't command his subjects to act in a way that's detrimental to their health. Obedience can't contradict fundamental human goods, health being one of them. Every human being has a right to pursue good health. A superior can't ignore this when he commands."

"Okay. That makes a lot of sense. Now for something more complicated. The Casa wants the bill paid and wants me out by Monday. I have no money. And Miles Jesu wants me back in the community."

"What's the status of your exclaustration request?"

"I submitted it to the Vicariate several days ago. Monsignor Moretti said the Vicariate would have an answer soon."

"Then, you just have to find a way to wait out the reply."

"Yea, I guess you're right." He confirmed what I knew. We made some small talk and bid our farewells.

Exiting the building, the doors swung shut behind me and the lights flickered dark. With the majestic Basilica looming behind, I started down Via Conciliazione toward the Casa del Clero. Distracted, deep in thought, I wandered forward. Tomorrow morning I'd pound out a serious letter to

Father Gelson. Considering the main points of the letter, I walked between four sidewalk tables overcrowded with boisterous, beer-drinking German tourists.

# CHAPTER THIRTEEN

The next morning, Saturday, May 19, 2007, Sean Brennan packed his bags for a morning flight to the States. He couldn't take the madness of Miles Jesu any longer. Droopy eyelids, uncombed hair, and a short-fused thinking process characterized a broken man. He mindlessly stuffed unfolded shirts and pants, clean and dirty, and a batch of homeopathic medicines into a black shoulder bag. Careless about neatness, Sean couldn't disappear from the apartment fast enough. Subdued by drugs, Father Duran slept motionless in the next room.

Nobody could talk with Sean or offer assistance. He was on his own. By custom, it was strictly forbidden to socialize with anyone leaving the community. Deserters were alienated and rushed out of the house quickly. Corruption had to be contained. Sean had given his resignation as a member of the general government. That took backbone. Nobody did that to Duran. Walking out the front door, the once darling of Miles Jesu would be stigmatized as a traitor. Brennan left under the pretext of needing time off, but the temporary arrangement would become permanent. His disgust with Miles Jesu and Duran ran deep.

Brennan had given sixteen years of his life to Miles Jesu. Now thirty-four years old, he suffered from ulcerative colitis. Three quarters of his large intestine was ulcerated. He'd struggled with this condition for the past eight years, sometimes successfully, sometimes squeaking by the doors of death. During the worst times Sean passed blood in his stool up to fifteen times a day. Perpetual sleep deprivation and nervous breakdowns didn't help.

His illness linked to a handful of causes. "Formation" by correction was one of them. Like every other joining member, Sean had been corrected for anything and everything, and then corrected for excusing himself, then for defending himself, then for showing a sour face about the corrections. The corrections didn't stop there; they turned vicious with the public accusations of members surrounding him in a group. These were followed by years of teasing, jabbing and public humiliations harping on mistakes made years ago. Duran swam in an atmosphere of breaking wild stallions, his quintessential mode of loving.

Sean's health condition also issued from his relentless care for Duran. For the past eleven years Sean Brennan had served either as Duran's secretary or personal assistant. He was practically chained to the man. He had shouldered the thankless job of satisfying Duran's every need. Sean cut the man's toenails, gave enemas, corrected members as instructed, injected Demerol, fetched cigarettes and alcohol, lied to Vatican officials, cooked, cleaned, and lost himself in a hundred more demanding details required by Duran.

But Sean's ulcerative colitis mostly stemmed from an ugly entrapment. From the first month of his appointment as Father Duran's personal secretary, Sean Brennan entered into the upside down world of sexual abuse.

Duran had craved intimate hugs and wet kisses. Erections, qualms of conscience, and an unending state of confusion followed. Duran emanated an air of powerful authority and Sean felt unable to oppose the fleshly advances of the man. Training had conditioned Sean not to lift a finger without Duran's explicit permission. Duran's lust grew into drunken sexual encounters. The publicly perceived saint would wake Sean at night, wanting to be held, touched, rubbed. Sean tried different things to cope with his dark secret. He drank to deaden his world of shame and hypocrisy. He sometimes fought off the beast, punching and pushing away Duran's perverse appetite.

The relationship between Duran and Brennan deteriorated into a sick dependency. Sean felt he needed approval for everything: using the bathroom, exiting the building, exercising, eating, making a phone call. Duran actually encouraged this and expected to exchange an approving kiss with Sean whenever the young man needed to leave his presence. No kiss meant a correction, or a dozen corrections for a few days. Sean became obsessed about Duran. He thought about him all day. Everything in his life revolved around Father Duran. From an emotional perspective, Duran was God. From a physical perspective, Sean's trauma targeted his large intestine

Brennan got an aisle seat on the flight to Detroit. At least he could enjoy a little sleep somewhere over the Atlantic. He didn't know what to expect when he'd meet his father and mother. Family ties had been severed for almost two decades now, following the Miles Jesu custom of breaking contact. Complicating matters, Sean would show up with unspeakable baggage. He wouldn't tell his parents the real story, not for a long time.

Brennan disappeared westward into the clouds. I sat at my desk at the Casa del Clero, finishing my letter to Father Gelson, unaware that I'd just lost Sean's critical support.

Saturday morning exploded with the vanishing of Sean Brennan, the glue holding Tespi together. Gelson stepped in to orchestrate Duran's care. He pacified the man with carefully crafted lies. He then organized and rallied Vasyl and Petro, the Ukrainian seminarians, to double their hours with Duran just as exam cramming became indispensable for academic survival. They were already teetering on the brink of their own emotional breakdowns.

Throughout the day, cloak-and-dagger meetings focused on resolving the problems created by Walsh, Brennan, and Sullivan. Gelson hit the phones and called in loyal, senior members to come to Rome from Chicago and Phoenix. He needed manpower and fresh thinking to handle the crisis.

That Saturday evening, Rick Wolowicz delivered my letter to Gelson. He and Walsh rolled to a stop near the entrance of Parco della Madonetta on Via Bruno Molajoli and waited in a gravel lot. A fading sun blanketed the grass field with twilight's glow. Matchbox cars lingered; young mothers pushing strollers made haste homebound.

Marcus Gelson and Anthony Sullivan coasted into the lot. The four men climbed out of their cars and gathered in a circle. Though the pairs represented a clash of two opposed paradigms, the encounter remained civil. Gelson and Wolowicz broke off and took a short walk.

Gelson had bags beneath blood shot eyes and operated with slow reactions. A trace of alcohol lingered on his breath. Ever the pharmacist, Rick asked about Marc's health. The priest dismissed any need for concern.

"Father Gelson, I'm concerned about you and Miles Jesu. The whole thing is going down and you're caught up in the middle of it. You're just as much a victim as everybody else."

"I don't see myself as a victim."

"But you are. A lot of people are getting hurt. It's time to go to the Church authorities and let them help us."

Gelson had a knee jerk reaction to this. He'd been conditioned by Duran neither to trust the Vatican, nor to permit external authorities to meddle in the affairs of Miles Jesu.

"No. It's not God's will. Miles Jesu is not falling apart." Marc jiggled a cigarette from its box and placed it between his lips. He reached into his pocket for the lighter.

"Yes, it is. Look at Father General. Look at you. You're sick.

Brennan's gone. There's no leadership. It's time to ask the Church for help."

"No! My health is fine." He lit the thing and took a drag. "There is leadership. I'm in charge!"

Oozing with denial, Gelson made the effort to stand with confidence and smile. His tone was not authoritative, but deliberately calming. He wobbled and blew smoke out of his nose.

"Everything will be okay, Rick."

"I don't think so."

"You'll see. Everything's going to work out." Gelson had no idea.

Wolowicz had done his best without insisting too much. He shook his head, looked into Marc's eyes, and surrendered a reluctant nod.

"Alright, it's up to you."

Wolowicz wanted to maintain a relationship with Gelson because he'd need the priest's cooperation to return to the States.

"It's your decision Marc." Rick held out my letter. "This is from Andy."

"Thank you." Gelson slid my letter into his breast pocket. He'd read it later.

Sunday, May 20, 2007. The reinforcements arrived in the morning. Father Omar Salido, a greying macho-priest from Chihuahua, Mexico, was ready to obey. He exuded the calloused character of a drill sergeant. Britt Curran, a virtual cyborg from Chicago, drained of emotion, known as the 'Hammer Man,' prepared to exercise his expertise.

Tom Walsh had been placed under house arrest in a carefully chosen bed and breakfast in Ostia. The romantic getaway was wedged slightly inland and obscured by a piece of forest, off the beaten path of beach tourists. Hot off the plane, Salido and Curran had been assigned to guard Walsh and interrogate him.

Anthony Sullivan had leaked the word to Gelson that Walsh made an appeal for an intervention. The general government panted for more information. It could only guess at the content of the appeal. Tom had assured the signers of confidentiality and persevered tight lipped. As hard as they tried, the inquisitors couldn't extract any useful information from the prisoner. With Walsh now neutralized, Gelson shifted his attention to me.

Gelson had read my letter. Somehow he could read now. The letter spelled out my moral and canonical grounds for refusing to return to community life. For health reasons, I asked for a special living arrangement, funded by Miles Jesu. What the hell, I'd raised almost a half million dollars for the community since living in Rome. I'd given twenty-eight years of free labor. I'd vowed my life to Miles Jesu. They now had the legal obligation to provide for my health. The letter also clarified that Cardinal Ruini had been informed of my circumstances and that I was waiting for an indult of exclaustration from the Vicariate.

Complicating matters, that Sunday evening I sent an alarming email to Gelson. Since twenty-four hours had passed without any reply to my urgent letter, I turned up the heat. I communicated that I'd return to the Vicariate and submit an additional appendix to my exclaustration request. The futility of my appeals for help from Miles Jesu for financial assistance would be exposed to Church authorities. The email ended with a few jabs. I expressed my judgment of Gelson's incompetence to help me and urged him to resign. I was desperate; the bill had to be paid in the morning. This curveball prompted a late night general government meeting, a written response, and an immediate plan to stop my recklessness as soon as possible.

Eleven-thirty, pitch black. The gravity of the situation demanded immediate action. Gelson got to the car first. He'd finished his transfiguration into the new acting General Director of Miles Jesu. He sat in Father Duran's blue Ford Sierra and flicked a cigarette butt out the window. The same cigarette brand puffed by Duran. After removing a cumbersome locking device connecting the steering wheel with the brake, Gelson buckled up and fired up the turbocharged engine. The thing purred like a kitten; Duran had pampered his four door sedan rescued from servitude as a taxi.

Driven by the sheer power of his will, it seemed that Father Marcus Gelson had done the impossible. He'd resurrected from the dead and embraced the quest to save the Institute. He had no choice. Nobody was left to carry the torch. The crucible of the weekend had triggered an extraordinary act of psychological repression.

Thud! Anthony Sullivan slammed the door shut and fastened his seat belt in the passenger seat. Gelson adjusted the rearview mirror, depressed the clutch, shifted into first, and jolted ahead. Anthony held the final version of the letter. They headed up Via del Mare toward the Vatican, sped past the horse racing track and the Pyramid of Caius Cestius.

Lights shooting up from its base, that ancient thirty-seven meter pyramid, built before Christ, must have witnessed countless emergencies racing in and out of the Eternal City. Chalk up another one tonight.

They reached the road hugging the Tiber and snaked their way northeast. As they drove, they discussed the fine points of how to influence me. By midnight, Father Gelson and Anthony stood at my hotel room door. The corridor was clear. I had just gone to bed.

That midnight showdown at the Casa del Clero marked the definitive breaking point between Miles Jesu and me. From Gelson's perspective, it represented a conquistador moment of rescue. The new General galloped into the fray; everything hinged upon his victory. His self-appointed mission was to save me from the fires of hell and defend the Institute from assault. But really, it wasn't my need that prompted his knocking at the stroke of midnight, but the preservation of the prestige of Miles Jesu.

I lived in a changed world and felt things differently. My defiance stood as an irreversible leap forward on the path to emotional maturity. After almost six-hundred daily meditations of receiving love I felt empowered by love. Knowing I was loved and lovable engendered security and confidence. Love had birthed maturity, and maturity defiance. I could now stand against corrupt authority because I'd outgrown an existential dependence on acceptance by my superiors. Yet, this didn't imply that I felt like a super hero. I didn't. I still felt fear, but it no longer paralyzed me.

No doubt, some of my confidence during that midnight clash derived from the certainty that Duran was incapacitated and that my exclaustration was just around the corner. Circumventing the authority of Miles Jesu and appealing directly to Cardinal Ruini had bolstered me.

Following that midnight confrontation, I slept late. The morning sun pierced the window and promised a bright day. Out of nowhere, the phone rang and catapulted me out of bed.

Monday, May 21, just after eight o'clock, a call from the Vicariate put me in a good mood. The Chancellor wanted to see Rick Wolowicz and me at ten. The dawn of liberation woke me up. I called Via Tespi and got Rick on the line.

"Rick, where the hell were you last night?" "What do you mean?" He didn't know anything.

"No, I can't get distracted right now. I'm calling because we have an appointment with the Chancellor of the diocese at ten. We're in a rush. He wants you and me. Can we meet at nine forty-five at the obelisk in front of the Vicariate?"

"Yes, absolutely. I'll have to leave right away."

"Will you have a problem getting out?"

"No, I'll make something up to get permission. And if I don't get permission I'll just leave anyway."

"That's the spirit."

"I'll see you soon, Sully."

I hung up and grabbed the letter Gelson handed to me last night. Addressed to me from Father Kroll, no letterhead, no signature, no seal of the Institute. What a joke. A cover your ass piece of crap. Gelson didn't want any paper trail leading back to himself. *Why couldn't you give me a real letter with a file number?* I stopped myself from crumpling up the thing and decided to scribble a response and leave it at the lobby desk on my way out. Gelson had promised that Kroll would show up to pay the bill. So, I'd leave him a note.

Grabbing a pen and piece of paper, writing fast, I informed Father Kroll that I had a meeting at the Vicariate and thanked him in advance for coming to pay the hotel bill. I reminded him that my health demanded I live alone. My emotions spilled onto the page and I scrawled a couple rebellious paragraphs.

"By the way, illegitimate absence does not begin until the sixth month as a reason for dismissal, otherwise I could possibly be corrected, but nevertheless remain a member in good standing. The responsible manner in which I removed myself from the community and my urgent and grave health need secure my rights as a professed member.

"Please do not put any more veiled threats of the community not being responsible for me financially. In my extraordinary circumstances I am aware of my canonical rights. Besides, it will only be a matter of days, even hours, before the terms of my exclaustration will be made clear, from external superiors over Miles Jesu."

Folding the letter, I stuffed it in an envelope, licked and sealed it, and wrote "Father Jerry Kroll" on the front. I scooped up the photocopied new appendix I intended to add to my exclaustration request and left the room.

After a rich coffee and fresh baked *rosetta* with cream cheese in the dining room, I left Kroll's letter with the pudgy concierge and caught the bus for the Vicariate.

Wolowicz and I greeted each other near the arched entryway of the Vicariate offices. I told him about Gelson's midnight visit. Rick was not surprised. We mulled over what we wanted to achieve with our meeting. Within fifteen minutes, we were escorted into the office of Monsignor Giuseppe Tonello, the Chancellor of the world's most illustrious archdiocese.

Tonello stretched a genuine but brief smile, shook our hands, and showed us where to sit. He looked at his watch and started the count down. The forty-three-year-old priest had a trim beard with greying streaks painted in it. His slightly bushy eyebrows hid behind wire framed glasses. He'd been a priest for fourteen years and already packed an impressive resume: a church rector, a judge on marriage nullity cases, the Chancellor of Rome.

He was born in Milan and this shaped the man's character. He lacked the spontaneous, passionate temperament typical of the lower half of Italy. Milan was a hop, skip, and jump to Switzerland and Germany. A straightforwardness and methodical efficiency seemed to pulsate in the blood of the Italians close to the northern edges of Italy. People joked that the vine dressers up there were part German. Monsignor Tonello had inherited the Milanese 'get down to business' attitude about him.

Before sitting, I leaned over the desk and handed my extra appendix to Tonello.

"Monsignor, I wanted to add this appendix to my exclaustration request."

He took it and nodded. "Thank you, Father Sullivan." Dumping the thing on his desk, he completely ignored it. He had other things on his mind. Maybe he'd read it later, but the Church bigwigs had already made up their minds about the Miles Jesu fiasco.

We pulled some chairs forward and lined up at the edge of Tonello's desk. He clutched a swivel chair, scooted it beneath his descending body, and looked us over. Beaten down, an anxious hopefulness read across our faces. Aware of our traumas, the chancellor seemed to take pity on us. We suggested an image of beaten puppy dogs with weepy eyes.

Tonello was stuck in the middle of another human disaster and he didn't like it. Ruini and Moretti had passed the buck and wanted him to fix everything. We expected someone, anyone holding the reins of authority to rescue us. Stroking his black beard, Tonello felt squeezed from both sides.

The Chancellor looked down at the crisp requests on his desk and a Miles Jesu file removed from an old cabinet. Tom Walsh's appeal for an intervention rested smack dab on the center of his desk. Father Tonello momentarily considered how to soften bad news. What the hell; he'd just say the truth.

"I've received and read your requests to Cardinal Ruini. He's assigned me to help resolve the issue of Miles Jesu." He glanced at the thick file. "The Congregation has known for many years that there was something wrong with Miles Jesu, but couldn't do anything about it."

Apparently, Miles Jesu had influential friends within the Vatican.

"The formal request for an intervention and your additional request for an exclaustration, Father Sullivan, now allow the Vicariate to pursue the appointment of a canonical visitor who could scrutinize the Institute. The accusations are very serious and must be investigated. We're already searching for someone who would accept an appointment. Unfortunately, it may take a while to find somebody. It's not the kind of job people want."

"A while?" I asked. "What do you mean it will take a while? Will it take weeks? Months?"

"Probably closer to months," said the monsignor.

"Months? Really?" Rick's voice rose. "What do we do in the meantime?"

"I'm sorry for your predicament; I'm sympathetic to your situations. But the bigger problem of Miles Jesu must be resolved before anyone's personal needs can be addressed. From a canonical perspective, only the major superior of an institute of consecrated life can grant exclaustrations or dispensations to its members. The Vicariate can't overstep its authority in this respect. After an investigation and after Miles Jesu would be capable of proper governing, only then can your needs be definitively settled."

"After an investigation?" I shook my head in disbelief.

Rick was mortified.

"Who cares about canonical procedure? Our superiors are crazy! We're having crises now. Right here and right now! How long will it take for an investigation to be completed and competent superiors put in place?"

Silence. Rick couldn't wait for an answer and blew up again.

"They're nuts! So we're stuck? The priorities are wrong! If someone falls overboard you don't fix the ship first! You rescue the damn people!"

Tonello stuck to the predetermined game plan. He ignored Rick's rant and answered the question.

"In a best case scenario, it might take a year to install competent superiors."

"A year! That's ridiculous!"

Both of us exploded. Tonello saw the desperation on our faces and felt our panic, and went on to say, "I know it is a difficult thing to accept. Are we not called to practice our faith a little?"

"Don't talk about virtue," I said. "I don't have that kind of virtue! I'm not a saint! I have nowhere to go. I can't go back into that place."

A surge of emotion erupted from deep within me. I placed my hands and head on the desk and began bawling. All the work, the secret consultations, the writing, everything seemed dashed to pieces. I had nowhere to go, nowhere to hide. I couldn't stop crying. Lifting my head, I sobbed in barely discernable words,

"I need help right now!" Tonello got mad.

"This is not supposed to happen in the Church!" His frustration echoed in the room.

I almost yelled. "Well, it *is* happening! This is Miles Jesu. It's the only way of life I've known in the Church. Maybe I should go to the press and speed things up!"

"No. That would only slow things down. Father Sullivan, I'm not saying that you need to return to the community." He back peddled a little. "We just need to find a place for you to live until things get better."

"Where? I have no money even if we found a place."

"There is a place for priests and I have a friend there. I can call him and see if there's room for you."

The diocese of Rome operated a discreet residence for problem priests, where broken men suffered crises of one kind or another. It sounded like a halfway house for ordained crackpots.

I dried my tears. We were making progress.

"If I can get in there it has to be kept a secret. Miles Jesu can't know where I am; otherwise they'll hunt me down and intimidate me."

Rick knew exactly what I was talking about.

"Yes, I'm aware of that," said Tonello.

Was he really? He had no idea.

He then turned his attention to Rick.

"You're layman. You can simply care for yourself as you wish. Until the Institute becomes functional, you can live as you see fit, wherever you want. At a later date you could apply for a dispensation to a new major superior."

The whole thing stank. Rick felt no support whatsoever. He fumed in silence.

Tonello focused on me.

"Father Sullivan, the Cardinal wanted me to specifically address your immediate needs. Can you please come with me? Rick, can you wait for us in the waiting area?"

Tonello jumped out of his chair. Rick didn't answer. We exited the office and separated in the corridor. Rick didn't want to wait anywhere. He turned to me, "Sully, I'll meet you near the obelisk when you finish." He shook Tonello's hand and disappeared down the hall.

"Come this way, Father Sullivan."

We scooted down the corridor without saying a word. Beautiful frescos of angles passed overhead. We entered an elevator, he punched a button, and we descended. Exiting, we hung a left and found a door with a blurry windowpane filling its entire upper half. Swinging open the door, we entered a small room crowded with priests and a few religious. A bishop with a silver chain around his neck stood in the corner. Fat and balding, he counted money pocketed in an envelope. Some people were standing in line, others walking out. Windowed service niches lined the back wall, with tellers assisting customers. My eyes opened wide: it was a secret miniature bank. What were we doing here?

Tonello cut through a line and greeted a teller he knew. He handed a bald and goateed man a slip of paper and without any questions the guy forked over a stack of euros. They each laughed at something. I didn't know what was happening. Tonello gripped the thick envelope and handed it to me.

"This is for you Father Sullivan," he said. My heart jumped. I couldn't believe it. "Here's three thousand euros. It's a gift from Cardinal Ruini, who is sensitive to your predicament. He wanted me to tell you this."

"Thank you, Jesus," I whispered to myself. "Thank you, Monsignor."

A wave of relief settled upon me. A habit took over and I counted the money. Two-thousand euros.

"Monsignor, didn't you say three-thousand euros?"

"Yes. Why? Is there a problem?"

"This envelope only has two-thousand euros."

He asked for it and counted it. Reaching the end, Tonello shook his head and went back to the teller. The Monsignor indicated the problem; a hand shot through the window with another thousand. I understood why a bishop had wedged himself in a corner and counted his money.

I thanked Monsignor Tonello again and asked him to pass on my gratitude to Cardinal Ruini. We walked out of the bank, hung a left, and strolled to the archway of the courtyard. Tonello assured me that he would convey my thanks, and that he'd have an answer very soon about the priest residence.

He then warned me to keep clear of Miles Jesu.

"Miles Jesu could serve you a letter of canonical warning to speed up your dismissal. You should do everything you can to avoid receiving such a letter. It would complicate things." I agreed. "And don't let anyone know that the Vicariate gave you money."

After goodbyes, we separated and each went our own way. He hiked to his office to extinguish other fires. I wandered to the obelisk and looked around. Rick had disappeared.

The thriving life of Rome surrounded me, the traffic, the deluge of tourists, the natives following their daily routines. Mixed feelings surfaced. I was disgusted that my exclaustration request had been dashed to pieces. What a colossal waste of time. But I felt invigorated to have three-thousand euros in my pocket. The terror and bliss of greater freedom sank in my gut.

I made a decision right then and there that I would survive Rome until psychotherapy finished. Then I made a mental checklist for the rest of the day. I'd start an aggressive fundraising campaign. I'd abandon the Casa del Clero as soon as possible.

That same Monday, Tom Walsh also experienced the cutting of Miles Jesu apron strings. Stuck at the bed and breakfast in Ostia, he woke to the intense glare of Britt Curran.

Curran had sandy brown hair, clipped short purely for reasons of convenience. A tight face, small lips, snooty nose, and penetrating eyes greeted Walsh as he tried to shake his slumber and recall his whereabouts.

Irish hardheadedness ran through Curran's blood. He seemed to thrive on conquering difficulties with the driving force of his will. This quality was both natural to his character and further ingrained as a habit from Miles Jesu training. Britt's tenacity had rewarded him with gradual success in a Chicago band before the bass guitarist had joined Miles Jesu. A hardened determination now dominated his personality. He moved with the intensity of a hawk swooping down upon its prey. Genuine Duran spirituality at work.

Walsh rubbed his chin and fleshy cheeks, squinted, and tried to plan his day. His first thoughts were about exam cramming, how, when, where.

Curran's voice interrupted Tom's thought process. The hammer man took the first swing of the day.

"Tom, the general government wants you to remain here and not go to school today. We'll be having meetings with you when we're ready."

Walsh's quick mind instantaneously translated the meaning behind the words. Of course, it didn't take a rocket scientist to understand: *Tom, you're a rat and we're going to squash you and get to the bottom of your treachery. Put on these handcuffs and obey!*

Walsh trembled with anger and it almost got the best of him. Curran waited for a reply. Whatever Walsh might say would be used against him. It took real courage for Tom Walsh to ditch seventeen years of indoctrination and answer.

"I'm not able to comply with that command."

Convinced that Curran and Salido wouldn't physically restrain him, Tom Walsh dressed, brushed his teeth, and gathered a few books. Everything was done in silence, though the atmosphere burned with shock and judgments against him. The rebel packed his school bag, swung it over his shoulder, walked out the door, and didn't look back.

The Miles Jesu veterans could hardly fathom the depths of Tom's disobedience. Seeing Walsh disappear in the distance, they likely remembered the golden quote from sermons, examinations of conscience, and even written into the constitutions of Miles Jesu: "Self-will, rebellion, pride and stiffness of the will are the unmistakable characteristics of the followers of the devil and his proud cry *non serviam*." Members heard it almost daily. It applied to anyone who exhibited the faintest thought or feeling of disobedience.

Tom Walsh viewed his actions differently. His pursuit of a Vatican intervention was not only a matter of conscience, but ironically an act of faithfulness to a fundamental prescript of the Institute's own constitutions.

The section on evangelical obedience spells out the proper course of action when community directors act autonomously of Church authority: "A director or directress who commands any particular point against the official teaching or discipline of the Church should not be obeyed in that matter and the case should be reported to a higher superior. And even more, any superior, even legally elected or appointed, who is not in communion with the Vicar of Christ must not be obeyed." This prescript was hardly foreseen to be actually applied, but it did look good in print.

Tom spent the day in the city, at the Angelicum consulting with Professor Molony, with Tonello at the Vicariate, with Murphy at the Vatican. His mind and body kicked against studies. He kept to himself and ruminated on the outcome of the intervention and his own destiny. By the end of the day, exhausted, he trudged back to Ostia, stepped off the bus, and walked to the bed and breakfast. Why did he come back? He just did. It was the habit of a life customarily trying to do the right thing.

Reaching the dreaded building, Tom inserted the key, swung open the hotel room door, and looked inside. Empty. Salido and Curran were gone. They were stuck in meetings with Father Gelson, absorbed in military strategy. At that moment, God granted Tom Walsh a special grace. The irreversible nature of the Vatican appeal and the barrenness of the room triggered a colossal life decision. He would leave and never return.

It was not a light decision. Swooping up a lousy piece of luggage, Tom gathered his few belongings and stuffed them until the upper flap barely closed. Nor was it a choice entirely spontaneous. Months of reflection had finally climaxed. The deception, coercion, fear, and ignorance that moved him through his commitments throughout the years had finally collapsed.

Walsh closed the door behind him, picked up the bloated suitcase, and found his way to the *Lungomare Duilio,* the main road cutting along the coast. Where would he go? Tom had no idea. The bald, overweight American deacon just walked, with his black cassock flapping in the wind. Nervous that the Miles Jesu goons might see him on the street, he cut a brisk pace.

It was disorienting to have to grab a few personal items, flee, and face an unclear future. Tom's thoughts turned inward. From a purely natural perspective he'd made a horrible mistake: living for seventeen years in a tragically dysfunctional Church institution. Yet, perhaps from God's per- spective, it seemed that providence had situated him in the perfect time and place to effect a change for the betterment of many people. He almost slammed into a pole.

An Italian family, no doubt a devout household, pulled to the side of the road. The white Fiat Multi-Wagon sat idling. Saint Christopher stood on the dashboard. A pious mother clicked down her window and called to the apparent priest. Tom walked up to her and the pretty woman asked if he wanted a ride. He smiled and laughed. "Of course I'd like a ride. Thanks a million." He climbed into the car and it sped into the darkness. They talked about Church stuff all the way into Rome.

That night, Walsh slept in the Hotel Galileo near the Termini train station. How fitting. Galileo had been ostracized and accused of heresy for confronting the status quo and introducing a new way to view the universe, both scientifically and theologically. Tom had bucked the system too; the Church didn't orbit around Miles Jesu, but the other way around. Tom Walsh suffered too, for discovering the truth.

Miles Jesu had around sixty incorporated members serving in ten communities. Within six months, eighteen guys would leave, eight from Rome and ten more worldwide. This exodus would represent a catastrophic blow to an already fragile institution. Over a longer period of time the hemorrhaging would slow to a trickle, but continue.

This thinning of the ranks resulted from two intimately related causes. The Vicariate and Vatican appeals were the first cause. Either personally or by email, I'd shared sections of my exclaustration request with selected members. This had opened the eyes of some. On a wider scale, while gathering signers for the intervention request, Sean Brennan and Tom Walsh had given a voice to long-concerned members. Springing from these sources, shock and discontent rooted and spread like a cancerous growth.

An authoritative reaction to the budding exodus was the second cause of even more membership loss. Gelson and crew adopted a radical procedure to arrest the spreading cancer. They would simply amputate the hopeless members corrupted by Walsh and Sullivan. Regardless of how many years a member may have served or the level of commitment reached, some malcontents would be surgically chopped off the body of Miles Jesu and sent home. The whole mess would also occasion the dumping of some members discarded and left to rot by Duran.

After thirteen years of life in Miles Jesu, Olha Klub was the first casualty of the purge. Three days after the denial of my exclaustration request and Tom Walsh's escape, Thursday, May 24, 2007, Olha woke up oblivious to her fate. She became the test dummy of the reactionary policy.

After Mass that morning, Olha accompanied Annemarie Kross on a few errands. A bright and breezy-faced member of the general government, Annemarie handled the Institute's finances. She told Olha not to bring her purse, not to dress in the religious habit, and that they'd be back before noon. The Angelicum would host a farewell party for students that afternoon. Olha didn't want to miss her much anticipated trip into Rome.

She and I had pre-arranged a secret get-together near the university that day. When the celebration would make headway, Olha would slip away and trek about two-hundred meters up hill to an unassuming family café across from the Piazza del Quirinale. The fountain with its horses and obelisk was the agreed upon landmark. We had counted the days, waiting for just an hour together.

The instant the two women left for the grocery store, Jeni and company ransacked Olha's belongings. Somebody removed clothes from the closet and dug through the pockets; another woman fumbled with the mess in Olha's dresser. A third scrutinized every item and scrap of paper in her purse, desk, and school folders. They searched for incriminating evidence and found nothing. It's a good thing Olha had burned my personal notes to her, just the previous day. A woman's intuition?

Two hours later, Annemarie and Olha rolled into the driveway in front of the women's apartment. Stepping out of the car, Olha noticed help descending down the stairs. She raised her eyebrows. Nice. Community members took hold of the grocery bags and went back inside the apartment. Olha was unexpectedly blocked and told to wait. She was not allowed to go up the stairs. What was happening? The same women now came back out of the apartment carrying Olha's purse and luggage. The orchestrated deception blindsided her.

A feeling of disbelief and violation made her head spin. Am I being kicked out of Miles Jesu? Like this? After thirteen years? The trunk slammed shut, a side door opened, Olha was told to get back into the car. Every woman wore a cool face. Olha boiled.

En route to the airport, with her stub nose and emotionless demeanor, Jeni Staus explained things.

"Olha, we're sending you back to the community in the Ukraine. You're not happy here. You'll do better there. Blah, blah, blah…"

The robot directress made up whatever shit she wanted. But the words made no difference. Everything was a clouded mess in Olha's head. She just sat there and listened. Why ask any questions? You'd just get lies anyway. The beautiful Italian countryside blurred past.

Thirty minutes later, Jeni, Annemarie, and Olha left the check-in counter with a boarding pass and passport. The bouncers kept hold of things. The three waited together for a while. Olha used the bathroom. She was escorted there, guarded, and watched on the way back. There was no such thing as dignity, respect, trust.

Eventually, the threesome reached the security point where only passengers could enter. Jeni approached a guard and asked if Olha could be accompanied to the gate. She made up some lame excuses. The handsome, bearded young man dressed to perfection almost laughed at her. He then voiced a firm denial to the request. Jeni had wanted to assure that Olha would actually board the plane.

Olha finally received her boarding pass, one-way ticket, and passport, and crossed the threshold into the inner section of the airport. Freedom at last. Was there any such thing as true friendship? No genuine goodbyes passed through anyone's lips, neither from Olha's nor from the women executing God's will. Jeni and Annemarie would hang around until the plane actually departed.

The inner airport paraded a brightly lit and clean atmosphere with colorful shops, indoor bushes, yellow gate signs, a wide and long walkway, and a sea of lightly padded grey seating. Olha immediately found a seat and checked the secret pouch in her purse. They missed it! She still had six euros. Just enough to make a phone call.

Sitting at my desk at the Casa del Clero, I answered the phone.

"Hello."

"Andy! Oh, I'm so glad I reached you! I called twice, but it was busy."

"I've been fundraising. Is everything okay?" She sounded distressed.

"No. I'm calling from the airport. They kicked me out!"

"What? What do you mean they kicked you out? You're at the airport? Who kicked you out?"

A crowd of disembarking passengers shuffled by and Olha had to raise her voice.

"I really don't know why they're sending me home. Jeni said I'm being transferred to the community in L'viv. I don't know what to believe. They're probably kicking me out of Miles Jesu."

"Nothing would surprise me, Olha. Tell me how it happened."

She told about her morning and explained how she ended up finding a phone to call me. The shopping trick; the obstruction from entering the apartment; the attempt to watch her through the departure gate; the whole story came tumbling forth. The final boarding announcement for the flight to Kiev boomed overhead.

"Those assholes," I spat out. Throughout the years, I'd played my role in kicking guys out and knew exactly what Olha was going through. "They have no idea how to treat a human being."

"Andy, I'm so sorry. It really helps to talk. It's a great relief to me. But I have to go."

"You're in a rush?"

"Yes, they just made the last announcement for my flight."

"Okay. Olha, listen my love. I will never abandon you. Do you hear what I'm saying? I will never abandon you, my love! I'll come visit you this summer, no matter where you are, as soon as I can."

"Thank you so much Andy. I'll wait for you."

We quickly confirmed each other's email addresses and said our goodbyes. "I love you, Olha."

"I love you, too." She hung up and dashed for the gate. I hung up and cried.

A few hours later, somewhere thirty thousand feet over Hungary, Olha did the forbidden. She had a glass of wine and thumbed through a racy looking magazine. Welcome to the real world, Honey. Her anger had dissipated and she now experienced a profound sense of relief. As far as she was concerned, the crazy life of Miles Jesu was over. The well-meaning witches had done her a big favor. She sat there embarrassed, still clothed in an ugly green work dress

Eventually, after a ten-hour journey by train, she arrived at the community property in L'viv. Upon arriving at the Miles Jesu house, she was soon taken by car to a bus stop and told to go home for three months. Another lie. They didn't want her in community where her corruption would spread. They said they had changed their minds. Olha knew better.

From Rome to her family home in the village of Dobrosyn, it took almost thirty hours. By the time she reached the farm the sun was near setting and Olha felt exhausted. She stepped up and dropped her suitcases on the porch. Her mother opened the front door and saw her daughter. What a shock! Confused, yet happy, she gave her long lost daughter a warm embrace. Olha was right back where she started thirteen years ago, wounded but wiser.

# CHAPTER FOURTEEN

Friday, May 25, 2007, I woke with love pounding in my heart. Olha was gone, yet grief didn't consume me. I opened my eyes and drew some deep breaths. Instantly, the presence of Jesus overwhelmed me. Feeling his head resting upon my breast, I burst out crying. The intensity of receiving love was unbearable.

"Come," he whispered. He stood, walked to the door, opened it and left. I knew where to find him. It was the same thing practically every morning.

It was the twenty-first morning of my stay at the Casa del Clero, the day I'd abandon the place. That early morning, waking by the sensation of love's inward rush, I dressed and soon made my way to the elevator. Exiting on the top floor, I walked down a long corridor, softly because everyone slept. Pushing through an unlocked glass door, I walked onto a spacious terrace.

The dawn enthralled up there and I'd miss it. The panorama of the whole city encircled me. The smell of fresh baked bread and pastries engulfed the building. The vibrant facade of Saint Peter's Basilica lit up the square below. Gurgling fountains, shimmering cobblestones, and cooing pigeons calmed the soul.

That last morning at the Casa I welcomed the sight and let it penetrate into my spirit. Homemade therapy had taught me not only how to receive love, but also how to absorb sensual beauty surrounding me. Let good enter and allow it to change you. Life was no longer about achieving. That seemed ages past. Life now embraced an unmeasured dose of enjoying, and I savored the moment.

In a flimsy plastic chair, the single-molded white kind you'd find near a swimming pool or at the beach, I adjusted my butt. Closing my eyes, I surrendered to an unconventional, some would say heretical way of meditation. I really didn't care about what others thought of my prayer.

The images and words were neither forced, nor planned, nor consciously pieced together. The scene effortlessly unrolled inside my mind and felt absolutely real, like Alice's wonderland or Dorothy's Oz. I visualized and felt a familiar world.

A quiet beach scene seemed to kick start every meditation. Waves lapped at my feet. A peaceful breeze caressed my skin and filled my lungs. While protected beneath a large blue and white umbrella, the sun heated the sand all about. The distant sounds of awakening street traffic and the tantalizing aroma of fresh Italian pastries gave way to the smell of salt and the discordant squealing of seagulls over sparkly waters. Momentarily, lost in a chair on the roof, I disconnected from the real world around me.

Jesus sat on my left. Without the trouble of words, we simply took pleasure in the rhythmic spell of the ocean, its infinite horizon, its soothing blue immensity. I experienced his loving presence and let it comfort me. After a while, he placed his hand upon mine and the entire beach scene instantly changed to the Miles Jesu chapel at Via Tespi. The meditation had a mind of its own and placed me where it wanted. No detail was lost in the scene replacement.

Shooting through a grand tinted window, the golden hue of a rising sun flooded the living room chapel. Sweet pungent incense drifted upwards in the air. Immobile members sat around the altar. I couldn't tell if they were meditating or sleeping. Some held books; probably meditating. Dressed in red vestments, Father Duran sat with his back to the window and basked in the dawn's light. He appeared young, the way I remembered him from my youth, but oddly non-responsive. Everybody seemed lifeless.

Sitting next to me, now wearing a white tunic, Jesus held a gift in his lap. A grapefruit-sized box wrapped in gold with a red ribbon. From past meditations, I knew that the gift symbolized an act of forgiveness and a connected blessing that would enrich me.

Next to him, I sat clothed in black except for the plastic white square of the Roman collar on the front of my neck. I stood, pulled the white flap from my neck, dropped it on the carpet, and stripped naked right there in the middle of the chapel. Nobody paid much attention. Even more surprising, I felt no shame. It seemed perfectly normal to be naked and I didn't question it. Actually, it felt wonderful.

I bent down and gathered up my clericals, walked around the altar, and stopped in front of Father Duran, who barely acknowledged my presence. I dropped the pile of clothes into his lap.

"You can have these back," I said. "You never asked me if I wanted them. I don't need them anymore."

Duran sat lifeless with an empty gaze. The man was incapable of grasping my words. Turning around, I walked back to Jesus. I fell on my knees and threw myself into his lap. Jesus embraced me. I choked up.

"I'm sorry. I forgive him," I sobbed. "I forgive him."

With my face buried in his lap, Jesus placed his right hand on the back of my head and spoke softly.

"Andy, my son, and what do you forgive him for?"

"For ordaining me a priest."

My soul intuited the truth that instant. Forgiveness is multi-dimensional, with many sides and layers to it. Someone may be forgiven, only to discover that a specific aspect of a relationship still needs more forgiving.

"Yes. Very good. You said it." He caressed the top of my head. "Now go back and tell him."

I returned and knelt before Father Duran; my tears dropped upon the priestly clothing still waddled up in the zombie's lap.

"I forgive you Father. I forgive you for ordaining me a priest."

He couldn't comprehend anything I said. His paradigm had no way of processing my words. Still crying, I rose, kissed him on the cheek, and returned to Jesus.

The mood of the meditation shifted to an atmosphere of happiness. Jesus beckoned me with a warm hug and then directed me to sit close to him. All attention, his and mine, focused upon the gift. He handed it to me. "Here Andy, this is for you." Instantly, the beach scene returned.

"Thank you." It felt like a heavy burden had disappeared. The wonderful feeling of forgiving invaded me. My tears receded and excitement grew. I grabbed the box and started to unwrap it. Jesus looked on with a flash of approval in his eyes. Suddenly, the entire scene filled with light; gentle, sparkling water flooded everywhere. These elements entering into a scene usually signaled the completion of an area of healing by an act of forgiving or acceptance.

Opening the lid, my heart jumped.

"Oh my God! Thank you Jesus."

I burst into tears, only this time out of sheer joy. I felt euphoric. Jesus smiled and put his arm around my back. It was such a shock to see. Resting on an elegant silk pillow, I beheld two gleaming wedding rings. Tears of happiness streamed down my face and actually woke me, as if from a dream.

And there I sat on a roof near the Vatican. My wet eyes blinked at the brightness of dawn. The sun had inched over the eastern horizon of the Eternal City and smacked Saint Peter's Basilica in the face. It was time to grab a coffee, finish packing, and disappear from the Casa del Clero.

With me launching the first salvo, cyber and paper wars erupted the next day. Emotionally charged emails and bulk mailings flew everywhere. On that first day of battle, from the safety of my new hide-out equipped with a spanking new Toshiba lap top, I clicked and whooshed a declaration of independence.

Addressed to Father Duran, I stated my decision to remove myself from community life and gave the reasons why. A Jesuit canon lawyer had helped me draft the thing. The superiors of Miles Jesu were 'incompetent, damaging, negligent, and unjust.' I needed time to heal from 'a harmful environment.'

"Stay away from me!" The email concluded with a clarification. "This letter neither means that I am not a member of Miles Jesu in good standing, nor that I forfeit my canonical right to be financially cared for by Miles Jesu in my grave emotional illness."

I rejected the influence of Miles Jesu but wanted the canonical link for financial purposes, to remain in Rome and continue psychotherapy. I also emailed an audacious letter to my two-hundred plus benefactors in the States. A few days later, Mom would print out the email, stuff envelopes, and kick the letter in the mail, with returned checks. It stated that Miles Jesu had harmed me, that I was seeking an exclaustration, and that in good conscience I could no longer raise money for the Institute. I declared a discontinuation of my monthly fundraising letter and added that if anyone wanted to help me they could contact my mother.

I'd hit the hornet's nest with a baseball bat. Take that! You wicked, legalistic, avaricious bunch of societal leeches! Why should I continue to raise thousands of dollars a month for Miles Jesu and struggle to survive?

I burned my bridges. Why did I act so recklessly? Had my indignation at their incompetence and pharisaical superiority reached a boiling point? Did my anger stem from years of pent up feelings? I don't know. Yes. Maybe I was just mad at what they did to Olha.

Gelson and crew wasted no time and retaliated with three nasty letters. The first circulated to all internal members of Miles Jesu, warning everybody about the rebellion. I knew about this letter because a mole had leaked it. Walsh and I were accused of "illegal absence, open disobedience, hostility, maliciousness, refusing help, undermining legitimate authority, and taking advantage of Father Duran's illness."

Henceforward, nobody was allowed to communicate with us. The Vatican supported Miles Jesu. Right. A high power attorney in Chicago was ready to hunt us down. "Please pray" for their "repentance."

The second letter went out to my benefactors. It was pretty much the same letter with a few twists. Demonstrating my irrational behavior, it claimed that Father Sullivan "is frustrating our attempts to get money to him and pay his bills." That sounded weird enough.

Father Sullivan "wrote to us to say that he deletes our emails without even reading them. We do not know where Father Sullivan is staying and are very concerned for his well-being. It is not good for him to be on his own."

Of course, they failed to mention that I was traumatized by Miles Jesu and that the Chancellor of the Diocese of Rome hid me away to protect me from them. They didn't know.

A dog systematically abused, if it can break away, runs away and hides. Such behavior exhibits an animal's internal mechanism of self-protection. Human beings have it, too. I had it. I didn't want any contact with Miles Jesu. I wanted healing. This human reaction to abuse is a somewhat universal reaction among ex-prisoners, divorcee's, battered women, ex-combat vets, and ex-cult members. I just wanted to find a hiding spot and lick my wounds.

The third letter also ended up in the hands of my benefactors. Signed by my brother, Anthony, it aimed at discrediting and neutralizing me. The letter explained the fallacy of my self-diagnosis and the damaging effect of my therapeutic self-experimentation. Father Sullivan, lost in a world of "subjectivity" and "confusion," refuses all help from Miles Jesu. *What the hell?* I was the person who thought clearly. The letter ended by soliciting prayer for me and by underlining the ultimate purpose of the communication.

The letter concluded. "Please take any future newsletter of communication that you may receive from him with a grain of salt."

In a healthy institute of consecrated life, superiors would not pit family members against each other. I never defended myself from the accusations of these letters. Side stepping the Punch and Judy frenzy of Miles Jesu, I cut my losses, lost my friends, and moved on.

While Gelson and the general government hatched a plan to serve me a canonical letter, I focused on hiding and healing. After Ambra Treichler refused to speak with Miles Jesu, they planned to stake out her psychotherapy clinic and ambush me whenever I might show up for therapy. Their letter demanded my return to community or else threatened my imminent dismissal.

Back at the broken-priest residence, where Tonello had placed me, I let daily life happen and allowed a slower pace in a changed environment to occasion further healing. Miles Jesu lived by force and speed, I deliberately chose the principle of receiving love at a snail's pace. Go slower and go farther. Life was not a sprint, but a marathon. My meditations had refined my receptive capacities and once in a new environment I now absorbed life itself.

Fresh human experiences now triggered further developments in the way I thought and felt. With a cold beer and plate of French fries, I watched an entire soccer match in the midst of wild fans in a bar. A first time experience. Somewhere toward the game's end, suddenly, my prejudices that held the world in contempt vanished. I was part of this world. It was a good thing and I enjoyed it. To the average Joe this may seem like nothing. But for me it represented a monumental breakthrough in my thought process: the instantaneous dumping of twenty-eight years of anti-world indoctrination.

Ordinary human realities triggered profound changes in my soul. Watching children playing in the park, I realized the beauty of paternity. Miles Jesu depreciated parenthood because it often lacked supernatural fecundity. Observing a wedding ceremony, I felt the goodness of a man and woman enraptured by love, surrendering every possibility of life to each other. The constitutions of Miles Jesu disparaged marriage. The Vatican had corrected Duran for his warped viewpoint. The damning Vatican memo lay buried in a file, hidden from the eyes of unaware members.

I attended a birthday party and would never be the same again. I relaxed at a festive table decorated with candles, flowers, and centerpiece crystal bowls of fresh cherries mixed with fine caramel chocolates. The restaurant popped with lavish strokes of sweeping streamers and an explosion of colored balloons. We just finished a steak and baked rosemary potato dinner for twenty-six hungry men. Everyone beamed with happiness and genuine interest in the birthday of their friend.

Sincere toasts, clinking glasses filled with local wine lit the atmosphere. The birthday boy, a twenty-seven-year-old priest from Sicily, felt the warmth and love of his parents sitting next to him. Singing broke out. A sheet cake aglow with twenty-seven candles and gifts landed before him. He blew out the candles and a burst of clapping and laughing filled the air. The young priest reached for the first present and the bellowing background voice of Pavarotti resumed. Unwrapping ensued. Love crowded around Father Paolo's slice of chocolate cake. Real gifts: an expensive watch, an iPad, a mini DVD player.

At that moment, absorbing beauty surrounding me, tears welled up in my eyes. Though I tried, I couldn't stop the flow. So this is a birthday party! So beautiful! I'd forgotten the reality existed. An uncontrollable wave of healing swept through my soul. I was blown away by the genuine celebration of a life, the sincere expression of respect.

Miles Jesu had corrupted the most innocent experiences of human life, including the celebration of birthdays. I couldn't stand them. No decorations appeared in the room. The birthday victim usually sat at the table and listened to a specially written song about him or her. It wasn't an uplifting ballad, but a funny concoction meant to expose and make fun of the person's character. Everyone would laugh and make merry of his faults, idiosyncrasies, mannerisms, habits. Nothing was sacred. It wasn't unusual for the lyrics to include stuff like picking your nose, burping, pulling up your pants, and farting. The custom was justified because it taught humility, illustrating that nobody should take himself too seriously.

Other than the song, nobody laughed at anything else. An edgy ambiance hovered over the table. You never knew when Father Duran might explode with a harsh scolding of anyone who thoughtlessly took a bite of ice cream before he did. Or he might just lay into someone for any reason whatsoever. More or less, the basement crowd ate in silence. Everyone really didn't want to come to the party, except perhaps to get out of evening prayers. The majority of mandatory party guests simply wanted to get out as soon as possible.

The mockery of the birthday boy continued with a specially designed card passed around the table. The card complemented the song with a visual of the victim's bad habits. A handful of wrapped gifts came, and each unwrapped present provoked a surge of amusement. The gifts were not gifts at all, but pointless items merely employed to goad laughter: an onion; a can of beans; toothpaste; a roll of toilet paper. They were things bought for the house anyway, now changed into laughter pranks.

Sometimes there might be a real gift mixed in the batch, like a pen or pair of gloves. A gift for someone else, perhaps arriving by mail months ago; now found its way into the hands of the birthday celebrant. Superiors redistributed the thing. Maybe you got something meant for someone else; maybe someone else would get something meant for you. This custom attempted to instill a spirit of detachment from worldly possessions. It also promoted the Miles Jesu custom of poverty. But in reality, the custom instilled the deep seated feeling that you were not worth a real gift.

I sat there at that birthday party and wiped my tears. Emotions flew helter-skelter. Overloaded with a barrage of mixed feelings, a swell of grief appeared out of nowhere and I cried for years of lost celebrations. I then felt hope that real birthday parties still existed. Maybe I could enjoy them later in life. My soul flipped and I cursed Father Duran. Although he exempted himself from the birthday treatment, he trampled on the human dignity of everyone else, in the name of his God. Sipping wine and munching on cake, my passions eventually calmed. The party left me with an open wound that needed healing and thrust me into another frontier of forgiveness.

The bomb dropped on the morning of June 7, 2007, a mere twenty days after Tom Walsh's request for an intervention. Monsignor Tonello arranged a meeting in his office between Miles Jesu and the newly appointed Canonical Visitor, Father Anthony McSweeney. Apparently, Tonello had cut through bureaucratic red tape and fast tracked the inquisition of Miles Jesu.

That morning, an ambush had been planned for me. Two gung-ho community members were just about to leave to confront me. They planned to hide near the psychotherapy clinic and pounce on me with a canonical letter when I showed up for therapy. Tonello's phone call to Miles Jesu postponed their mission.

That mid-morning meeting announced the upcoming investigation of Miles Jesu. Father Gelson, Father Omar Salido, and Father Jerry Kroll sat clueless and listened to the historic pronouncement. McSweeney cleared his throat, eyed the three lawbreakers, and spelled out the dreaded scenario. Wearing stoic faces, twitching in their chairs, the three priests braved a communal spanking.

Anthony McSweeney emanated the good-humored aura of a leprechaun, never mind his tall stature and Australian accent. His amiable face lit up with a big chin, laughing eyes, and wide grin that stretched to sharp points on each side of his face. His usual soothing voice sounded different this morning, like a barking dog, at least to the ears of the shocked clerics.

Fingering Cardinal Ruini's declaration, the Aussie let loose the game changer:

"It is decreed that the Ecclesial Family 'Miles Jesu' be subjected to a canonical visit, *ad inquirendum et referendum* (for inquiring and referring), with provisional suspension of the powers of all the organs of government presently in act, none excluded." Gelson swallowed hard.

Tonello clarified how things would work.

"The investigation will officially begin on the eighteenth of June, but the suspension of governing powers will take effect immediately. These developments should be made known to all the members."

Salido clenched his teeth. Speed bump veins bulged on his right temple. He had a history of migraine headaches. Kroll stared at his feet. McSweeney paused, kneaded his white goatee, and continued.

"The inquiry will tend in particular to ascertain the well-foundedness of the alleged violations of canonical discipline, to verify the ways in which the Ecclesial Family is being governed and the real functioning of its organs of government, as well as examine the community life of each religious in all its aspects—including the relations between them and with the Superiors—and the administration of goods, in special way those constituting the stable patrimony of the Ecclesial Family itself, with the drawing up of a detailed final report to present to the Ordinary of the Diocese of Rome, as well as to the Congregation for the Institutes of Consecrated Life and Societies of Apostolic Life, for those measures that will be held to be appropriate and necessary."

The document went on to strip Gelson of his authority, authorize McSweeney as the provisional head of Miles Jesu, waive the Institute's constitutions, and demand the sincere collaboration of every member during the course of the investigation. The decree equipped McSweeney with the authority to access all documentation in the Miles Jesu files.

It concluded with a warning not to deter the members from participating in the investigation, not to hinder visits to the Canonical Visitor.

"Any act eventually carried out in violation of the present decree by the above mentioned organs of government is to be considered radically invalid."

You could have sliced the silence in the office with a knife. It seemed the hands of the clock stopped ticking. For the first time in its history, Miles Jesu faced an inescapable house cleaning. The three priests scurried out the door as soon as possible, like cockroaches scampering for cover at the instance of light.

After Miles Jesu left, Tonello and McSweeney continued hashing over the logistics of the investigation. Father Anthony McSweeney was the perfect point man for the job. He looked an energetic seventy. The man's background included ten years teaching theology; two terms governing as a Superior General; and twelve years heading the Union of Superiors General, making him an *ipso facto* member of the Vatican's Congregation for Consecrated Life. He was an astute observer of human nature. The man knew every trick in the consecrated life playbook. No, he didn't.

Six weeks later, the empire struck back with a six page, single spaced, small point personal appeal to Cardinal Ruini. Gelson had recruited a hotshot canon lawyer, an old friend of Father Duran's and churned out an audacious epistle. Turn the other cheek? No way! This round, the Aussie would take a few blows. Duran would have been proud.

With briefcase in hand, fetching the document from the Vicariate, Father Anthony McSweeney twisted up the stairs of his general house in Rome. The building reflected a territorial castle of old, except for the absence of a moat and boiling oil. At Largo Aprile XXI, the well maintained, puke-yellow structure towered on a coveted piece of real estate. Tall walls protected its interior. Within the compound, a pampered garden, chapel, comfortable living quarters, and spacious administrative building flourished.

McSweeney kicked off his shoes, pulled out his Roman collar, unbuttoned his shirt a bit, and dug into the black briefcase. From the safety of an upper floor, the former general sat at his desk and combed through the Miles Jesu appeal.

*Your Eminence,*

*Blessed be the name of Jesus.*

*We are appealing personally to Your Eminence with matters concerning the current visitation and not to the Visitor, Fr. McSweeney, for reasons we shall set forth.*

The bottom line: they asked the Cardinal to cease the investigation and to restore their power to govern because the entire request for an intervention was based on a deception orchestrated by a few disgruntled members. They detailed and documented, they believed, a handful of reasons that supported their exceptional request. The letter manifested a meticulous construction of arguments, with panic lurking behind each paragraph.

McSweeney stretched and rubbed his eyes. He glanced out the window at the piazza below, and the twelve-meter statue of the tax man staring up at him. Who in his right mind would create a monument honoring the tax collector? Benito Mussolini. The art was fine; it was the idea that raised eye brows.

The priest shook his head, licked his thumb and flipped to the last page. By the third reading, the Canonical Visitor had boiled down the Miles Jesu defense to a few statements. Father Gelson employed three thousand-five hundred words to elaborate nine points: Although eccentric and ill, Father Duran is innocent. Miles Jesu is constitutionally sound. The community should solve its own problems. Walsh, Brennan, and Sullivan are liars, malicious too. Sullivan should be put in a chokehold and forced to apologize to the benefactors. The Canonical Visitor is biased and already believes Miles Jesu guilty. McSweeney smiled when he read this. Don't touch our constitutions! Don't insert an outsider to govern us! We need to move on and elect our next general.

The epistle was signed by fourteen members, adding the information that most other members agreed with everything said. Not one member of the general government signed the letter. Next to the signatures a note indicated how many years each signer had lived in Miles Jesu. The accumulated total reflected two-hundred and forty-six years of community life. Apparently, they wanted to demonstrate a spontaneous and unified uprising of grass root members.

The leprechaun's mug turned pensive. He dropped the letter on the desk and gawked at the crucifix on the wall. Miles Jesu preached blind obedience and docility in unparalleled fashion, but apparently relished a bloody fistfight with the Church. Strange. It didn't match. Character assassinations. Public judgment of consciences. Who were these people? Soon overcome with weariness, he stretched, yawned, rose, and hobbled to his bed for the sacred afternoon nap.

While the Canonical Visitor slept, Miles Jesu weaved its spider webbed stratagem. Backed with a document from a doctor stating his incapacity to govern, Duran had already been transferred to an undisclosed location in Spain. They'd already recruited a lawyer and puppet signers for their appeal to Ruini. They'd next fight for the election of Gelson as the new general director of Miles Jesu.

Constrained by the technicalities of canon law, Cardinal Ruini soon yielded to part of Miles Jesu's appeal. He acknowledged that the Vicariate had overstepped canonical provisions by suspending the authority of the Miles Jesu government.

Although the properly appointed canonical visitor would remain in place and the investigation would continue, the governing apparatus of Miles Jesu would be restored, at least provisionally for matters of ordinary functioning. However, extraordinary matters would still need the approval of higher authorities. This victory shifted Miles Jesu into high gear for the election. And who really cared about the fine line distinction between ordinary or extraordinary governing? Wasn't the election something ordinary? They'd advance their plan regardless.

# CHAPTER FIFTEEN

**W**hile Miles Jesu scrambled to survive and Ambra Treichler indulged in a deserved vacation, I jumped on a flight and flew to Timisaora, Romania. I'd promised Olha that I'd never abandon her. A connecting flight pressed northeast another eight hundred kilometers. Olha left her family in Dobrosyn and endured a marathon ten-hour trek by train toward Russia. After a two-month wait, we met with laughter, teary eyes, and a warm embrace in Kiev, Ukraine.

Freedom! It felt so good! Lost in that beautiful city, we discovered the summer we'd each missed in life. Miles Jesu had snatched us from youth. Now, snapping the leash of the cult, life resumed. Head over heels in love, Kiev offered a refuge and romantic playground.

From July 24 to September 3, 2007, Olha and I lived together in a dingy flat near Maidan Nezalezhnosti. With its exquisite statues and huge glass dome bulging out of the ground, Independence Square pulsated as the heartbeat of Ukrainian sovereignty. This showpiece of national pride embodied a personal meaning for us.

Cocooned by majestic buildings, Olha and I enjoyed strolling and watching the wonderland of sidewalk artists, break-dancers and magicians. The gurgling fountains, walkways, stairs with overflowing waters skipping downwards, fresh cut grass, and protective angels on pillars cradled and gave expression to our own inner joy of liberation. The apartment and square provided a moment of calm in the eye of the Miles Jesu hurricane and the chance to deepen our friendship.

We laughed while feeding monkeys at the zoo. Watching landscapes ease by, we leaned into one another as we took a river cruise and our excursion ship churned ahead on the Dnieper. Snuggling at movies, winning stuffed animals at amusement parks, praying in Byzantine churches with their onion and golden domes glistening in the air, napping upon each other's tummies, holding hands while gazing upward at fireworks; every crack of dawn welcomed a fresh adventure. Each evening ended at our fa-vorite spot, teasing chocolate shakes in a McDonalds on the northeastern corner of Maidan Nezalezhnosti.

Relaxing at a secluded table, kicking off our shoes, we'd talk animatedly about everything under the sun late into the night. We felt like innocent teenagers, with the added wisdom that only age and suffering could gift. A sense of urgency prevailed upon us. It was time to seize a new life.

Those intimate talks exposed the deepest parts of our souls to one another. No topic was forbidden. Nothing was taboo. An atmosphere of complete openness abounded. Love enraptured us, taught us about each other, fused our lives, opened our eyes to a possible future together.

Thunder and lightning invaded the epicenter of the city and everybody scattered. The heavens ruptured with a downpour upon the Square. Olha and I sat watching, snug in a cozy cubicle in a busy McDonalds as veins of water ran in rivulets down the window.

She wore a flowered dress with a subdued color pattern. Blue, violet, and crimson blooms blended without sharp contrasts. The outfit matched her unassuming personality. Olha didn't like showy and loud appearances. She preferred a low profile, a quiet place in life, focused on substance over symbolism. A meat and potatoes farm girl.

Drenched teenagers waited in line, gazing up at the menu translated into the Cyrillic alphabet. The Beatles' *Let It Be*, and indiscernible chatter muddled the atmosphere.

"Suppose we'd get married Olha; doesn't it concern you that I'm sixteen years older than you?" The smell of burgers and fries filled the air.

"No. I really don't care. It's not an issue for me."

"Really? Why not?"

She placed her chocolate shake on the table.

"God has brought us together. We love each other. I feel that we're meant for each other."

"I feel that too. But I'm concerned that I'll age, while you and the children stay young."

We had already shared our mutual desire for children, a few sooner rather than later.

"Really, it makes no difference to me." Her answer begged the question.

"Then what would be important to you in a marriage?

"A husband who is responsible and not an alcoholic. A husband who'd be a good father. A best friend who'd live my faith with me, who'd be faithful to me."

"Do you think I'm that kind of person?"

"Yes. I know you are." I let the good feeling sink in.

The rain beat upon the window as we picked at the mound of fries. No appointments. No Miles Jesu spies. No rush. No worry in the world. The conversation drifted to lighter things.

I burst out laughing when she described the memory of her two-year-old brother terrorized by a chicken. The hen pecked the toddler's pee-pee and all hell broke loose. We both cracked up when I told the story of trying to climb over the neighbor's fence when I was five. I slipped and ended up hanging upside down by my underwear for it seemed an eternity. After swapping a few more childhood memories and finishing the fries the conversation casually returned to the dream.

Olha paused, looked me in the eye, and spoke her mind.

"Realistically, a lot has to happen before marriage is even possible for us, the way we want to do it. My parish priest told me that it takes years to leave the priesthood."

"I don't know how long it takes. I just know that we want to live our faith and do things the right way. Before marriage you have to receive a dispensation from your promises in Miles Jesu, and I have to finish my psychotherapy and get a dispensation from the priesthood."

"I agree. I'll wait for as long as it takes."

"I know you will Olha." She really meant it. I took her hand and squeezed it.

The rain subsided. Quaint streetlamps lit up the fountains and beckoned us to a leisurely walk on damp shimmering pathways. After a lap around the sights, arm in arm we sauntered homebound.

For six weeks we lived together, slept together in the same bed. And although love consumed us, we withheld from passion's ultimate carnal expression. We never had sex, not even once. We came close at times. We felt the fires of attraction. But we'd agreed beforehand that we would save sex for marriage, and we kept our mutual promise. Somehow, when she was weak I was strong; when I was weak she was strong. We deliberately lived on the edge, hurled ourselves into the risk of life, and nurtured a greater respect for each another.

One night, in the pitch darkness, as we lay facing each other, wrapped together, I whispered into her ear.

"Honey?"

"Yes?"

"Help me. I want you like crazy."

She laughed. Teasing me, she stretched and gave the faintest little peck on my lips. That drove me wild. Did she know that? Blood rushed through my body and I vibrated with sexual tension, everywhere. She hugged me tightly.

"Andy."

"Yes, my Love."

"I think it's time to go to sleep."

"Yeah. You're right."

Lingering a while, we kissed, said goodnight, and turned our backs to each other, with our butts touching. It took a while for the magnetic pull to weaken, for my body to calm down.

"Good night, Honey," I said. "I love you."

"I love you, too."

By strange coincidence, Kiev magically lured not only Olha and me but the regrouping leaders of Miles Jesu. Coming to reclaim our lives, Olha and I believed we'd left the cult behind. But the inner circle of Miles Jesu had come in secret too, to take back their tinsel empire. Of all the places in the world, polarized destinies converged at the same time in the same city. Olha and I took sanctuary in a cheap apartment. The general government retreated into five bedrooms in an anonymous hotel a few metro stops south of Independence Square. Hidden from Rome's scrutiny, Miles Jesu would proceed to elect a new general director.

They occupied the perfect nondescript hide out. West of the Dnieper, southwest of the city center, the five story whitewashed hotel looked like any other dull soviet construct. A furniture store, travel agency, notary office, and bank occupied the ground level of a rise named *Mir*, meaning "Peace."

At the forefront of the building down a flight of stairs, an expansive patched and potholed walkway accommodated crowds of busy nobodies heading for the always busy bus services and metro. A newspaper kiosk and makeshift vegetable market attracted the curious and hungry. On the other side of the noisy street a small park welcomed a few souls with enough time and sense to wander away from the rat race.

Besides the bedrooms, Miles Jesu procured the use of a meeting space for its desperate act. At a bargain price the management provided a lackluster room with a cheap but spacious table and a dozen red padded chairs. Two large windows fitted with vinyl vertical blinds brightened the egg-shell white walls and spotless grey carpet. Kicking off the initial meeting, each of the seven electors placed his or her hand on the Bible and swore to secrecy. Deliberations boiled before the actual vote. Two additional women members shopped and cooked for the elite.

Everything predetermined the election of Father Marcus Gelson. Duran had wanted Gelson to follow him and for years stacked the deck in favor of this outcome. The voters were basically a rubber stamp committee ratifying Father Duran's prior determinations. Nobody could last for long within the Miles Jesu inner core of leadership who didn't agree with Duran. Other than Gelson, Duran had publicly trashed all other possible general director candidates. A paranoid apparatus for a predestined transference of power had long been in place.

Father Gelson carefully chose an election location that warded off external interference. The vote should have happened in Rome where the Institute held its primary juridical footing. The city of Kiev, Ukraine was chosen to play the advantage of overlapping ecclesial jurisdictions. Miles Jesu could freely elect its general within the chaos of the Catholic Byzantine Church, where a preoccupied hierarchy couldn't juggle anything but the most pressing catastrophes at hand. The Patriarch with the Colonel Sanders mug and imperial head gear had little time for Miles Jesu games.

The constitutions of Miles Jesu mandated the presidency of the local bishop or his appointed delegate at the election. For one reason or another, this didn't happen. Gelson restricted everyone from answering a phone because Rome could have intruded and opposed the proceedings.

Yet, not everything behind closed doors remained a secret. At some point within the discussions a flash of internal fighting reared its ugly head. Father Omar Salido didn't believe Father Gelson capable of leading the Institute. Calloused with many years of experience in Miles Jesu, he saw that Gelson was a broken man, and said so. During the heat of the moment Salido even accused Gelson of operating as "a predator." What did he mean? How much did the war-hardened Mexican priest really know?

Once the doubled-creased slips of paper were unfolded and tallied Father Gelson won hands down. The dysfunctional deed was done.

Following a low key celebration, Gelson and Jeni Staus decided to take a quick trip to Spain to update Father Duran on the latest development. They hopped on a plane and disappeared for a few days before boomeranging back to Rome.

Oddly enough, twenty-eight months later, an important ecclesial superior would journey to Spain to inform Father Alphonsus Duran that he was no longer the General Director of Miles Jesu. Blindsided. Duran had absolutely no idea.

He yelled, "You have no authority to tell me that! I will oppose it!"

Had the Spaniard lost his mind? Pretty much isolated in a top-secret location, had the sickly man ever been visited by Gelson and Staus? Or perhaps most likely, had Duran been victimized by his own Frankenstein creation? Had he succumbed to a manipulation aimed at pacifying and stringing him out? Had Father Gelson shrewdly managed the volatile priest?

According to the newly revised 2004 set of constitutions, the General Director is elected for a twelve-year term. Father Gelson's reign would last a mere twenty months before the implementation of the investigation would catch up with him and dismantle the entire general government. Meanwhile, Gelson would buy a new Miles Jesu headquarters in Rome, rally the remaining troops, and pretend the ongoing Vatican and Vicariate intervention hardly existed.

Olha and I learned of the presence of Miles Jesu and the election in Kiev about half way into our summer getaway. The information had been leaked to Olha by an insider who'd tried to leave Miles Jesu for many years. The unwelcomed news inserted some reality back into our relationship. A slap in the face, the newsflash sobered us at first. It then colored the remaining days we spent together. Straightforward talks brought us down to earth. Miles Jesu still threatened our happiness. But the menace helped us focus. By the time we departed Kiev, our resolve to dodge the dragon and grab hold of the future crystallized.

The Catholic Church is made up of two types of members: ministers and the pew-sitting laity: the ordained and the non-ordained. Among the ordained there are deacons, priests, bishops, cardinals and the pope. Among the lay faithful there are husbands and wives, singles, even habited celibates. This grand distinction stems from a fixed theological doctrine that characterizes ordination as an irreversible consecration. So goes the vernacular maxim: once a priest always a priest.

It logically follows that there is no way out of the Catholic priesthood. Strictly speaking, this is true. No matter whatever administrative procedure or wave of a magic wand, the cleric may be made to appear and function like a lay person, but deep in the core of his soul he remains a priest forever. The Vatican driven process of repackaging a priest as a quasi-layman is called a laicization.

Laicization divests the priest of the licit use of his irrevocable priestly powers. Complementary to this primary end, the laicized priest is deprived of title, office, and clerical garb. He loses priestly privileges and surrenders priestly duties. In many cases, the laicized priest is dispensed of celibacy and consecrated vows. By the time the laicization process concludes, the priest may marry and operate in the Church and society as any other Tom, Dick, or Harry.

Laicizations come in two different forms: involuntary or voluntary. Intended as a punishment for wicked behavior, Church authorities may strip an unwilling priest of his ministerial functions. Otherwise, a laicization may be granted as a favor by voluntary request. The Vatican dishes out five-hundred laicizations a year, more or less.

After returning from Ukraine, it took about two months to identify and hunt down the 'Wizard of Laicizations' in Rome. I wanted the best guy possible to help me.

Father Peter Heisner grew up in New York and now worked as a procurator general of a huge consecrated institute in Rome. He operated as a hotshot lawyer with the expertise and Vatican connections to flip laicizations like hot cakes. His proficiency turned heads. A few years down the road, the Pope would elevate the 'Wizard' to a prestigious Vatican post where his administrative magic would be fully exploited.

Father Pete welcomed me into a sprawling office and immediately apologized.

"This is not my idea of an office, but it is what it is."

The left side of the room supported an elevated deck with a costly oak desk surrounded by floor to ceiling volumes of law books. A pile of portfolios sat beneath the glow of a gooseneck desk lamp. Descending from the office recess and passing between two Corinthian pillars, the larger part of the room spread out with exquisite Breccia marble and chandeliers. A circular arrangement of plush black leather furniture occupied the open space.

Mimicking a museum, each wall presented superb artwork from varied cultures spanning the globe, missionary procurements. Beams of light shooting from the ceiling lit up each unique object: a Baoyueping vase from China; a Bellflower Lladro from Spain; a Byzantine icon from Russia.

Wedged in a corner, an antique cedar liquor cabinet displayed a variety of half-filled crystal decanters. Father Pete joked about the nook, calling it "the water hole for the yaks," referring to bishops.

"So, where ya from Father Sullivan?"

We walked to the luxury area and got comfortable.

"I'm originally from California."

Pete looked somewhere in his early fifties. He had a full head of curly black hair, complemented with a bushy beard. A flattened boxer's nose and sunken black eyes conveyed a rugged past with a bare minimum of sleep. During his late teens and early twenties, he'd racked up twenty-eight wins as a middleweight marvel.

"California? I'm sorry about that, the land of fruits and nuts."

He chuckled and shook his head a bit.

"I'm from the best borough of New York: Brooklyn. We gave the world the baseball hat and hot dog. Who could beat that?" He nodded, with his hands dancing in the air.

The priest wore black pants and a cuffed white dress shirt. I wore my penguin suit. Following a few minutes of light talk, Father Pete crossed his legs, leaned back, and let his practical nature take over.

"So, how can I help you?"

"I want to pursue a laicization and need some advice about how to do that."

"A laicization? Are you sure you want that?"

"Yes, I'm sure."

"Of course, I'm obliged to ask if there's any way to persuade you otherwise. Father Sullivan, the procedure is like a vasectomy. It's hardly reversible."

"I'm sure I want it."

He stared at me, leaned forward, and massaged his beard. His voice softened.

"I'm genuinely sorry that your situation in life has brought you to this decision. Respecting your resolve now; what's your story?

Knowing your background will get you better advice."

So, I told an abbreviated version of my story from joining Miles Jesu to escaping and the highlights in-between, including my captivity, suicidal disposition, exclaustration request, and on-going healing of emotional immaturity and trauma.

"Sounds like you got a weasel deal from this wannabe group." "A what?"

"A weasel deal is a sour arrangement that robs you of what was promised."

"Yeah. I'd agree."

Father Pete felt confident about the win. An emergent curiosity reflected in his eyes.

"Father Sullivan, if that's all true, which I have no reason to doubt; you have a slam dunk case. I've done hundreds of laicization cases and haven't seen one this certain."

"That's good to hear." It was wonderful to hear. I tried to hide my jubilation. "Really? Father, this is all new territory for me. Bottom line: how do I get a laicization then? What are the concrete steps? What do I have to do?" Now I was speaking his language.

He stood up and let his energy lead him. Waving me off, Pete's pragmatism ignited.

"Don't get up Father Sullivan. Above all else, you need to focus. You don't need that exclaustration anymore. Ask yourself what you really want. Do you want to be tied to Miles Jesu for another three years? And then tied again for another two while seeking a laicization? Or do you want real freedom? As soon as possible?"

"I don't need the exclaustration?" My eyes followed the slinking cleric.

"Priests ask for laicizations from every possible circumstance. I just submitted one from a monsignor who is now an insurance agent in Florida, married civilly, raising two kids. You see: an exclaustration is not necessary."

"So I drop the exclaustration request?"

"Yes. Focus. I'd be careful about sending your superiors mixed signals. Then you get a case manager for your laicization request. Your superiors, whoever they are, have to assign a manager for your case. Only a delegated manager can prepare the required portfolio and submit it to the Congregation for Clergy for you. The idea about a case manager is to insert impartiality into the appeal."

"What kind of person would make a good case manager?"

"An anal retentive type, otherwise the thing could get bogged down for years. You need an attentive mind that can follow the directions of the Congregation. Once the appeal is submitted it goes to the bottom of the pile. When it finally sees the light of day, if documents are missing or defective they need to be done over. And then your appeal goes back to the bottom of the pile again."

"What else? Can I do anything even before I get a case manager?"

"Yes, you could write your curriculum vitae. It's one of the thirteen documents you'll need."

"And what's that?"

"It's a two- or three-page account of the reasons why you're asking for a laicization. Then you can write your letter to the Pope. One page. You need to make a personal request to him for a laicization. Your curriculum vitae and letter are the only documents you prepare; everything else, including testimonials from witnesses and your superior's two cents, belongs to the case manager to collect and present."

Pete circled around the back of the couch and plopped back into his chair.

"Okay. Going back to the curriculum vitae, what should it show? What kind of things should be emphasized?"

"This is important." He pointed at me. "About ninety percent of the Congregation's interest concentrates on your preparedness to be ordained. They'll want to have a good idea of everything leading up to ordination: your discernment process, candidacy program, evaluations, anything indicating your suitability and level of maturity. They'll also want to know about your capacity to live a life of celibacy and if you possessed interior freedom when you decided to be ordained. In your case, it wouldn't hurt to show the incapacity of your superiors to make a good judgment in your regard. In the end, if they determine that you were obviously not ready to be ordained, you'll get your laicization."

Silence fell. He wanted the advice to hit home. I wanted to remember it. Leaning back, he added an afterthought.

"And the tone is important. You should come across as a humble beggar. Show haughtiness and you'll pay for it."

"I've begged for food and money my whole life. That shouldn't be a problem."

But I hid my true thoughts. After all the injustices I'd suffered, why should I have to kiss anyone's ass to reclaim my life? I sighed and kept going.

"Father Pete, so you think I have a good case?" He tilted his head and raised his bushy eyebrows.

"You got more chance to get a laicization than I have hair on my head."

I looked at him. Hair everywhere.

"Okay, great," I said.

"But the mechanics are the easy part, Father Sullivan. Just as you had to fight to get out of your community, you'll have to fight to reclaim your life. The hard part will be learning how to live as a layman again and finding your footing in the Church. Do you comprehend that nobody will understand?"

"I'm just taking one step at a time here. I'll deal with the future as it comes."

"You know that you'll lose everything."

From somewhere deep within, a wave of despise for Miles Jesu surfaced. But I held the emotion at bay. He didn't know everything.

"But I have nothing to lose. No bank account, savings, pension, insurance. I've never held a job. No work history. No credit history. Nothing. I don't even have pastoral experience as a priest. In seven years, I've done one baptism on the sly. Hell, I spent my last three and a half years in Miles Jesu imprisoned in an apartment. Yes, I know. I'm ready to lose everything."

"Good point." He nodded his head in agreement. "I'm just hinting about your future, encouraging a thought process. I'm not saying to back away from your choice. I do understand that risk is the catalyst of a genuine life."

Father Pete glanced at the grandfather clock near the right pillar.

"If that's it, I'm needed at another meeting. I'm sorry but my time is limited Father Sullivan."

"Sure, Father. Thank you for your advice."

"A word of wisdom here. Your superiors may try to obstruct you by saying you can't demand a grace from the Church. Although it's true that a voluntary laicization is a favor granted; it is equally true that you have a right as a priest to present your case. Don't forget the difference. You may need it."

We rose and started for the door.

"Once you get a case manager, if he doesn't know what he's doing, send him to me and I'll coach him, for your sake."

The boxer pointed in my face, wagging his finger.

"I really shouldn't do it."

"Thank you Father Heisner. I'll be in touch."

"You can't tell anyone that I met with you and that I'm helping you. This is important. Nobody can know, except you, me, and the case manager."

"Yes, of course."

He moved close to my face, as if he was going to punch me.

"You know I really mean this."

"Yes."

"Good. See ya later, Father Sullivan."

I turned my back to him and heard the thumping of the door behind me. Light glistened in my eyes. A smile appeared. Olha wouldn't mind knowing the latest. I hurried to the international phone stalls.

Friday, January 18, 2008, I emerged from the Laurentina metro south of Rome. This modern transportation hub linked the city to spider-webbed bus routes spreading throughout the beautiful Mediterranean countryside. Up the stairs, hanging a right, I headed for *Friends Alimentari*, a voluminous produce and dry goods store across Via Vigna Murata. The immigrant owners felt no reservations about combining English and Italian words together.

Plastered with Hindu scribbling on the facade, the family store accommodated for rushed travelers, but catered to Indians. Up front, the industrious souls from Calcutta sold plenty of grab and go items like chips, candies, sodas, and the like. The deeper part of the store morphed into a mini-warehouse sheltering an assortment of spice packed barrels, bulk water cases, and gunny sacks of basmati rice. A dozen international phone booths stretched parallel to a pallet line of Indian imports. I'd come to call Father Tonello.

Scattered clouds, damp streets, and crisp air should have encouraged a refreshing walk. They didn't. My mind was completely absorbed in the only choice left to me. Numerous attempts to get a case manager for my laicization had resulted in failure and I now had to demand attention. Either confront the Chancellor and force some kind of movement or languish in an eternity of waiting.

I peered through the window of booth number seven and waited for the secretary to transfer the call to Tonello's desk.

A self-assured voice shot through the receiver.

"Hello?"

"Father Tonello?"

"Yes?"

"Hello, this is Father Andy Sullivan. How are you today, Father?" "I'm fine."

The priest took a sip of coffee and waited for the purpose of the call.

"I'm calling to see if there's any progress with the Vatican about my case. Father McSweeney told me that you two were seeking an immediate solution."

Right away, his impatience boiled to the surface. The lumberjack was sick and tired of the whole Miles Jesu mess.

"An immediate solution? To what?"

"I've requested five times in writing to submit my case to be laicized, and still have no official reply."

"Look, Father Sullivan, it's extremely complicated. We can't show any partiality to anyone who left Miles Jesu, otherwise the intentions and procedures of the intervention may be called into question. You know this."

"How is partiality shown by relieving suffering and submitting a laicization request? I've reached the end of my patience. What do you want me to do? Wait a couple of years for everything to be fixed before I move on in life? This coming Monday I'll meet with a well-known canon lawyer to explore the possibilities of making a legal case against the Vicariate for obstructing my right to seek a laicization."

"What! That's ridiculous!"

I meant it and already had the meeting arranged with a sly Jesuit.

"This is not an idle threat. I'm calling to inform you that I'm finished waiting."

Tonellos's secretary poked through a crack in the door and the bearded priest waved her away.

"I'm the one with no patience here! Listen to me, Father Sullivan. You're in a very dangerous situation. Don't attack the only friend you have. Don't forget that we helped you more than anyone else."

"You've helped me in the past, Father Tonello, and I'm grateful for that. But today I'm taking control of my life."

"The Vicariate is not obstructing you. We have no power to give dispensations. We have no power to appoint a case manager for you. And we're totally unaware if and when there might be a Commissary for Miles Jesu."

"I've been assured that the Vicariate would intercede for me."

"The Vicariate? No, that's impossible. Who told you such a crazy idea?" McSweeney did; but I kept that to myself.

"Are you sure, Father Tonello?"

"Of course I'm sure. The Congregation told the Vicariate that Miles Jesu possesses full governing power. Only Father Gelson can appoint a case instructor for you."

I stared at an Indian family gathering potatoes from a bin, and shook my head in disbelief.

"So, Gelson's authority is not in question?"

"No. You'll have to go to him. He only needs to inform the investigator of his decisions."

"And when did this happen?"

"It's been the case from the beginning."

"Really? That's not true. You guys changed your mind and left us hanging in the wind."

Apparently, once Father Gelson had reclaimed his power the Vicariate adopted an internal policy of showing absolutely no appearance of collaboration with the dissenters. In my case, I'd been left in the dark and didn't even know it.

"Well, now you know," he said. "You should watch yourself, Father Sullivan. A laicization is a grace that can't be demanded." "You're missing an important distinction."

"Yes. And what's that?"

"It's a grace regarding its reception, but a right regarding its presentation. You're a canon lawyer, Father Tonello. You should know this."

The Chancellor didn't like that at all. He fidgeted in his chair and changed the subject.

"Nothing's been decided about a Commissary for Miles Jesu. That's premature. We're just investigating. You must to go Father Gelson for your needs."

"I'm glad I called. Thank you for clarifying things."

"You're welcome."

He hung up before I could say anything else. My head spun. I'd wasted months barking up the wrong tree. Now I had to crawl back to Father Gelson and ask for help. Just the thought of it made my stomach turn.

With autumn long past, winter gave way to spring in Ukraine. Rolling hills burst forth everywhere with signs of life. Wrestling free from the bondage of dark and cold, foliage, sprouts, and buds of all kinds pushed upward through the rich soil. Everything was not dead after all.

Olha Klub experienced the same kind of progressive resurrection in her own life. She'd been out of Miles Jesu for a year now. May marked the completion of her initial year of healing.

Detaching from a make believe world and trying to clutch reality, post-cult recovery is a rude awakening. Olha suffered through this crucial adaptation in a small farming village named Bishky. Her younger sister offered Olha a room in an old farmhouse and let the woman have some privacy, as much as possible. The sister, Luba was an energetic and attractive blond with a happy face. Always busy, she juggled a husband, three girls, the demands of a farm, and a job in a mushroom production center.

Physical separation from a cult implies the struggle of a wounded soul still straining to escape the tentacles of an inhumane paradigm. Olha suffered months of insomnia, disorientation, depression, loneliness, and grief. Miles Jesu had no idea of the damaged human beings it left behind. Anger would flare up from nowhere. She had lost thirteen years of life. Who wouldn't be mad? An overwhelming feeling of displacement haunted her. She felt like she didn't belong anywhere. A discarded misfit. Life was starting over again, this time with no meaning.

But there was a ray of hope, and that was me. Olha and I shared our souls with each other every Sunday afternoon. Every thought and feeling flew, the good, the bad, and the dreams, sometimes nightmares, sometimes fantasies of a better life. Hope survived.

We earnestly anticipated our Sunday chats. I'd place the call from a phone booth at *Friends Alimentary*. Waiting in her shack with a light bulb dangling overhead, she'd snatch up her blue Nokia cellular and answer. For a year we talked about our experiences of recovery and celebrated the breakthrough moments: her first job and paycheck; my conclusion of psychotherapy; her reintegration into family life; my latest dump of documents at the Vatican.

"Hello? Andy?"

It was May 4, 2008, and rain fell upon the thin grey tiles overhead and dripped down the unpainted wood slates outside her window. A cool ten degrees Celsius kept Lisko the work horse and Krasula the family's beloved black and white cow huddled in the adjacent barn. Beneath the window, Ebbi, the family's yellowish mutt lay curled in his muddy dog house.

"Hello, Olha. How are you, my love?" I sat on an elevated bar stool in booth five.

"I'm okay. Thanks for calling."

"How could I miss our call?"

"It's so nice to hear your voice."

She lay down on the bed and got comfortable.

"Thanks. Tell me what's new, Honey. How's your situation at work? Is it any better?"

During the past month Olha had bumped into the underworld of work politics, gossip, back stabbing and jealousies at her job: the normal ebb and flow of a not so perfect work environment at the mushroom production center. At thirty-one years old, the harsh interchange of post-soviet labor relations was a new experience in Olha's life. We commented on the latest incidents and moved on.

Peering through the window at a bin of coconuts, I couldn't hold myself back any longer.

"I got some big news for you, Honey."

She flipped off her shoes and pulled the tiger blanket up to her neck, the cheap electric space heater proving ineffective.

"What happened? Tell me."

"My request for the laicization was finally submitted this last Friday."

"Really? That's great news. Who submitted it?"

"Miles Jesu did; believe it or not."

"So, Father Gelson really did help?"

"Yeah, in the end, he wouldn't give an exclaustration to recover my health, but didn't seem to mind helping remove me from the priesthood. I guess it was a convenient way for Miles Jesu to wash its hands of me."

"That makes sense. Doesn't surprise me. Did the Congregation say how long it will take?"

"Well, remember what Father Heisner said. The request will go to the bottom of the pile and then take one to two years."

"Two years!"

"He did say that my request would probably take shorter than longer."

She didn't seem to hear that. Olha closed her eyes and let out a sigh, indiscernible by phone. Frustration invaded her soul. It seemed that each victory always ended with another impossible hardship.

"How much longer will Miles Jesu continue to mess with our lives?"

I pressed the handset to my lips and almost whispered.

"Don't worry Olha. Just a little more patience and it will all happen."

Of course, I shared the same exasperation, but focused on the positive.

She paused, stared at the ceiling, and absorbed the comforting words. Resigned, she started talking again.

"Andy, so what's next?"

"What's next? I'm finished here. It's time to come to Ukraine and wait it out. I need to tie up a few loose ends and say some goodbyes and then I'll be on my way."

"But shouldn't you go back to your family and spend time with them for a while?"

"No, I won't do that. You are my life now."

Her heart skipped a beat. She persisted with the question and then gave up without pressing too hard.

"Yes, come. Come soon. It's hard to be alone. Thank you. I love you so much!"

The call lasted about an hour. Imagining our future, the goodbyes echoed with happiness.

I hung up and sat there for a minute, and ruminated over an idea I'd had a thousand times. Whenever I could leave Rome I wouldn't flee to my parents and my past; no, I'd run to Ukraine and seize my future. I wouldn't let it get away from me this time.

# CHAPTER SIXTEEN

L iving within the commune of Rome since February 1995, I ached to abandon the place. Thirteen years. That was enough. I just wanted to flee and embark upon my own life now, truly, freely chosen. But a monumental task remained.

Somewhere in the belly of McSweeney's general house Tom Walsh and I sat at a spacious black table in a poorly lit room. Document mounds bulged before each of us. Half shut window blinds permitted slivers of sunlight to pierce inside. McSweeney sat there too, looking frayed but still grinning. I fingered a cheap Bic pen from my left breast pocket; the Canonical Visitor leaned back and assumed the role of a witness.

Father Anthony McSweeney had consumed a year to interview, raid files, write his analysis of Miles Jesu, and recommend a course of action for Church superiors. By spring, 2008, I'd seen McSweeney's masterpiece basking on a table in Father Tonello's office in the Vicariate. The Chancellor had proudly indicated the hundred-page achievement and waved his hand over the three, twenty inch towers of supporting documents. Tonello had a big mouth, and I appreciated the inside information.

Although McSweeney's study and recommendation had already been submitted to the Vicariate and Vatican, he recognized the value of fortifying the supporting document stacks with sworn testimony. When Walsh had volunteered to upgrade his testimony with sworn statements, Father McSweeney jumped at the chance. Subsequently, I asked if I could do the same.

Page by page, I signed and re-dated my previous submissions, now including an addendum:

*I, Andrew Lee Sullivan, do hereby swear that the following testimony is true, and I am prepared to testify to it in any future ecclesiastical tribunal.*

I grabbed the first of eighty-nine pages and began skimming. Holding a document given to McSweeney six months ago, scanning gave way to reminiscence. What's the rush? Chewing gum, flicking my pen between forefinger and thumb, I eased into a leisured read. I felt like an artist stepping back for a moment to admire his work.

*I have now been removed from the Miles Jesu community environment for six months. In that time, an adaption to a non–Miles Jesu world accelerated my emotional growth and opened my mind to a greater extent. A distance from Miles Jesu, continued psychotherapy, study, solitude and reflection, hindsight, and first time experiences in human life, sharpened my understanding of Miles Jesu. Seeing the light, as it were, helped me comprehend the darkness.*

*Miles Jesu is a cult in orthodox clothing. It only takes a study of the nature of cults and a familiarity with the internal nature of Miles Jesu to arrive at this conclusion. I believe that this viewpoint provides a framework that harmoniously fits together the puzzle pieces of Miles Jesu's systemic dysfunctionality.*

*To avoid ambiguity, I would like to define what I mean by the term cult. Adopted at a 1985 conference of scholars and policymakers, the International Cultic Studies Association uses the following definition of a cult:*

*'A cult is a group or movement exhibiting great or excessive devotion or dedication to some person, idea, or thing, and employing unethical manipulative or coercive techniques of persuasion and control (isolation from former friends and family, debilitation, use of special methods to heighten suggestibility and subservience, powerful group pressures, information management, suspension of individuality or critical judgment, promotion of total dependency of the group and fear of leaving it), designed to advance the goals of the group's leaders, to the actual or possible detriment of members, their families, or the community.'*

I flipped off my penny loafers beneath the table. Momentarily, I eyed Tom Walsh eagerly devouring the contents of his own documents. Father McSweeney sat with his back against a wall of wood closets. He kept himself occupied with his own pile of things to do. Dead silence. My eyes adapted to the poorly lit room and remained focused on the document in my hands.

*Accordingly, when I state that Miles Jesu is a cult I hold that Miles Jesu fits the above definition. Take note, as defined above, a group is a cult not by beliefs but by methods and behaviors. On that account, even if they believe Catholic doctrine, Miles Jesu's methods and behaviors alone make them a cult. And, typical of a cult, through deception, manipulation, coercion and isolation from the outside world, Miles Jesu exploits the faith, commitment, trust and good will of each and every member. Ultimately, each member, is gradually emotionally traumatized, intellectually indoctrinated and defaced as a human being.*

*Of countless examples I could choose from, three decades worth, I would like to offer a simple example that demonstrates the above. Consider the Miles Jesu charism of availability, often meaning the following: abandoning all personal interests, hopes and dreams; putting aside your natural talents and dispositions to do what you are totally unfit to do; never again going back to school; never again visiting your family or friends; linking your dreams to the General's; surrendering any sense of a social life; never developing any personal job or project because of continuously being assigned something new; living in a state of detachment so severe that everything can change overnight, i.e., where you live, who you live with, what you do, etc.; giving up what you thought was your vocation and replacing it with a new idea; being only focused and concerned about doing what the General says; ignoring all your own needs, wants, hobbies, etc.; surrendering all sense of privacy. In short, Miles Jesu availability ultimately means sacrificing your future, truly and entirely, on the altar of blind obedience. Miles Jesu's ideal of availability is so angelic it is inhuman. Its practice creates uneducated and underdeveloped individuals only concerned about obeying.*

I paused and laughed, remembering how I'd coined the phrase "The Green Beret of the Catholic Church." That said it all. McSweeney peered at me over the top of his reading glasses. I cleared my throat and ignored him.

*But it gets worse. The Miles Jesu ideal of availability also means the following: going to countries to live without required visas; deceiving new recruits; kicking out members without affording them any sense of dignity and justice; offering bribes to government officials; being indefinitely removed from school just as exams begin; harshly correcting people when you know they are innocent; living in inhumane conditions; accepting absolutely impossible assignments without access to the means to achieve them; slandering people who left Miles Jesu before their family, friends, benefactors and community members; surrendering any right to privacy in regard to letters, emails, phone calls; not being able to take a walk alone; surrendering access to your own passport.*

*In my opinion, cult dysfunctionality diffuses into the very blood stream of Miles Jesu from the person of Father Duran, as from the principle artery. I am certain that Father Duran had a chronic psychological sickness known as Anti-social Personality Disorder, not uncommon among cult leaders. He was neither diagnosed nor treated as such because this disorder, not unusually, often requires close observation to detect. Superficially, among those with no education in such a matter, Father Duran appeared 'normal.' Yet, as the Founder and General Director of Miles Jesu for forty-four years, Father Duran was able to elude the scrutiny of both Church authorities and qualified psychiatric professionals capable of administering any genuine and thorough psychological evaluations.*

The document at hand referenced sociopathic behavioral characteristics common to cult leaders. Excerpted from the book *Take Back Your Life*, an attachment described Alphonsus Duran with uncanny precision: erratic life style; rage and abuse alternating with love and approval, difficulties in peer relationships, irresponsibility and unreliability, totally oblivious to devastation inflicted on others.

Other relevant factors mentioned were: glib and charming, great capacity to destroy detractors, unable to recognize the individuality and rights of others, highly manipulative, possessing tremendous feelings of personal entitlement, forceful expression of personal views as well as a lack of remorse, shame and guilt.

Other giveaway characteristics would include: deep-seated rage probably linked to childhood abandonment, perception of others as targets and opportunities, inability to enjoy a genuine friend and a tendency to either make victims or accomplices. Such a person would see himself as an ultimate moral arbiter.

Sociopaths exhibit spontaneous outbursts, callousness, voids of empathy, unawareness of personal boundaries and unrestrained desires that allow nothing to get in the way. Such tormented souls find it difficult to give and receive love. They entertain a propensity to embarrass and harshly test their followers.

A sociopathic cult leader indulges in blaming and scapegoating with a ritualized procedure. Promiscuous sexual behavior is not uncommon. Instability regarding purposes and constantly shifting objectives flourish. Yet, at the same time, a self-perception of superiority by divine inspiration emanates from his or her personality. An amazing summary of Father Alphonsus Duran's bizarre character.

The first three pages, I agreed with everything, swore upon my soul, and signed away. Bring it on. I was willing to testify before any robed court. The Church should know what kind of man the system had allowed to slip through the cracks and govern. Father Alphonsus Duran was a Doctor Jekyll and Mister Hyde enigma. Publicly, he could dazzle like a saint; privately he could behave like a monster. And he had imbued his Frankenstein creation, Miles Jesu with his own disconnected personality. Near a wall mounted crucifix, a simple black-rimmed clock ticked away. Reading and signing advanced; hours passed.

Although I didn't think of it that moment, I'd become a new me. I'd grown up. The habitual reception of unconditional love had transformed me into an emotionally mature human being. Eighty-nine signatures flowed. Black ink gushed from a secure love unmixed anymore with desires for approval and acceptance. Mature love had birthed boldness against evil.

Psychotherapy hadn't changed me. It had merely observed and confirmed my own unstoppable march to maturity. In my case, a psychotherapeutic friendship had served as an educated encouragement that tweaked my own inner journey. Ambra Treichler had never seen any client grow up so fast, nor even read of it. She'd never witnessed anyone's navigation of Jung's process of individuation so intensely and masterfully. But it was Jesus, not Jung's archetype, but the real Divine Person who had changed me. The Lover of Man, as Eastern theology calls him.

Sure, there may be a power within the soul that can self-orientate and lead to a highly personalized destiny. But this doesn't prove there's neither God nor communication with Him. God created us with the natural internal apparatus to grow emotionally and psychologically, and resume growth if needed. And He's ever free to intervene and tinker with his marvelous creation for our benefit.

My eighty-nine signatures that day represented a mere stepping stone in a divine landscape: not the Vatican's but God's intervention in Miles Jesu. My stand against evil gradually unfolded from a divine work of love nurtured in a distressed heart long ago and far away. The remote principle of the Vatican's intervention in Miles Jesu really traced back to Todd Scott.

I'd recruited Todd into the Miles Jesu Chicago house in Lincoln Park, Illinois in 1989. On a humid summer evening close to midnight, Todd had begged God to reveal which path in life he should follow. That instant, I'd called and urged the young man to join. For me, the telephone call was just another name on the hot list of possible vocation candidates. For Todd, the call was a heaven sent sign, a clear answer to a desperate prayer. He soon quit his job and journeyed to the Windy City.

At twenty-three years old, Todd was a pious and industrious neophyte, a real keeper, a regional trainer for seven Taco Bells. Fit and trim, the innocent and happy-faced recruit from Minnesota abandoned family, friends, and everything he owned to join the community.

After many long years in Miles Jesu, Todd had been discarded by Father Duran and vanquished to the island of misfit members in Puerto Rico. Duran routinely dumped throw away members into the Institute's parish down there, not knowing what else to do with them.

On a sweltering summer night in Puerto Rico, Todd Scott lay upon his back grappling with graphic sexual temptations. Searching for a way to battle haunting pornographic fantasies, Todd deliberately constructed a mental picture of the face of Jesus. The static image helped at the outset but soon lost its sway to the impure thoughts dancing about in his head. So, Todd tweaked his approach.

After a couple weeks of trial and error, yielding to the prodding of grace in his life, Todd had discovered a prayer experience powerful enough to vanquish the temptations. A static face wasn't enough. He imagined an interactive Jesus not stuck in history but right next to him in a contemporary setting, fishing at the boundary waters of Minnesota.

Then something amazing happened. Jesus turned to him and smiled. Todd didn't consciously construct that experience; it just happened. That smile went straight to Todd's heart and launched a grand prayer adventure brimming over with moving images, shared emotions, and vivid conversations. Before long, Todd felt a torrent of love and freedom from sexual temptations.

That smile ignited an inextinguishable fire that gradually transformed Todd, rehabilitated other discarded members, spread to Rome, and sealed the fate of Miles Jesu. Although Todd Scott was labeled a heretic and forbidden to give spiritual direction, his secret, underground spirituality became unstoppable.

Written off as pathetic nonconformists, Duran had also dumped John Quigley and Father Michael Dietrich in Puerto Rico. Todd had befriended these throwaways and introduced them to his prayer method. Their lives had transformed, too.

Before Todd had finally escaped from Miles Jesu he'd stumbled across a book in the house library: *Healing the Unaffirmed: Recognizing Emotional Deprivation Disorder* by Conrad Baars, M.D. and Anna Terruwe, M.D. He skimmed it and recognized the close alignment of the book's principles with his own innovative way of praying. Like a baton handed off to an approaching runner, the book, the time bomb, found its way into the hands of John Quigley. Meditation inspired Todd to flee the cult; he packed his bags and returned to Minnesota.

A workaholic hot head from a broken family in Michigan, John Quigley devoured the book. Page by page, familiarizing himself with the symptomology of the disorder, he finally understood himself. The favorable judgments of Pope Paul VI and Pope John Paul II regarding the work of Baars and Terruwe further convinced John of the book's value.

Harmonizing the book and prayer method, Quigley and Dietrich advanced a provisional, in-house treatment toward the cure of their own emotional deprivation disorders. Given the isolation of the cult, it was the best they could do, short of actual affirmation therapy. To the imaginary passive reception of affirming love, they added daily walks. Not really by intent, these encounters became substitutive therapy sessions. They'd share their meditative experiences, accept each other unconditionally, and assimilate the therapeutic principles and practices advocated by Baars and Terruwe.

Then came my miracle. Father Duran had shut down Puerto Rico and sent me to Chicago, where Father Dietrich and I crossed paths. He handed the baton to me and flew to Phoenix.

I returned to Rome with the fire, and soon spread the prayer method to Tom Walsh. He and I enjoyed hundreds of intimate walks and became best friends. We shared our meditations, talked about emotional deprivation and its treatment, and gradually arrived at a thorough understanding of the truly damaging nature of Miles Jesu. We caught up to Todd's judgment.

Truly, Todd's prayer method and its therapeutic adaptation by Quigley and Dietrich ignited the Vatican intervention. At the right place and time, Thomas Walsh and I found healing and power in that prayer, and enough inspiration to turn the world we knew upside down. I believe that God was behind it all, from the instant of that casual smile of Jesus in Todd's soul many years past.

I finished signing page eighty-nine, scooped up the papers, and joggled the bunch on the table until the edges lined up smoothly. Feeling like a student completing an exam, I walked up to the Canonical Visitor and handed him my sworn testimony.

"I hope this will help. Something has to be done to stop Miles Jesu's damage of people."

He looked up, smiled, and shook his head slightly. McSweeney knew he shouldn't agree or disagree.

"Thank you Father Sullivan."

Inadvertently, faintly raised eyebrows gave him away. I picked up my briefcase and we said our goodbyes. Exiting the castle, I met Tom Walsh waiting outside.

"How about lunch, Andy? I'm springing today."

"Sounds good to me. I'm starving. Let's get the hell out of here."

We strolled down Viale XXI Aprile toward Piazza Bologna, enjoying each other's company and a cloudless afternoon.

Toting his own briefcase, Father Anthony McSweeney headed west to the Vicariate. He'd bolster his document stacks in Tonello's office and take the rest of the day off. The fate of Miles Jesu now rested in the hands of the Vicariate and Vatican.

Stopping at a *trattoria* invading the sidewalk with quaint tables and blue umbrellas, we pulled up a couple chairs, sat down, and ignored the menu. A beautiful face and low cut blouse came by and we ordered two bowls of carbonara permeated with rustic shavings of cured bacon. Americans were clueless about making decent, *al dente* pasta.

The food arrived, though the smell of it came first. We thanked God and twirled the pasta with our forks. Between bites, we chewed the fat about Tom's upcoming return to New York and my imminent flight to L'viv, Ukraine. Roman life had reached its end.

Our genuine friendship had resulted from the radical prayer life and countless walks we'd shared. Miles Jesu had discouraged particular friendships because they threatened the harmony of the community, even its survival. Nobody was supposed to have a special friend, a particular preference or affinity for one person over another. Tom and I had smashed through that rule long ago. We'd come to believe, and heaven forbid, feel otherwise.

A few days later we said our goodbyes. I flew east; he west. Within a couple years Tom would earn a Ph.D. in Theology, land a decent administrative and teaching job at the diocesan level in the States, discover his marital vocation, and become the proud father of a beautiful baby girl.

An endless ocean of farmlands seemed to explode with myriad shades of green. I studied the fertile terrain thousands of feet below. Rolling hills, trees, streams, and matchbox houses traced a patchwork quilted paradise. I made it! Home at last! Though it wasn't my home, that's what it felt like. I had no home. Creeping along in the sky, zooming to L'viv, the anticipation of a brand new life made me feel wonderful. I could hardly wait to see Olha.

Resting my head against a cabin window, my eyes gobbled up the beauty. Thoroughly relaxed, the magical flow of land made me reflect on fresh meditations. Characteristically, my meditations hit hard with vibrant, unforgettable images that rippled for days, begging for reflection. The view blurred and my mind replayed the images of the last two days.

I stood near the edge of a towering cliff where a rocky, lifeless, desolate landscape stretched behind and to my sides. A stunning panoramic view unfurled a bay and setting sun. Golden-yellow rays raced over deep blue.

Far below and ahead, a vast sandy beach spread beyond measurement in both directions. No people at first. No movement. No fear.

In the middle of that calm ocean inlet, a shipwreck lay submerged except for its tortured bow and snapped mast jutting through the lapping surface. The right rim of the bay hosted a modern dock berthing a sizable, white vessel. Then I noticed ants on the beach; tattered shipwreck survivors huddled around a campfire. A few young men waded through the waves toward the shore. Far to the left in two beach chairs, two specs unwound and observed. I couldn't make out identities, yet intuited Ambra Treichler and Tom Walsh.

I felt the presence of Jesus behind and to my right. His left arm and hand came to rest upon my back and neck. Then I felt his face near my right ear. "It is finished," he whispered. Feeling a distance from Miles Jesu, my soul readily agreed. The image froze. The vision took hold of me and I beheld the finality of a passing chapter in my life.

The next morning's meditation picked up where this one left off. I turned around and saw an enormous church towering on a steep hill. A winding stairway flowed downward twisting and turning, pinched by huge boulders, ending at my feet. It seemed like a football field length climb. I took one step upward and suddenly stood at the church entrance. Jesus appeared at my right side. Massive doors opened to a dark interior.

Jesus then bowed his head, motioned with his hand, and beckoned that I enter while he remained outside. Inside, I saw my mother kneeling in a confessional niche. I approached her and she rose. "Mom, I forgive you." We hugged and cried. It gave me great satisfaction to forgive. We then walked back through the doorway, stood outside, and faced the faraway bay.

Olha appeared and I introduced my mother to my fiancée. Surprisingly, Mom seemed happy to meet her. Olha never said a word. I turned and directly faced my mother. "Mom," I said. "I want you to love me as your son, not as a priest. But this does not mean that I don't love you. I love you." We embraced and cried again.

Jesus whispered into my ear, "I'll take care of her." He took her by the arm and comforted her. While he walked her into the church, Jesus paused and turned to Olha and me. With penetrating eyes, wordless, he nodded. I understood a world in that gesture. It felt like he said, "I got this. I'll take care of her. The first part of your life is over. You and Olha go live your new lives." His glance said everything. Jesus turned, tightened his grip on my mother's arm, and disappeared into an almost cave-like church entrance.

Olha and I stood alone. We grasped each other's hand, walked to the edge of the descending staircase and paused. We tightened our hands and took a step forward, but didn't drop downward. Our feet never touched the first stair. We floated and took off flying in the air toward the sun. Squeezing each other's hands, pure exhilaration enveloped us.

The flaps dropped. Rushing wind swept over the wings. The plane jerked forward and the cabin filled with sounds of slowing down. Clicking my tray table into place, I pulled at the seatbelt strap and leaned back. A landing announcement cackled, yet I made the effort to focus on the meaning of the meditations. Before landing, I wanted to make a mental summary.

By the time I stepped into the airport bus adjacent to the airliner, the two meditations had boiled down to a simple truth: goodbye Miles Jesu and hello Olha Klub. God seemed to be encouraging my pursuit of a new life. It was up to me to seize that new life with a sense of responsibility. I already felt the gratitude.

From a birds-eye view, the two most recent meditations fit into a third stage of prayer. From the day Father Michael Dietrich had taught me the ways of therapeutic prayer, thirty-two months and a thousand meditations had passed. In hindsight, looking at the experience as a whole, three distinct stages of prayer had gradually evolved.

The initial stage had rescued me from suicide and gently walked me into a deeply satisfying, love-filled relationship with God. This beginner's stage encouraged the emotional experience of genuine trust and friendship, both with God and man. It taught me how to forgive and how to receive healing from traumatic memories. Even more, it brought on a dramatic shift in the way I thought and felt about practically everything. Love had awakened my heart, seeped into my brain, and affected my judgment.

The middle stage had plunged me in overwhelming love and precipitated a profound psychic birth. I'd discovered the real me, lovable, valuable, worthy unconditionally. This led to an abatement of fear and growth in feeling secure. Real self-confidence and risk-taking appeared seemingly from nowhere. Resistance against abuse and an assertion of independence followed. My confrontation against Miles Jesu was a direct result of this personal development.

With emotional growth and healing as a foundation, the third and final stage of affirmation meditation dealt with integration into normal human life. Less intense and waning, meditations seemed oriented to the proper use of independence, an exploration of marital life, and adjusting to a non-cult world. The meditative energy that had once hurled me forward like a runaway freight train slowed to an easygoing roll. As meditative trances weakened, nocturnal dreams made their way back into my life. Ambra Treichler would have been pleased. Throughout psychotherapy she had wanted subconscious dream material; but I could only offer otherworldly meditations.

These three stages did not start and end abruptly; they overlapped and bled into each other. Yet, they manifested differences by a predominance of distinct themes and changing intensity levels. But the enduring image of receiving love a thousand different ways had always remained constant from beginning to end.

Once I passed through customs, there she stood in the crowd, dressed in daisies. She looked so pretty with her bright smile and beaming eyes. Her feminine curves and golden hair absorbed my embrace. The kiss, the smell of rose perfume, the touch of her skin broke my imagination and pulled me into tangible reality.

"Hello, Olha! It's so nice to see you! You look wonderful!"

She really adored me. But honestly, I don't know who treasured the other more. Hadn't we rescued each other? My eyes searched her face and I couldn't find trauma. Only happiness. Of course, trauma still lingered, I just didn't see it at that moment.

"You're finally here," she said, and hugged me tightly, again. The long wait was finally over, but not entirely.

From the airport, we took two bumpy bus rides and chatted about a hundred different things until arriving in Zhovkva an hour later. She heard the latest about my sworn testimony in Rome. I learned the latest about her mushroom nursery and housing adventure. Olha had fixed up a room in a hundred-year-old house owned by her uncle Zenik in Zhovkva.

Not far from a forest at the west end of town, Olha's uncle actually owned two houses on the same property. No farm for him. He didn't want one. The good-humored workaholic was a passionate carpenter. He and his wife, Nadie, and their two teenage daughters lived in the new house, a veritable construction project. The original dwelling had been abandoned years ago. Thanks to Zenik's hospitality and a little persuasion from his sister, Olha's mom, we had a place to live.

The discarded house looked a dull grey with cracks and missing plaster. Construction materials, an old red fence, sheet metal leaned on the side of the unkempt building. Weeds grew all around. Warped asbestos roof tiles needed replacing. Huge spider webs sagged beneath the overhang.

Inside, the place lacked running water, plumbing, sinks, a bathroom, and conventional heating. The house divided into two large rooms. Zanik used the left room for storage: old furniture, disco equipment, construction materials, jarred meats, vegetables, fruits, discarded school stuff, clothing, mice poop.

We got the old bedroom on the right with a creaky sofa that unfolded to mimic a bed. No other furniture except for a table and two chairs. The bedroom did however have a functional brown *pietz*: a ceramic seven-foot tower used to burn wood and heat its interior bricks to warm the room. A faint double-smell of ash and marigolds hung in the air.

Olha and her mom had invested a lot of time and energy to make this room acceptable. They'd cleared the room, repaired and painted the walls, painted the floor, scrubbed and curtained the windows, laid out a new carpet, and washed and freshened up the sofa with new bedding. A brand new flower-molded light fixture hung from the ceiling. Olha's luggage sat in the corner.

Yes, I did feel at home. I squeezed her and let my feelings speak.

"It's just right, Honey!"

"You like it?" she asked, wanting reassurance.

"It's perfect. Thank you for all the work you did."

Big grins stretched across our faces. Without doubt, the excitement of living together swayed our judgment. The place had a lot of inconveniences, but our love was enough to make up for the deficiencies. I suppose a tent and campfire would have sufficed.

As the months passed, we continued to fix up the place and prepare for winter with a colossal mountain of wood. Learning a multitude of ways of loving without sex, we resumed our wait for the blessing of marriage and children. Life taught us how to replace begging with earning income, an indispensable psychological development for each of us. She sold strawberries; I gave public lectures. We pinched pennies and lived poorly.

We lived on hope, waiting for the Vatican to grant my laicization. We couldn't imagine what we'd do if it didn't come through.

From the declaration of the Vicariate's and Vatican's intervention, it had taken a year to complete McSweeney's inquisition and labored recommendations; a year to hunt down and appoint a provisional commissary to mop up the ecclesial disaster, and another four years to eventually elect a new general director from the internal ranks of the Institute. That's a six-year investment to salvage the Miles Jesu shipwreck.

I'd like to believe that investment worked. I don't know. It's easy to slap fresh words on paper, indicate new directions, forge new constitutions. It's an entirely different reality to change a person's heart.

From a sweeping perspective, the phenomenon of Miles Jesu represented a mere pebble in a Church mosaic of struggling, post Vatican II consecrated institutes. Focusing on a recent twenty-year period, the landmark study of Giancarlo Rocca had counted almost eight hundred new forms of consecrated life, eighty of them already extinct. That's a ten percent mortality rate of newborns. Put fairly, most Church people had no idea of the great suffering brought on by the failed experiments of consecrated life.

The research of Luis Oviedo, OFM dug up the causes of the extinctions. Each newborn community faced the challenge of transitioning from an excessive dependence upon a charismatic founder to an organized institution respectful of the comprehensive welfare of every member.

Numerous obstacles prevented this absolutely essential transition. Often, the founder had profound defects that transfused into the membership. In many cases, succession proved too difficult. In many more cases, the membership couldn't survive internal divisions as it attempted to define an essential identity and mission. Some groups simply flopped at recruiting. Some groups couldn't operate harmoniously with the Roman Catholic Church as a whole. The list of mortal blows mounted.

The quandary of Miles Jesu fit into this wider context. Knowing the full picture, the Vicariate and Vatican faced the decision whether to suppress Miles Jesu or attempt a radical repair job. Like a chameleon with changing colors and eyes looking in opposite directions, Church superiors convolutedly opted for both solutions.

While McSweeney's appointment grew old, Cardinal Ruini retired. The ageing prelate was replaced by Cardinal Agostino Vallini. He quickly, formally concluded the canonical visitation and simultaneously appointed Father Barry Fischer as the Commissary of Miles Jesu. The deputized fix-it man.

The full force of the intervention hit with the removal of Father Marcus Gelson as the General Director of Miles Jesu. Trapped in Tonello's office, Marcus absorbed the pronouncement with calm and dignity. Stone-faced, he just listened. His worn visage exhibited every sign of proper form and etiquette. Expecting a twelve year first term, Father Gelson's twenty-month reign evaporated into thin air. There seemed to be nothing the drowning man could grip to save his dignity. His physical and emotional melt down would gush forth a few weeks later. Invested with undisputed powers, Father Fischer grabbed the bull by the horns.

While remaining active and engaged in his own religious order, Father Fischer wouldn't live in Miles Jesu communities. Perhaps, the priest wanted to preserve his sanity. He intended to keep a healthy distance and rule from the edge of the field, like a coach orchestrating from the dugout.

Immediate moratoriums swept through the communities: no new members; no further commitments; no new seminarians; no new priests. The message was clear. Stop the train! A few abrupt go-aheads hinted at radical changes to come. You could now travel and take walks all by yourself, without feeling guilty. Members could visit their families, without the fear of corrupting the Institute and losing their souls.

The bald priest with thin, black rim glasses had plenty of experience backing his game plan. He'd slogged in the missions of Latin America for twenty-six years and governed in Rome as a superior general for two terms. Rome's oversight man, full-faced and clean shaven, still retained his hub of activity at a spirituality center in Salzburg, Austria. That was the deal. From his heavenly wonderland, catching international flights here and there, he juggled the affairs of the Missionaries of the Precious Blood and the reconstruction of Miles Jesu. Apparently, the authorities believed he could tackle the job as a part-timer, removed from the inner Miles Jesu environment.

Fischer's Vatican-backed marching orders apparently focused on the re-founding of the Institute. Pulling up his sleeves, filled with zest, the missionary-blooded Commissary embarked on a long journey to rebuild practically everything. Evidently, Father Anthony McSweeney had recognized that Miles Jesu retained good human material at its core. Granted, this had always been the treasure of Miles Jesu: good-willed, highly idealistic, completely dedicated human beings. The ranks included saintly souls, sadly exploited and misled, but capable of reeducation. Father Barry Fischer built from there.

He set out to rewrite the constitutions, rediscover the original but lost praxis of Miles Jesu spirituality, initiate a vocation discernment program, design a formation procedure, reorganize financial and governmental structures, educate members, and from top to bottom revise all the practices and customs.

Perhaps the biggest challenge: he'd attempt to detach Miles Jesu from Father Duran and reattach the corporate body onto another head. This head transplant demanded innovation because the Catholic Church expects every religious to imitate not only Jesus Christ, but the founding head of his or her particular institute of consecrated life. Franciscans become holy by imitating Saint Francis; Jesuits by Saint Ignatius; Dominicans by

Saint Dominic. The problem: the Church no longer wanted the members of Miles Jesu to emulate the way of life of Father Alphonsus Maria Duran. Perhaps the membership could preserve a few acceptable, foundational concepts from Duran, but not much more. Father Fischer had boasted to me that when all would be said and done, he'd be considered the true founder of Miles Jesu.

After seventeen months of exposure to Miles Jesu, Father Barry Fisher posted a long overdue statement on the Institute's official website. His concise eight hundred and fifty-three-word rocket shot into cyberspace. Years later, it would vanish from the Miles Jesu site altogether. But at the time of Fisher's statement, a tight-lipped, sanitized disclosure finally appeared in electronic print. From the initiation of the Vatican's intervention, it had taken three years for a church superior to address the public regarding the problem of Miles Jesu.

The Commissary noted Rome's intervention, McSweeney's fact-finding mission, and his own mandate to hit the restart button. The statement disclosed a handful of summary ideas:

*During the Apostolic Visitation a number of irregularities and questionable practices came to light in the sworn testimonies of many members. Also, the behavior of Fr. Duran in regards to certain questionable conduct and his exercise of authority came to light. The conclusion of the Apostolic Visitation was that an outside person should be called in to work with the Ecclesial Family in order to correct these situations and to work with the members in the renewal of the Institute.*

*.... In time it has become clear and undeniable, that the Founder, Fr. Alfonso Duran, presented erratic behaviors that were totally beyond the scope of the powers given to him. Some members have identified wounds caused by the inappropriate exercise of authority under his leadership. The mistaken sense of allegiance and obedience instilled in the membership facilitated his behavior, which was totally unacceptable and not in accord with the discipline of the Church nor supportable in any way by a healthy sense of consecrated life.*

*Members who challenged his actions or behavior were often ostracized. The internal discipline and customs of the Institute provided protection for the Founder. It must be said in justice, that most of the members had no idea of the improper conduct of the Founder. Some of the allegations against Fr. Duran are hearsay and have not been verified. However, many are factual. It is important for all that the truth be disclosed, which is the reason for this public statement....*

*In my personal contact with Cardinal Vallini, I perceive that he wishes to assure the membership and also the lay associates ("Vinculum") of his concern and of his assurance that he accompanies them in this process with his prayers and with his conviction that the membership today has a right to a future....*

*As Commissary and in the name of the Church, I wish to express my deep concern for all those members, former members and family members who may have been hurt in the past due to the manner in which authority was exercised. I also am personally grateful for those members who had the courage to solicit the intervention of the Congregation of the Institute of Consecrated Life and Societies of Apostolic Life, thus bringing to light the situations under question.*

*Though this communication may come as a surprise and be painful to many members, Vinculum members, and friends of Miles Jesu, the truth cannot be hidden. Only in truth can a better and healthier future for Miles Jesu be achieved.*

This statement circulated a selective version of Miles Jesu madness for public consumption. It authenticated the delinquency of Father Duran, the deformity of Miles Jesu, and redeemed the good names of the signers behind the intervention. It underlined the importance of transparency.

Words. Words. Words. Fischer omitted critical information. The full truth remained concealed.

He didn't state that the Church gave him the power to dissolve Miles Jesu and the freedom to exercise that power. His mandate included not only possibly re-founding, but definitively dissolving if deemed appropriate after testing viability.

As it turned out, Father Fischer preferred to salvage and rebuild, but not without threatening to dissolve whenever the cooperation of his new council proved crucial. The ever present menace of dissolution was a convenient sword to rattle as needed. Tired of the threat, a council member confronted him and demanded to know if the Catholic Church really wanted Miles Jesu or not. Fischer wouldn't answer. He just gave a blank stare and then changed the subject. That said everything.

Father Fischer's statement also omitted Duran's sexual abuse of members. To his credit, Fischer had confirmed this discovery in the original draft of his statement. But Barry Fischer was a team player subject to the discretion of higher superiors. Cardinal Agostino Vallini had scrutinized Fischer's original draft and played the editor. He instructed Fischer to scratch out the recognition of Duran's sexual abuses. A Miles Jesu member who'd been recruited to serve on Fischer's council of renewal heard the narrative, related by Fischer himself.

Omitting the existence of the hundred-page study, the statement diverted attention away from Father Anthony McSweeney's chief findings. Writing in general terms, Fischer instead based his assessment of Miles Jesu on his own personal exposure to the members. The nitty-gritty content of McSweeney's study remained a secret both to the public and to Fischer's own council. His council, the future leaders of Miles Jesu, had no access to McSweeney's conclusions and unfiltered recommendations.

Father Fischer's statement unveiled a half truth to the public. The complete truth hid within the omissions. Why not tell everything? Why perpetuate the cover up? Perhaps superiors judged the full truth intolerable to public sensibilities.

In my opinion, the Church stumbled upon its worst nightmare in the Pope's own diocese. Miles Jesu, an approved champion of orthodoxy, was a cult operated by a sociopath and sexually perverted founder and director. Duran had escaped forty-three years of ecclesial scrutiny. Somehow, by the sheer power of his charisma and manipulative nature he secured his directorship without election for the first thirty-eight years of the Institute's existence. Then he passed through a rubber stamp election after returning from drug rehab and an in-house punishment for sexual abuse. Father Duran left behind a group of broken leaders indoctrinated in a non-Christian way of operating. Things were so bad, church big wigs decided to dissolve the group, but perceived expediency in passing the buck to Fischer, letting him make the decision.

Why would the Church authorize dissolution and rebuild at the same time? Giving the benefit of the doubt, maybe it was a last ditch effort to save members from tragic displacement. Maybe it was a nod to orthodoxy, showing mercy to a group of innocents who wanted to do better.

Or perhaps the chess move was political. It seems to me that the suppression of Miles Jesu by high ecclesial authorities in Rome would have backfired. Dissolving the champions of orthodoxy would have triggered an avalanche of questions. Why? A persistent search for answers would have led to McSweeney's investigation and the skeletons in Duran's files. Eventually, the truth would surface: a crazy man and sexual deviant ruled an institute of consecrated life. Many bishops and cardinals, even the Pope himself had said wonderful things about Miles Jesu. They'd all be dragged into the outrage. Scandal of scandals! Church superiors would look complicit, irresponsible, incompetent, duped.

A noisy and direct suppression was therefore out of the question. It would be better to sweep everything under the carpet and discreetly authorize dissolution. The real solution may have been for Church superiors to simply wash their hands, cover their asses, and let Father Barry Fisher take the blame or credit.

After four years of Fisher's overhaul, Miles Jesu finally elected a new general director from its own internal ranks. Father Robert Nicoletti won the vote, a man neither involved in Duran's governing, nor in the cover up. Fisher still observes in the background as the appointed Religious Assistant. He functions as the Vicariate's training wheels.

The fate of Father Alphonsus Maria Duran remains deliberately clouded. He lives somewhere in Madrid, Spain. Only a select few superiors of Miles Jesu know the details of his whereabouts. Although his name, image, and historic connection to Miles Jesu have been cut to a bare minimum on the official website of the Institute, Duran's good name and reputation for holiness persist within the Miles Jesu network. Duran's records of sexual perversion were conveniently destroyed in a basement flood.

During the Fisher years, Father Marcus Gelson came to his senses. Burdened with severe PTSD, the razed victim of sexual abuse finally accepted psychotherapy. Father Barry Fisher helped the broken priest find his way. After a year of prayer and discernment, Gelson requested a laicization from the Catholic priesthood. He discovered that Duran was not an isolated anomaly, but a standard product of the dysfunctional clerical culture of the Catholic Church in Rome. At last, Gelson abandoned Miles Jesu with a sanctioned $100,000 "gift."

My blood brother, Anthony Sullivan, remains in Miles Jesu, ironically because of me. Many years past, Anthony had decided to leave Miles Jesu but I'd prevented it. He'd secretly vanished from the Miles Jesu apartment in Rome. When Anthony didn't show up for morning prayers, Duran had gathered some members in a makeshift situation room. As a member of the rescue team, I played a vital role.

During that crisis, Duran instructed me to persuade my mother not to wire money to Anthony so he couldn't leave Europe. Contriving to shock my mother into collaborating, Duran ordered me to call her and elaborate on Anthony's alleged sexual addictions. I obeyed and stressed Anthony's need to remain in Miles Jesu. She didn't buy it and decided to wire Anthony's air fare through Western Union.

Meanwhile, before Anthony could get his hands on the money, another member and I hurried to Rome's Termini train station to hunt him down. Miraculously, I found him waiting at a phone booth and confronted him, as gentle as possible under the circumstances. I lied and told him that Mom wouldn't be able to wire money until tomorrow. Defeat and shock froze in his eyes.

We slithered into a greasy diner, where he barely agreed to talk. For two hours, I passionately pleaded with Anthony to stay in Miles Jesu. He finally capitulated, and together, we returned to the Miles Jesu apartment at Tespi. He felt like a dog with his tail between his legs. Duran greeted Anthony with a compassionate hug and a few chocolate bars.

Anthony's still in there and I've gradually come to terms with it. Not really. I wish I could have a good relationship with him but the saga of Miles Jesu frustrates and complicates the possibility. It's taken a long time for me to let him go. I still struggle with it. I repent of harming him. I repent of obeying Father Duran.

Of course, this incident says nothing of Anthony's presumed innocence. It speaks volumes however of a sociopath's willingness to tear a family apart.

# Chapter Seventeen

A nippy Monday twilight, October 27, 2008. Zipping up my suede jacket and adjusting a grey flat cap, I descended from the post office in Zhovkva, Ukraine. I had just got off the phone with Father Giuseppe Tonello. Withholding details, he'd sent an email a few days earlier asking me to call.

Miles Jesu had submitted my laicization request five and a half months ago. Olha and I had been living together for four months now. Father Marcus Gelson still enjoyed his power.

The eight degrees Celsius temperature and two kilometer walk felt wonderful. Or was it the good news from Rome that put the smile on my face? I enjoyed the road that stretched directly into a colorful sunset. House after house, smell after smell, baked bread, chimney smoke, fried potatoes shepherded me back home. Relief, gratitude, happiness. What a phone call! I floated on clouds. I could hardly believe it. Passing our mountain of firewood on the left, I stepped up to an unlocked front door.

Dressed in a plain white apron, Olha stirred the pot of borscht simmering on the banged up stove. The mouthwatering smell welcomed me. Closing the door, hanging up my jacket, my lungs filled with potatoes, shredded cabbage and beets, onions, garlic, carrots and bite-sized chunks of pork. Every ingredient shouted freshness from the Klub family farm, including the meat which had romped about in a barn only a few days past.

"Hello, Honey," I said.

She pulled her hair back and walked up to me. We embraced and gave each other a kiss.

"Hello, my love."

Olha could hardly contain herself. "What did Tonello say?"

I asked if we could sit down and she readily agreed. We pulled out chairs and sat at a wobbly wood table covered with a checkered red and white vinyl cloth. The covering emitted a picnic atmosphere. I moved the salt and pepper shakers to the side.

"You won't believe what just happened," I said.

"What? Come on!" She had little patience for drama.

"The Congregation for the Clergy gave me the laicization. I'm not a priest anymore."

"What!"

"Yep. It just happened."

"I don't believe it. It's only been five months."

"Yeah, even Tonello was surprised at how fast it came."

"Really?" Shocked, she paused and shook her head. Our life, our world had just changed.

"But isn't there some kind of document?"

"Tonello said the Vicariate will mail the rescript tomorrow."

"Rescript?"

"The Vatican's official response to my laicization request."

"What else did he say?"

"He informed me of the laicization and asked if I could come to the office to get the document. I told him that I'm living in Ukraine and that it would be impossible to visit his office. So, he said that he'd mail the rescript."

Olha was percolating now. She looked at me with a puzzled face.

"But you'd told me that the Congregation's response had to go to the case manager, Father Kroll. How did Tonello end up with the document?"

"That's right. And I asked Tonello the same question. I reminded him that the procedure emphasized that the official response had to go to Father Kroll. He agreed, and then said that the Congregation didn't trust Miles Jesu. So, they bypassed Kroll and sent the document directly to him."

Olha and I burst out laughing. After the countless times Duran had peddled the Vatican's praise of Miles Jesu, the Congregation's true thoughts gave us the giggles. After regaining our composure Olha dried her tears and continued.

"They finally got it right! Miles Jesu can't be trusted."

She jumped up and asked me to wait a second. After turning off the fire beneath the borscht, Olha hurried back and reclaimed her chair.

"What else did Tonello say?"

"Not much more. I asked him if the laicization depended on my response or signature. He explained that it takes effect upon notification and that I'm now officially notified and laicized. I'm supposed to sign the rescript as a matter of acknowledging my acceptance of the fact and send a copy back for his files. He didn't want to spend a lot of time on the phone. I gave our address and he said I'd have the document in a few days."

"So, you're really laicized! I can't believe it."

She got up, reached her arms behind her and re-tied the apron strings. Olha scooped up two bowls from the cabinet and asked me to get the sour cream from the refrigerator. Then a distracted thought popped into her head.

"You didn't tell him we were living together?"

"Yes, of course I did, and explained our sleeping arrangement too."

"What!" The dishes almost hopped from her hands.

"Really? You said that!"

She stopped in her tracks and stared at me with an expression of disbelief. A few seconds passed. Then the dam broke with our smiles and laughter.

We enjoyed our borscht, fresh baked bread, and an excited heart-to-heart about how to prepare a wedding on a shoe string budget. None of my family would be there. Not enough notice, too expensive, way too far away. Besides, after twenty-eight years of Miles Jesu my family relationships still suffered from atrophy. Her family would encompass a small crowd. It seemed that we could do everything, including the dress, priest stipend, rings and vodka for three hundred dollars. After the dishes we watched our usual Russian edition of Law and Order and went to bed.

Several days later I woke up at the crack of dawn, grabbed a cup of coffee, and printed out an English translation of the rescript. You can find anything online. Olha kept sleeping. I always got up early. I wanted to take my time and understand the document.

Fingering the rescript, the barely yellow paper felt thick, textured, graceful. In soft red ink, the elegant papal tiara and crossed keys topped the page, dead center. In bold red, *Congregatio Pro Clericis* appeared just beneath the insignia. Holding the letter up to the rising sun cracking through the frosted window, I noticed a water mark. The keys again, with the words *Officia Sanctae Sedis*. Down to the embossed seal, the paper radiated the authority of the Pope.

The rescript was a personalized form letter from Pope Benedict XVI through Cardinal Claudio Hummes, the Prefect of the Sacred Congregation for the Clergy. With a file number and addressed to me, the opening lines announced that the Pope, on the 10th day of October 2008, had granted my request for laicization. Latin filled up the front and back of the single page, concluding with a line for my signature.

I placed the original rescript and indispensable translation side by side and this clarified everything. My Latin was terrible. Priestly duties and privileges, beside my vows of poverty, chastity, and obedience disappeared by a grand dispensation. The document even specified that I may marry, but *discreetly handled without pomp or external display*. That looked strange.

I quickly noticed that the rescript went beyond an unqualified dispensation. It wasn't that I just couldn't say Mass and wear a Roman collar. While exhorting me to live my faith and give edification to others, it declared a concrete list of norms that delineated my participation in the Church henceforward. Surprise! I couldn't lead a ministry, teach theology or religion, direct church functions, run a parish, preach, distribute communion, read from the scriptures at Mass, exercise pastoral leadership, work in a seminary, or even serve as an altar boy. Wow! And the rescript made clear that my signature confirmed an acceptance of the regulations. Tonello had been silent about that.

Though the rescript allowed me to impart sacramental absolution to anyone dying, the litany of restrictions turned my stomach. Nobody had told me that laicization came with leprosy. That's how it felt. It seemed that the Church wanted me to live my faith, but from the distance of a back pew. A twelve-year-old girl had more right to serve at the altar than me. Why? Most likely, the Church intended to contain the scandal of my "defection," as described by pertinent documents.

I'd read enough. *I didn't defect!* I stared out the window at the rising sun and tried to digest the new rules. My life had just changed again. Now, most of the rescript felt like a punishment for doing something wrong. But I'd lived in a cult that had manipulated my choices in life! That cult had recruited me by deception, omitted a process of true vocational discernment, and coerced my commitments. None of this mattered. As far as the Church was concerned I'd defected. By a form letter, I'd be lumped together with all other defectors. Father Heisner was right. Nobody would understand. Not even me.

Taking up a pen, I closed my eyes and whispered a prayer. The presence of Jesus pulsated next to me but the visualization was blurry, as if the magic had worn off.

"Thank you Jesus for giving me a new life. These rules are hard to accept."

A solitary tear rolled down my face.

I didn't intuit words from Jesus. Perhaps his silence affirmed my solitary act of independence. But I did have a thought: freedom has its price. Mixed feelings swirled inside me. I felt bitter about the unexpected conditions, the sudden restrictions imposed upon me for the rest of my life. They seemed outdated and overdone; too cautious, too careful, too fearful of the sentiments and thoughts of whomever. I still had much to offer needy souls, but the Church wanted me to sit on the bench for the rest of the game. Simultaneously, I felt a surge of triumph. Surviving many bloody battles, encouraged by Jesus, I'd won my freedom. Without pressure or prejudice I could now freely choose my own way in life. I bowed my head and signed.

The ink flowed with a curly speed, and began drying. Andrew Lee Sullivan. My signature represented a dual reality. While the Miles Jesu ordeal lacked the power to break my bond with the Catholic Church, the laicization now piled on and intensified my feelings of distance, cautiousness, and distrust of ecclesial leaders. I begrudgingly accepted my new status as a leper and found it heartbreaking. But there was a flip side, a payoff. After all was said and done, I felt a real relationship with Jesus that would last forever. And that was worth everything.

A few weeks later, Olha and I were married on a frozen, quiet Tuesday morning. No music with instruments of any kind, no guest list, no invitations, no entourage, no wedding dress, no tuxedo, no decorations. The radiators had been drained to prevent the pipes from freezing over. The inside of the church was colder than the outside. Yet, despite the absence of the bells and whistles typical to a wedding, that November 25, 2008 was the happiest day of my life.

It fell on the feast of Saint Josephat, the great martyr axed to death because he'd promoted the cause of Church unity. We didn't consciously choose his memorial day when planning things; it simply appeared that morning. Oddly enough, eighteen months ago, in the confessional next to the body of Saint Josephat in Saint Peter's Basilica, I'd discovered that I could marry. Josephat's feast also towered as a special day of celebration for Miles Jesu. It felt like God had turned the feast on its head. That day took on a new meaning for us, a day of unity between husband and wife.

The wedding or 'crowning ceremony,' as Eastern Orthodox Christianity called it, took place in the village Church of the Elevation of the Holy Cross, where Olha had been recruited to join Miles Jesu. During Communism this Dobrosyn landmark had been chained up and prohibited from use. Renovated, it now thrived. Its interior breathed the classic atmosphere of a poor, Byzantine, rural church in Western Ukraine.

A giant wall separated the common people from the holy of holies where the priest presided. The wall exhibited five levels of icons, each image couched within arches, gold trim, and white pillars. Grand golden gates completed the strict division between the ordained and non-ordained.

The main body of the church displayed a sea of icons with hanging lamps, chandeliers, lit candles, and walls painted with colorful symbols. Layers upon layers of rugs with incongruent patterns attempted to welcome the cold feet of weary farmers planted for hours at a time during liturgy. Copious amounts of incense habitually clouded the church and impregnated the walls with the pungent and sweet smell of prayer.

About twenty-five grandmas and a few men attended the wedding. The women wore thick and long winter coats with veils stretched over their heads. Their cracked hands and wrinkled faces hinted at harsh work and hard earned wisdom. The men wore black leather jackets and looked like the mafia. Nobody had received a formal invite. The small crowd resulted from word of mouth exchanges in the village. Although anyone could have come, half the attendees were related to Olha's family. The other half represented devout church mice, lingering after the end of morning liturgy.

The cheery grin of Olha's mother stood out within the bunch of villagers. Her round, plump face, pointed nose, and high cheek bones with a reddish hue distinguished her. Otherwise, almost everyone wore the same humdrum garb and white veil knotted beneath the chin.

I wore a deep grey suit with tiny pin stripes and a tie with shades of beige running diagonal. A mini-bouquet of microscopic flowers pinned on my right lapel and silver-looking cufflinks marked me as the groom. A few drops of jell darkened the grey hair. Clasping my hands as tight as possible, amusing myself with thick freezing puffs of breath, my eyes flashed giddy playfulness.

Thirty-three years had passed since I'd begged Jesus to let me marry and now I felt like a six-year-old in a candy store. I felt no fear of commitment, no reservations. I accepted and valued all the suffering in my life for the fullness of love I now enjoyed, both divine and human. It was all worth it. Suffering had broken me down and opened me up to receive God's love. That transforming fire climaxed with the gift of this loving woman at my side. Everything had come together in my life, matured me to be a good husband and father.

Olha looked stunning. Glistening with sparkles and flowers, golden hair curled everywhere. Gold embedded pearls swung from her neck and ears. Imitation jewelry of course, but wonderful enough for us. A brown, soft leather coat exploded with fur that surrounded her head and rested upon her shoulders. Her natural smile, sincere face, and pleasant laughter emanated an aura of irresistibility.

Just before the priest opened the gates, the church echoed with a soothing archipelago melody. While villagers positioned themselves for a decent view, Olha and I turned to each other. Our eyes locked and everything around us seemed to fade away. We clasped our hands together and gazed into each other's soul.

"Are you ready, my love?" I whispered, wanting the privacy. Nobody within ear shot understood English anyway.

"Yes. I'm ready." A soft but confident response.

"Thank you for waiting for me."

"You're welcome."

Closing her eyes, tears of joy squeezed forth and rushed down her face. I dried them with my fingers. "Don't do that. They might turn into ice." She giggled, and I laughed too.

Unexpectedly, the presence of the priest shook us from our distraction. Dressed in a beautiful white vestment he approached holding a golden paten with two, five dollar rings resting upon it. He blessed the rings, held them to our lips for a kiss, and then placed them on our fingers. This opening ritual was called the betrothal, by which Olha and I pledged ourselves to one another.

Following the exchange of vows, the rest of the ceremony unfolded with a series of meaningful symbols of realities to come.

From behind us, gold leafed crowns were held floating over our heads. They symbolized the kingdom of marriage, ruled by a partnership of love and fertility. The crowns anticipated the birth of our first son, Andrew Nicholas, ten months later. Immediately following Olha's C-section, I'd receive the newborn upon my naked breast and cry like a baby, for sheer joy. Two more years down the road, Michael Daniel would follow.

Next, we stood upon a beautiful embroidered towel. The many colors woven together symbolized the many aspects of married life: family, tradition, faith, work. It would take a couple of years for these facets of life to congeal for me. Eventually, at forty-nine years old, I'd land my first salaried, full-time job as the spiritual counselor of a hospice. Olha and I had taken the risk of marrying before we were financially stable, trusting that God would care for us. Love came first; no matter what. God provided.

The miracle of therapeutic prayer had taught me to surrender everything to the passive reception of God's love. Healing from trauma, emotional development, friendship, enlightenment, courage, risk taking, and the capacity to effortlessly give love followed. And now marriage! Life can change!

Toward the end of the wedding, Olha and I took our first steps as a married couple. Holding onto his white stole, the priest led the way around the entry table of the church. The walk represented our faithful journey, traveling through life while attentive to the solicitude of the Church. This symbolic journey would turn real when we'd immigrate to the United States. After twenty years in Europe I'd travel with a wife and baby to a changed country.

After the final blessing, Olha and I bundled up, held hands, and walked to the church entrance. A thoughtful old lady jumped ahead and opened the doors before us. Light rushed into the church and fell at our feet. Without skipping a beat, we walked into the brightness, passed beneath the threshold, stopped in our tracks, and stood in awe before a winter wonderland. Snow! It filled the sky and floated everywhere, unfurling a blanket of endless whiteness. The unexpected explosion of beauty took our breath away.

Pausing, enjoying the moment, we kissed.

I turned and adored her face. "I can't believe it! We're married! I will love you forever. My wife!"

"And I will love you forever!"

We held each other tightly and moved forward to the edge of the descending stairs. We had no idea of our future. Belief was enough to move forward. Stepping downward, we didn't fly away, but landed on the first step of a new world.

# AUTHOR'S NOTE

There are Cinderella truths the world needs to hear. Love begins not by giving, but by receiving. Human growth begins by love received. These truths are both human and Christian. My story offers an insight for the emotionally immature and traumatized, for anyone stuck in a cult or abusive relationship. Learning how to receive God's love can be your way to emotional and spiritual growth, and freedom.

Regardless of the many responsibilities you may juggle, each Catholic bishop must effectively monitor the new forms of consecrated life within your jurisdiction. Innocent souls who want to surrender to God deserve your protection. Defend their rights. Scrutinize the founders of innovative upstarts. My story underlines what can happen when an unsuitable superior eludes supervision.

I neither intend my memoir to advance the married priesthood nor argue against the western tradition of celibacy. I do hope that it calls attention to the importance of human maturity and love-enriching prayer.

Followers of Christ, discern not only God's purpose in your lives, but the formative, human environment where you'll live. May my story encourage the good judgment of each neophyte as you discern your vocation.

I share a testimony of darkness, light, and love. Exposing the human side of the Catholic Church doesn't negate the heavenly side. I'm still a practicing Catholic, praying in the back pew. If someone is scandalized by what I've written, just try living it. Don't get stuck in the darkness. The heart of the story is about the power of Jesus's love.

It's important to say a few things about Miles Jesu. I used the real names of Father Alphonsus Duran and Miles Jesu because I wanted to indicate a true, historical point of reference. Church superiors can refer to Duran and Miles Jesu as an example of a once harmful way of life. Anyone contemplating commitment with the group should know the back story. A fiancé deserves to know the true past of his fiancée before marriage.

It's fair to make a distinction between the Miles Jesu of the past and the present. I lived in a Miles Jesu that was a rogue cult. Then, the investigation and recommendations came. After years of oversight by the Vicariate of Rome, admittedly, Miles Jesu enjoys some positive changes. I neither know how much Miles Jesu has changed, nor the depth of rumored reforms. It's easy to change paperwork, another thing entirely to change decades of entrenched paradigms and habits.

Granted, there's a lot of Church incompetence, corruption, and abuse. My story highlights that sorry world. But I hope the reader can see beyond the tragedies and focus on the heart of my testimony. I received Jesus's unconditional love and changed like crazy. I pray that my testimony may introduce you to your own epiphany of life.

Andrew Lee Sullivan

Vatican Intervention
P.O. Box 43012
Phoenix, AZ  85080-3012
vaticanintervention.com
https://www.gofundme.com/heal-spiritual-abuse

Write a review. Please share your reading experience at Amazon.com.

# ABOUT THE AUTHOR

Andrew Lee Sullivan is a Catholic priest, laicized by Pope Benedict XVI. In 2007, he helped expose a rogue Catholic cult to the Vatican. Sullivan is happily married and the father of two young boys. He and his family live in Phoenix, Arizona, where he works as the spiritual counselor of a hospice and a specialist in grief recovery.

Made in the USA
Columbia, SC
14 May 2021